THE ROMANCE REVOLUTION

THE
Romance Revolution

Erotic Novels for Women and the Quest for a New Sexual Identity

CAROL THURSTON

University of Illinois Press   Urbana and Chicago

1 2 3 4 5 C P 5 4 3 2 1

This book is printed on acid-free paper.

Library of Congress Cataloging-in-Publication Data

Thurston, Carol
  The romance revolution.

  Bibliography: p.
  Includes index.
  1. Erotic stories, American—History and criticism.
2. American fiction—20th century—History and criticism.
3. Women—United States—Books and reading—History—
20th century. 4. Sex role in literature. 5. Women
in literature—United States—History—20th century.
6. Women—United States—Social conditions. 7. Popular
literature—United States—History and criticism.
I. Title.
PS374.E75T4   1987   813'.085'09   86-30759
ISBN 0-252-01247-X (cloth)
ISBN 0-252-014421-1 (paper)

Contents

CONTENTS

Preface

During the past six years the question What do romances have to do with the mass media (or with international communication, or with media policy research)? has become all too familiar. Yet I have continued to be at least a little surprised each time it is asked, perhaps because the reason for studying these popular novels and their readers seems so obvious to me. All mass media both affect and are affected by the cultural milieu in which they exist, and certainly the romance novel as we know it today constitutes a dynamic and popular mass medium. The erotic romance in particular is a uniquely female form of American popular culture, which emerged and then evolved during one of the most turbulent periods of social, political, and economic change in this century—change that by the early 1980s had affected the lives of all American women.

On occasion I have responded to the question by pointing to my long-standing interest in trying to design and adapt empirical and quantitative research methodologies to what have generally been considered qualitative questions. I have also resorted to numbers, explaining that romance novels attract an American audience of more than 20 million women, that by 1984 one out of four adult women in this country were reading them (at an average rate of four or more per month), and that hundreds of paperback romances are being translated and sold by the millions in at least twenty other countries around the world. In spite of such "telling" numbers, however, my personal experience is that very, very few of my academic and social peers, male or female, have any knowledge at all of this mass medium or its audiences. And most of them are proud of it. Certainly the tenacity of our society's gender socialization was brought home right at the outset of my research when one of my academic colleagues (perhaps the most deeply and consciously egalitarian male I have ever had the good fortune to work with) volunteered to act as a reader-coder for the historical romance content analysis reported in chapter 4. Halfway through his first title, however, he confessed with some embarrassment that he simply could not force himself to read any further.

My investigations were stimulated more directly by a growing awareness of two conflicting realities: descriptions of the popular romance novel and heroine as inherently conservative and unchanging, as opposed to personal experience and scholarly observations of the role of the sociopolitical milieu in shaping the content of mass media. As it turned out, my initial research question was only a door-opener, and others soon flowed from it. The questions multiplied precisely because popular culture is the product of the symbiotic relationship between a cultural artifact, its producers, and its consumers, all set within the context of a specific time and place—and to examine only one piece of this complex puzzle is as inadequate and inaccurate as trying to ascribe the flavor of a delicious stew to just one ingredient.

Along the way I had an enormous amount of help—from (female) students, friends, and colleagues who volunteered to read and code content; from editors, authors, and booksellers who supplied information about the romance publishing business; and from more than 500 romance readers who gave generously of their time and attention to answer my questions. I had just completed the historical romance content analysis when I first met with authors Rita Estrada and Rita Gallagher, who were organizing the first Romance Writers of America meeting in Houston in 1981, and they gave generously of both information and support. It was soon after that conference that Star Helmer, then an editor at Richard Gallen, wrote to volunteer her help, initiating a two-year association and a lasting friendship.

There were weeks, during both 1982 and 1985, when the high point of my day was when the mail came. The survey responses I received from readers were often entertaining, sometimes humorous, at other times sad, but always packed with information, much of it unasked for and unexpected. When the available white space on the questionnaire was used up, some of them wrote letters and sent those along. A few personalized their contributions via the telephone. Equally unexpected, however, was the more subtle message that emerged from all of the reader information taken as a whole—one that left me with an immeasurably enhanced sense of shared female experience.

Barbara Doscher, my colleague and long-time friend, has from the beginning been an invaluable contributor and the one I could always count on, whether as reader, sounding board, critic, or crutch. Beginning at least a decade ago, long before the word "romance" became part of my daily vocabulary, discussions with Ilya Prigogine were stirring thoughts about a social system analog to his theory of how new organization or structures are generated in chemical systems, and he has kindly reviewed the material presented in chapter 10. Cheris Kramarae and Maurice Charney added their unique insights and helpful suggestions on the original version of the manuscript, which served to sharpen the focus of my own thinking and, ultimately, the organization of the text. George Thurston contributed photographs and figures, adding a certain clarity and dash of seasoning, both of which he also brings to my life.

THE ROMANCE REVOLUTION

Introduction

THE ROMANCE NOVEL
AS POPULAR CULTURE

Traditional Verities or a New Synthesis?

[Because of acid paper] whole genres routinely dismissed by scholars and critics as trivial may be lost to the future. . . . [Even] the least skillful writing can still convey a powerful sense of what it meant to be alive — thinking and feeling — when that work appeared.
Books are not only things we own, they are surrogate memories that reveal the values and concerns of those who wrote and read them.

Lane Jennings, "Why Books Will Survive"

*R*omantic fiction today is an entertainment medium that is both *mass* and *dynamic*, though both characteristics often are ignored or go unrecognized by casual observers and scholars alike. Paperback romances are being read by at least twenty million American women of all ages and all socioeconomic levels, yet they are rarely included in anthologies dealing with images of women in the mass media or popular culture.[1] Generally written about and commented upon in newspapers and popular magazines by people who know next to nothing about either the books or the women who read them, romances are seldom taken seriously, even when the latest sales figures for this half-billion-dollar industry are being reported.

A modern mass entertainment medium that rivals popular television programs for audience size and repeat exposure, the new paperback romance novel came to full bloom between 1972 and 1982. In the process it contributed to innovative changes in the production, packaging, promotion, and distribution strategies of many publishers, which, along with radically changed earnings expectations, have in turn contributed to today's widespread emphasis on "commercial fiction." The huge popularity of the new romance provoked shifts in the acquisition and space allocation policies of public libraries, gave used/exchange bookstores a new lease on life, and fed the expansion of two of the largest bookstore chains in the country, Walden and B. Dalton.

Informal communication networks developed among readers, most of them for the purpose of exchanging books but also capable of word-of-mouth indictment or praise that could make or break a book. In addition, a broad array of parasite enterprises came into being, from romance review magazines and special Trivial Pursuit games, to writers' organizations and conferences, and a great outpouring of instruction manuals on "how to write a romance."

Popular culture is by definition a social phenomenon that changes with time. That the paperback romance is popular culture is attested to both by the numbers (books and readers) involved and the fact that it is constantly being reshaped, not only by authors and editors, but also by consumers and market forces. In spite of this, the conventional wisdom on "pulp" romance novels among most literary and popular culture scholars is that they reinforce traditional social norms and values, and that all romances are essentially the same and have remained fundamentally unchanged through time, especially when it comes to the patterns of behavior associated with sex roles and the so-called power relationship between men and women.

Whether overtly stated or not, these underlying assumptions are so broadly accepted that many students of the genre freely indulge in words that long have been anathema in the world of rigorous research and scholarship—all, always, and never.[2] Though often disowned as "literature," this popular fiction nonetheless has been relegated largely to literary analysis and criticism, where the focus has been on patterns in texts that demonstrate universality and continuity rather than diversity and change, and on consensus rather than pluralism. Kay Mussell, in the preface to her 1984 book, revealed such a traditionalist-universalist orientation in the sweeping statement that "romances rarely challenge the social order, and they do not urge women to recognize oppression or to revolt; instead, they reinforce the value of traditional roles in a changing society" (p. xi). As Mark Levy and Sven Windahl (1985) observed, scholars influenced by the notion of mass society and critical theory tend to see the audience as overwhelmingly passive, manipulated, and dominated from above, with the mass media acting as a powerful agent of ideological control.

Literary analysis also has rarely concerned itself directly with audiences (or with the media organizations that produce texts), but instead has relied on the texts alone to reveal who readers are and what they think. Kathryn Weibel (1977, 38), for example, concluded that "since the working hero has been continued, though new professions have been added, however, it seems likely that readers of the Harlequins are primarily working-class wives. On the other hand, readers of the 'Gothics' and the historical romances, who are presumably already married to professional men, dream of life among the idle rich"— which is not only speculative but inaccurate, judged alongside the demographic information about readers presented here, gathered from a large, nationwide sample.[3] Detailed analyses of so-called situational transformations within the text also do not tell us what impressions readers en masse carry away, or what they thought was said and done by what kinds of characters.

Though the recent popularity of reader-response theory and criticism is evidence of a new interest in audiences among humanities scholars, it appears to be a case of rediscovering the wheel. Criticizing a literary criticism that searches for plot parallels and repeated images, myths, structure, and points of view, Norman Holland (1975, 12) observed that when "the marks on the page become characters and events they do so because the reader plays the part of a prince to the sleeping beauty. He [*sic*] gives them life out of his own desires. When he does so, he brings his lifestyle to bear on the work. He mingles his unconscious loves and fears and adaptations with the words and images he synthesizes at a conscious level." Stanley Fish (1980, 13–14) voiced a similar thought in observing that interpretive strategies "give texts their shape, making them rather than, as is usually assumed, arising from them," and that a reader's strategies derive from the "interpretive community of which he [*sic*] is a member." Both observations echo Joseph Klapper's (1960, 8) mediating factors theory and his now famous statement that "mass communication ordinarily does not serve as a necessary and sufficient cause of audience effects, but rather functions among and through a nexus of mediating factors and influences." Similarly, when Janice Radway (1984) asked "what real readers do with texts," she was echoing the words of sociologist Elihu Katz, who suggested in 1959 that "What do people do with the media?" was potentially a far more productive research question than "What do the media do to people?" Katz's question stimulated an extensive body of research based on what came to be called the "uses and gratifications" approach to examining how the mass media function for audiences.[4]

Literary analysis also lends itself to psychoanalytic interpretations of characters (Modleski 1982) and reader behavior (Radway 1984), which are not only subjective and speculative but lend support to a body of thought that has been, and continues to be even in its derivative form, largely derogatory, hostile, and damaging to females, from birth to old age. As historian Lawrence Stone (1985, 30) pointed out in

5

terms that are much too kind, "Clinical Freudianism, with its stress on penis envy, early incestuous experiences (real or imagined), and the Oedipus complex, looks increasingly like the product of a Victorian, central European, middle-class, male chauvinist society."

John Cawelti (1976, 42) predicted that "the coming of age of the women's movement will invent significantly new formulas for romance," yet most scholarly critics insist that the romance novel remains fundamentally unchanged, portraying traditional power relationships between men and women, and domestic solutions for women, even after a quarter of a century of rapid and dramatic social change. Notable exceptions are Helen Papashvily (1956), Nina Baym (1978), and Josephine Ruggiero and Louise Weston (1977). Baym, in the introduction to her analysis of nineteenth-century "women's fiction," stated that "there is, clearly, general evidence of all sorts that women's lives were in ferment during the nineteenth century and that women were increasingly aware of their situations as gender determined and increasingly demanding of themselves and the world. But clearly too this phenomenon had multiple causes, and to assign a specific percentage of the cause to the novels they read is impossible. The novels might as much be evidence of a change as cause of it; or, like so many other things, the novels may have been both a sign of change and a contribution to it" (p. 21).

In the only two studies of the "modern gothic" that can be characterized as systematic (Ruggiero and Weston 1977; Radway 1981), the authors, though reaching different conclusions, found feminist elements in the texts, which indicates that female characters were at least in transition. In fact, in the face of overwhelming testimony to the contrary among literary scholars, sociologists Ruggiero and Weston were bold indeed to suggest that modern gothic romances might even be considered forerunners of the new women's movement.

The data, analyses, and conclusions about popular romantic fiction and its readers presented here follow in this heretical tradition, questioning and challenging the traditional verities, and suggesting instead that under certain conditions popular culture acts in concert with other social forces as a powerful agent of change, especially during periods of social and political turbulence, precisely because of its power to legitimize. The evidence indicates that one new and very popular type of romance narrative, the erotic romance, has been moving away from traditional sex-role portrayals and values for more than a decade. Indeed, rather than functioning as a stronghold of conservatism, this type of novel has traced the evolution of the "liberated" American woman with a responsiveness unmatched by any other mass entertainment medium, changing as both its most articulate consumers and the marketplace changed. In so doing, it was reflecting the existing social norms and values of some women at a given moment in time, while acting as an agent of change for others, especially those still holding to traditional sex-role definitions — and it was this process of *evolution* in readers, texts, and the market that brought about fundamental changes in some of the most tenacious conventions of the traditional romance formula.

As the romance market grew bigger during the 1970s and then more competitive, the symbiotic relationship between readers and publishers became increasingly complex, more so, for example, than the one commonly existing between such products as toothpaste or beer and their consumers. It was primarily during the latter half of the 1970s that romance readers became critics rather than simply fans. Feedback from readers to publishers, both sought and volunteered, began to produce changes in sex-role portrayals (in thoughts, words, and deeds), which, in concert with other forces in society, contributed to further change in readers, which in turn produced still further change in the romance texts. These modified stories then began to attract consumers from outside the existing universe of romance readers, fueling still more change in both readers and texts as distribution widened and sales continued to increase.

The neofeminist romance texts that emerged from this period of evolution put qualifications on the *kind* of love that overcomes all problems and obstacles — according to John Cawelti (1976, 42) the defining fantasy of the romance — qualifications that are inextricably intertwined with the full development of the heroine as an individual in her own right. These new role models and social norms were repeated in story after story, printed by the hundreds of thousands of copies, sometimes by the millions.

Though yet another transformation now appears to be underway, the popular romance genre since 1972 has been divided into two basic types — the sweet romance and the erotic romance — with the fundamental difference between them being the presence or absence of specific sexual behavioral norms and explicit sexual activities. Sexual content is the most important classifying characteristic, however, because of the kind of sex-role portrayal that came to be associated with it. The result of this evolutionary change is that today most erotic romances not only challenge the traditional power relationships between men and women but depict a more balanced power alignment as natural and expected—in other words, as the norm.

Other story characteristics (contemporary or historical settings, for instance) create secondary divisions in the two subgenres, but it was a specific kind of sexual activity, more and more explicitly described as the 1970s progressed, that created the first and most significant division within the genre. Indeed, the erotic romance ultimately sparked a veritable revolution in the genre by fundamentally changing the way women are portrayed in this popular medium.

First in the erotic historicals and "bodice rippers" of the 1970s, plus a few scattered pioneers that preceded them in the 1960s, and then in the so-called sensuous, or erotic, contemporary romances of the 1980s, the portrayal of the heroine as a whole person became a romance convention. In her fully evolved state the female persona is no longer split between two archetypal female characters: the plain-naive-domestic-selfless-passive-chaste heroine and the beautiful-sophisticated-worldly-selfish-assertive-sexually active Other Woman. Instead, the New Heroine is both good and sexual, and she possesses a passionate drive for self-determination and autonomy. These narratives by their very classification as erotic deal with the heroine's sexual self-awareness, whether just awakening or well-developed. They also increasingly depict the relationship between a developing sense of self and sexual awareness and satisfaction. In the early 1980s, given new opportunities by contemporary settings, the typical erotic romance heroine also was exhibiting a drive for economic self-sufficiency and individual achievement beyond that of any domestic role, while the typical hero aids and admires her success in whatever enterprise she requires for self-fulfillment. As one reader said of the New Heroine, "These ladies make it happen even before the guy walks in. The romance is just the icing on the cake—it's not the cake. And that's realistic."

Because she is no longer needed and because readers found her contrived and incompatible with the New Heroine, the Other Woman has almost disappeared from these narratives. Transformed from negative to positive attributes, some of her stereotypical traits have been assumed by the heroine, particularly her sexuality and attention to her own needs and aspirations. The heroine's major challenge in life is either external or a combination of the external (career) and internal (domestic), making competition over the hero either unnecessary or much less important than it was in the traditional romance. In addition, the heroine almost always has at least one close female

8

friend, and a male friend or two is not unusual. If a second male love interest appears in the story, perhaps to enhance the suspense as to which man the heroine might choose, readers today know without having to be told that the one who wants her to sacrifice her own career in order to serve his is not going to be the hero.

A second significant result of changes in romance novels and readers over the past decade has been the emergence of an entirely new form of popular culture—erotica for women. The erotic heterosexual romance, with content that is sexually appealing and stimulating to a large number of women, came into existence during the 1970s, when the social climate combined with a distribution strategy that put these romances into retail outlets that legitimized them for mass consumption by women—the American supermarket, discount store, and drugstore. Their legitimacy was further enhanced by the fact that stories were allowed to evolve as erotica without much notice and under the guise of a different label—romance.

Because of the heavy focus on the so-called Harlequin romance during the 1970s—studies in which "Harlequin" often was used synonymously with "romantic fiction," feeding the assumption that all romance novels are alike—most scholars either ignored or overlooked the bodice ripper. Conclusions drawn from these Harlequin texts and readers tended to be generalized to the entire genre and to all readers. The bodice ripper, however, was a strictly American phenomenon initially, and it is likely that Peter Mann (1979, 35), a sociologist at the University of Sheffield in England, was unaware of its existence when he concluded that "romantic fiction is always changing gradually to reflect the views of its readers, but it rarely attempts to go beyond the more conservative mores of its period. . . . Immoral behavior, especially pre-marital or extra-marital sexual liaisons, either do not happen or, if they do occur, are clearly labeled as wrong and likely to result in unhappiness"; "the dominance of the male in the relationship is accepted with hardly any questioning." Noting that his own research was limited to "the readers of modern romantic fiction [Harlequin/ Mills and Boon]," Mann (1981) later commented, "I have not come across an equivalent in the modern genre of the historical 'bodice ripper.' I have always been a bit surprised that that sort of historical so-called romance had that much of a market as I would not have thought it would have appealed very much to women at all."

In his monograph on sexual fiction, Maurice Charney (1981, 164) concluded that "much more remains to be written about the differences between male and female perceptions of sexuality. For one thing, we need a much larger and more autonomous body of sexual writing by women and addressed to specific aspects of the feminine experience. If it is true that literature is created out of literature—out of conventions and models and genre assumptions—then women have only a male literature on which to base their own attempts at a distinctive form of female sexual expression." More than simply being socialized by male literature, women have existed for centuries in a total cultural environment shaped by the masculine worldview, making it highly unlikely that any female sexual expression could suddenly appear in all its full-blown glory. Though women have written erotica and pornography in the past, more often than not they have done so under male pseudonyms, projecting male sexual myths and fantasies for male consumers.

Sold by the multimillions of copies, formulaic in character and therefore coherent in structure and organizing action, erotic heterosexual romances constitute the first large and autonomous body of sexual writing by women addressed to the feminine experience. That they may not fit perfectly Charney's (1984, 5) definition of sexual fiction —"all narrative material that makes important and open use of sexual activity as its subject matter, in which interest in sexuality is continuous throughout"—speaks to the very point he made about female sexual expression. Whether interest in sexuality is open and continuous or not is surely a matter of interpretation, since women often find certain passages in a novel inherently sexual that men do not. Aside from the model provided by the male example, as Charney suggested, why should we expect female sexual fiction to mirror either the definition or the conventions of its male counterpart?

Seventy-seven percent of the romance readers surveyed in 1985 agreed with the statement "Many of the love scenes depicted in romance novels are sexually stimulating," attesting to the fact that erotic romances contain fantasies that many women can and do relate to sexually. Furthermore, most readers consciously perceived these novels as erotica and said they use them for sexual information and ideas, to create a receptive-to-sex frame of mind, and even to achieve arousal. "Reading them helps me think of myself as a sexual person," one reported; others said, "They put me in a good mood for sex with my husband" and "Reading them makes me feel amorous." These responses are compatible with the data of Emory University psychologists Claire Coles and M. Johnna Shamp (1984), who found only two statistically significant differences between two groups of women they surveyed in 1978: the frequency of sexual intercourse reported by erotic

10

historical romance readers was twice that of nonreaders, and readers reported significantly greater use of sexual fantasy during intercourse than nonreaders.

Today, the most evolved erotic romances portray a feminine consciousness that has to do not only with sexual liberation but also with economic self-sufficiency, the cornerstone of all other meaningful kinds of autonomy. Contrary to the voices of doom warning that romance novels are the opiate of the female masses, operating both to subvert the women's movement and to condemn addictees to a derivative, vicariously experienced life, these tales of female becoming appear to have played the role of unsung and often unjustly maligned heroine to the feminist movement's macho and often sadistic hero, reaching millions of women most feminist writing, whether fiction or nonfiction, has not.

The Focus and Organization of This Book

Because they have been the primary locus of change in sex-role portrayals since 1972, and because their steadily increasing popularity forced important changes in most other adult heterosexual romance narratives and characterizations as well, erotic romances and their readers are of greatest interest and are the central focus of this book.

By 1983, 50 new series romance titles were appearing on the market each month, at least 30 of which were erotic romances, most of them with contemporary settings. This amounted to 4–5 million copies of erotic series romances per month, or about 55 million per year, a conservative estimate based on an average print run of 150,000 copies (though print runs for some romance lines are known to be as high as 500,000, especially Harlequin and Silhouette, both of which have large foreign sales, and even higher for bestselling authors). Assuming a return rate of 50 percent (see chapter 9), this amounts to annual sales of 25–30 million copies of brand name or series erotic romances per year, which does not include the 30–40 single-title erotic historical and contemporary romances published each month, also with print runs of at least 100,000. Even run-of-the-mill series titles were selling at the rate of 50,000–200,000 copies, most of them with a shelf life of only one month.

Lesbian romance novels have gained some popularity in recent years but do not come close to the numbers associated with heterosexual romances, whether erotic or sweet. Naiad Press editor Barbara Grier (1985) reported that Naiad's most popular romance novel, Katherine V. Forrest's *Curious Wine*, had sold 40,000 copies since publication in May 1983, and "the contemporary novels of Sarah Aldrich certainly fall in [the romance] category and they do comfortable trade paperback sales of 25,000 or so, over a period of time." In 1985 Naiad's list contained 7 titles by Aldrich. By comparison, in 1985 the combined total of series plus single-issue titles, both sweet and erotic, amounted to around 150 new adult paperback romances each month.

Titles in the Harlequin Romance and Presents lines are not included in the quantitative analyses presented here, nor are they included in the count of erotic series romances (above), even though they have to some extent been influenced by the erotic romances (i.e., some explicit sexual content and career-oriented heroines). With a few notable exceptions, however, the character of male-female relationships portrayed in these two lines remains unchanged; they are still, for the most part, unreconstructed domestic stories bearing Harlequin's 1970s trademark—the incomprehensible/cruel hero and the insecure/masochistic heroine.[5] This description does not apply to all romances published by Harlequin, however, and titles from four other Harlequin lines—Temptation, SuperRomance, American, and Intrigue—are included.

The data that inform the text were gathered using four research methodologies: systematic content analyses of more than 100 romance texts published between 1972 and 1985; assessment by readers of the personality traits of heroines and heroes, in both erotic historical romances and erotic contemporary series romances, using a set of semantic differential (opposing adjective) scales; two mail surveys of a national sample of 600 romance readers, conducted in 1982 and 1985; and personal interviews with selected authors, editors, and publishers.[6]

Blumler, Gurevitch, and Katz (1985, 258–59) suggested that it is time for a convergence of uses and gratifications research with other research paradigms or traditions, and they cited three "shared postulates" about the nature of the mass communication process that now make that possible: entertainment is, or may be, political; media impact is a product of the interplay between content features and audience dispositions; the relationship between media discourse and the surrounding social order is complex rather than simple or direct. The assumption of an active audience is inherent in media gratifications research, while investigations of the agenda-setting function of mass media assume that the media both reflect and act as agents of social change (see, for example, McCombs and Shaw 1977). Both of these fundamental assumptions underlie the research questions and methodologies described here, which constitute an examination not only of content and the reciprocal relations of audience motivations and media content recommended by McCombs and Weaver (1985), but also of the relations between producers (media organizations) and audiences. These microlevel data (from individual audience members, about text content, and about interactions between audiences and producers) are placed within a new theoretical framework — the evolutionary paradigm — which allows them to be viewed in the larger context of social system transition.

Chapter 1 is a chronological review of some of the events that contributed to the American sociopolitical environment during the period in which the erotic romance novel emerged and evolved, along with romance novel excerpts that reflect social change that took place during this time. Chapter 2 touches briefly on some of the antecedents of today's romantic fiction. Chapter 3 is a detailed history of the development of the erotic romance as a distinct, large, and popular subgenre (beginning in 1972 in the United States, when it emerged as a type). Also included in this chapter is a calendar which details publishing activity in the romance genre from 1960 to 1985.

Chapter 4 presents the results of a systematic content analysis of more than fifty erotic historical, single-title romances published between 1972 and 1981, as well as readers' assessment of personality traits of heroines and heroes in this type of romance. Chapter 5 presents data from a similar content analysis of more than sixty erotic contemporary series romances published between 1980 and 1985, and readers' assessment of characters portrayed in these kind of texts. Chapter 6 describes the who, what, how much, and why of romance reading, including the demographic characteristics of 500 readers, their reading-buying behavior, and their attitudes toward some of the most significant-to-women issues of our time. Chapter 7 considers the erotic romance as erotica for women, based on the testimony of readers which indicates that these texts serve some of their needs for both sexual information and sexual fantasy.

Chapters 8 and 9 present interviews with specific romance authors and editors, a brief description of romance publishing as a business, and addresses some of the problems inhibiting the effectiveness of the product-consumer relationship that developed during the 1970s and early 1980s. The latter part of chapter 9 examines the changing social and political milieu of the 1980s and the evidence indicating that the romance market is again in a state of transition. Chapter 10 suggests an evolutionary conceptual framework for the study of popular culture and then places the events described here—the evolution of the erotic romance, its readers, and the market and the kind of relationship that developed among these three elements—within this framework. (Readers interested in a more detailed description of the statistical analyses should consult the Appendix.)

Notes

1. For example, Katherine Fishburn's *Women in Popular Culture: A Reference Guide* (1982) gives short shrift indeed to twentieth-century romances, citing only two articles dealing with the modern gothic romance (Russ 1973; Mussell 1975). It seems curious that Fishburn mentioned every other medium Kathryn Weibel (1977) examined in her monograph on images of women in popular culture but made no mention at all that Weibel included modern gothic and Harlequin romances, nor is Harlequin indexed in Fishburn's book.

2. Joanna Russ (1973, 684) concluded that the modern gothic romance heroine "is precious to the Super-Male simply because she exists (like a child) and she is *never* independent"; Kathryn Weibel (1977, xiv), that "romance heroines would *never* make a verbal, much less physical, advance"; Tania Modleski (1982, 65), that "the Gothic heroine *always* feels helpless, confused, frightened and despised"; and Kay Mussell (1984, 11), that "*all* romances share a common perspective. The narrative unfolds from a woman's point of view." A number of ideological position papers also have appeared in popular magazines, such as Martha Nelson's 1983 article for *Ms.*, in which she claimed, "This mingling of pain and love, of humiliation and rapture, is a key element in *all* romance fiction" (p. 98), reinforcing the notion that women are by nature masochistic. (Emphasis added in all examples.)

3. All reader data and comments used throughout this text are drawn from two surveys of a national sample of readers conducted by the author in 1982 and 1985. Demographic and other information about readers is presented in chapters 6 and 7, and in the Appendix.

4. See, for example, J. G. Blumler and E. Katz, eds. (1974), *The Uses of Mass Communications: Current Perspectives on Gratifications Research*, Beverly Hills, Calif.: Sage Publishers; and Karl E. Rosengren, Laurence A. Wenner, and Philip Palmgreen, eds. (1985), *Media Gratifications Research*, Beverly Hills, Calif.: Sage Publishers.

5. Most romance review publications now label Harlequin Romances and Presents as "classic" romances and tend to be highly critical of them. *Rendezvous* (April 1985, 6) commented about *The Only One* that "our hero is a little less cruel than the usual type we see from Ms. (Penny) Jordan"; and Kay Thorpe's *No Gentle Persuasion* "is complete with the offensive Other Woman, arrogant hero, and bewildered heroine." *Romantic Times* (Summer 1985, 40)

was even more negative in its judgment: "Lillian Cheatham demonstrates the unfortunate tendency of this line to confuse violence with sensuality in *Lady with a Past*. Ms. Cheatham is a skilled author who has written very satisfying romance in other forms of the genre; it seems a great pity to waste such a strong talent with this type of book which has less and less appeal in today's market. . . . There is a great deal of violence, both mental and physical, throughout this book, with distasteful protagonists to boot. One wonders when Harlequin will realize that this is not romance at all."

Though shared to some extent with the Canadian office today, editorial control of the Romance and Presents lines remains primarily in England, where it has been since 1957, when Harlequin began publishing Mills and Boon romances under its own imprint. Frances Whitehead ("Market Update," 1986), an editor in the British office, says the "traditional, unsophisticated, naive" Mills and Boon heroine is stronger now, reflecting her American counterpart, and the hero's arrogant behavior has been modified "somewhat," though he is still harder to understand and less open than the usual American hero. Whitehead sees the basic difference as, "in an American romance if the hero were to leave the heroine she would carry on," while "the reader of a Mills and Boon romance must believe that the heroine's life will be totally devastated if she doesn't get her man by the end of the book."

6. Muriel Cantor and Elizabeth Jones (1983) carried out a content analysis of fiction in two women's magazines, *Redbook* and *True Story* (one aimed at middle-class and the other at working-class women), and also obtained information from authors and editors in an attempt to discover how content and writers for the two magazines differed, as well as how the fiction was selected for publication. In contrast with the audiences of these two magazines, the romance readership (as is evident in the statistics on income, education, and employment presented here) cuts across socioeconomic class lines.

Chapter One

WOMEN AND THE
PAPERBACK ROMANCE

The Quest for a New Sexual Identity

At about the same time that the act was passed that
gave votes to women, a solicitor's letter fell into the
post-box and when I opened it I found that my aunt
had left me five hundred pounds a year forever. Of the
two—the vote and the money—the money, I own,
seemed infinitely the more important.
    Virginia Woolf, *A Room of One's Own*

A woman's struggle to define herself against stereotyped images is a theme of current feminist novels and
of fiction affected by feminism.
    Rachel Brownstein, *Becoming a Heroine*

*P*ublished in slowly increasing
numbers throughout the 1950s and 1960s, paperback romance novels
blossomed during the 1970s into a mass entertainment medium that
by 1985 accounted for about 40 percent of all mass market paperback
books published in the United States, with twenty million readers and
close to a half-billion dollars in annual sales.[1] These mostly women
readers say they use romantic fiction for relaxation and entertainment,
fantasy and escape, and, to a lesser extent, information. Certainly
fiction provides more fantasy, escape, and entertainment than other
kinds of literature, but why do these women read romantic fiction in
particular, and why so much of it?

The stage was set for this wunderkind of publishing largely by the
coming together of four sociopolitical phenomena during the 1960s:
the civil rights movement, the new women's movement, the so-called
sexual revolution, and the national debate over the Vietnam War, all
of which stimulated widespread challenges to traditional authority,
institutions, and values. It was a time of foment that produced a social
climate characterized by a sense of moral responsibility for the welfare
of every human being on this earth, indeed, for the welfare of the earth
itself. And the cornerstone of this developing moral code was equality

of opportunity, which would make self-determination possible for everyone, whether black or white, Hispanic or American Indian, rich or poor, able or disabled, male or female—a creed that was given concrete form in civil rights legislation and in the job training, welfare, and consumer and environmental protection programs of the sixties and seventies. It also was reflected in changes that took place in the conventions and assumptions of the traditional romance novel formula.

The birth control pill, introduced in 1960 and frequently cited as the sole provocateur of the sexual revolution, turned out to be an instrument of equalization of the most fundamental kind, becoming both mechanism and symbol in the fight for social and sexual equality, and ultimately political and economic equality. Taking the Pill was a private act that freed women from the bondage of unwanted pregnancy and from control by others, and it caught the imagination of women in a way no other form of birth control had ever done before. It inspired country-western singer Loretta Lynn to express in her own unique way what "The Pill" meant to women everywhere: "All these years I've stayed at home while you had all your fun. . . . There's gonna be some changes made right here on nurs'ry hill. You've set this chicken your last time 'cause now I've got the pill."

Whether myth or reality, the idea that most women were at least sexually inhibited if not actually inadequate had been reinforced by statistics that indicated only a small percentage of women were experiencing orgasm with any regularity during sexual intercourse. Now, armed with the security of an easy-to-use, reliable method of controlling their fertility at a time when equality for women and minorities was high on the national agenda, women began to explore the pleasure to be found in sex, up to now considered primarily a male prerogative. It did not take them long to discover they were woefully uninformed and unprepared to take advantage of this newfound freedom, and that much of the literature reputed to contain "sexual" material was no more than a lesson in anatomy, though to a great many women even that came as something of a revelation. *Our Bodies, Ourselves*, a pioneering work by the Boston Women's Health Book Collective that provided detailed information about reproduction, rape, venereal disease, abortion, and birth control, first appeared as a seventy-five-page newsprint volume in 1966. Expanded and published in hardcover two years later, it was available in seventeen foreign languages and had sold three million copies by the time *The New Our Bodies, Ourselves* appeared in 1985. Denounced by the Moral Majority as "secular humanist garbage," *Our Bodies, Ourselves* put information that women wanted and needed into their own hands, at the same time sending the message that women should and can have a say in their treatment by a male-dominated profession that continued to practice nineteenth-century medicine, at least when the patients were female.[2]

It also did not take most women very long to decide that what was widely reputed to be sexually stimulating to men—particularly pictures of women's bodies—was not stimulating to them. In addition, as Herant Katchadourian and Donald Lunde (1976, 17) wryly observed, "The sight of the female genitals is probably as nearly universal a source of excitement for men as any that exists. Paradoxically viewing the male genitals does not seem to excite women as much, even though men fantasize that it does." Neither prudery nor some inherent inability associated with their function as incubators of the species kept women from responding to material that "turned men on" sexually. It was simply that there was little material of any kind available that spoke to the needs of women.

The Kinsey reports of 1948 and 1953, followed by those of Masters and Johnson in 1966, 1967, and 1970, opened the door to information and public discussion of both male and female sexuality. Research on sexuality blossomed in a number of university and medical settings across the country, employing methods that were nothing short of revolutionary compared with previously accepted protocols. Still, there was little material available that helped women deal with a growing awareness of their own sexual needs, or that women found sexually stimulating. If their physical capacity for sexual response was equal or perhaps superior to that of men, as some sex researchers were suggesting, why was their self-awareness and experience of sexuality so vastly different? For all too many women, the Big O was as elusive as ever. Though the sexual-social climate was changing, the male sexual response and what stimulated it were still the norm, and the primary sexual organ of the female, which was central to women's satisfaction, continued to be something of a mystery, at least to their male partners.

The time was ripe for something to fill the void, something that would provide both a testing ground and a sense of sexual sisterhood, of peer consensus and approval. That is why, when it did emerge, it came from women themselves, in the form of fiction, personal memoirs, and pop psychology dealing with female sexual fantasies, behavior, and needs, such as Erica Jong's *Fear of Flying* and Nancy Friday's *My Secret Garden*, both published in 1973; Shere Hite's *The Hite Report* and Karen Shanor's *The Fantasy File*, in 1977; Irene Kassorla's *Nice Girls Do—and Now You Can Too!*, in 1980; and Sandra Kahn's *The Kahn Report on Sexual Preferences*, in 1981, which compared male and female responses to the same questions. Helen Gurley Brown resurrected a dying *Cosmopolitan* magazine by hyping female sexual activity—continuing the philosophy she put forth in her 1962 *Sex and the Single Girl*, a manual of sorts on how to have and enjoy love affairs—and during the 1970s *Cosmo* became one of several voices treating sex as social prescription rather than a matter of individual choice. Perhaps the most widely read body of writing for and by women, however, and the most consistently overlooked contributor to consciousness-raising among women at the grassroots level, were the popular erotic historical romance novels published during the 1970s.

By 1972, the same year Congress passed the Equal Rights Amendment (first introduced in the early 1920s), women were ready and waiting for what came to be known far and wide as "bodice rippers," a tongue-in-cheek sobriquet said to derive either from the bodice-ripping sexual encounters described in these stories or the hyperventilation women suffered while reading about them. Just as other methods of birth control had been available before the Pill, so other romance novels were being published before these erotic novels burst on the scene, some of them quite similar in character to the bodice rippers. But now thousands of women were ready to explore all kinds of new territory, and a great many of them did so, at least in part, through these lusty tales about feisty heroines who broke over traditional social and sexual traces to embark on high adventure, far from the paths followed by their traditional sisters, only to discover their own sexuality.

The result was that what began as a small brushfire in 1972 with the publication of Kathleen Woodiwiss's *The Flame and the Flower*, quickly raged into a conflagration of passion, possession, piracy, and rape, portraying high-spirited women who ultimately won not only love but more respect and independence than the times in which they lived commonly allowed their sex. These erotic stories about heroines who tried and often succeeded in challenging the male-female power structure were the flip side of the traditional sweet romance (à la Harlequin and Barbara Cartland), and there were very few crossover readers. When sales of erotic historical romances began to soar, several other publishers suffering the effects of a "soft" economy developed or renewed their interest in romance novels, and the number of titles on the market quickly mushroomed.

If the sixties were a time of civil and social disorder, the seventies were the years when the energizing effects of that turbulence came to fruition. The Supreme Court ruled abortion legal in 1973, and women began to pressure state legislatures to ratify the ERA. Two out of every ten marriages ended in divorce that year (Sanoff 1983), and a little more than a half-million unwed couples were living together ("Census Figures," 1982). About 44 percent of all women sixteen years of age or older were in the work force, on the average earning fifty-eight cents for every dollar men were paid.[3]

As more and more women began to question and protest sex-related inequities and injustices, their deepest feelings were echoed with increasing regularity in exchanges between heroes and heroines in erotic historical romance novels, the most avidly consumed form of entertainment for millions of women during this period.[4] When the hero in Lynn Bartlett's *Courtly Love* (Warner Books, 1979, 115) reprimands the heroine for masquerading as a man in order to participate in a jousting tournament, and then asks why she tries so hard "not to be a woman," he gets this heartfelt response:

> "Is that what you think—that I wish to be a man? . . . Perhaps in some respects you are right. I would have others respect me for myself, not merely because I have a passable face or because my body induces lust in some. I have a mind—I think and feel the same as does a man. Do you think the jests of your men and the old lord's family when I came here did not hurt me? They did. . . . To be treated like a possession—an object to be used at someone else's whim, 'tis a degradation I hope you never feel, m'lord. A woman has as much pride, as much honor as a man, but she is treated as if she had none!"

Bartlett's hero also reveals the thoughts such a woman provokes in the man who learns to love her:

> He was trying to understand, but he could not. Every woman was content to be a wife; to be protected, to worry about nothing more pressing than what colors to choose for the tapestry she was making, or whether her new gown should be trimmed in fox or ermine. What need had Serena for more? No other women Gyles had known had troubled him as did Serena, no other had tried to reach his mind rather than his loins, and in doing so Serena had confused him as badly as she herself was confused. (p. 116)

A number of historical romance heroines were articulating their resistance to the idea of marriage, especially in stories set in medieval England, a place and time when the legal structure allowed women some measure of economic independence. When the hero in Grace Ingram's *Gilded Spurs* (Fawcett, 1978, 107), asks the heroine, " 'Don't you wish to marry?' " she responds,

> "Why should I?"
> "But—but do not all women wish—?"
> "To be handed over with a parcel of land to some heavy-fisted lout who fancies the bargain? . . . I've never yet encountered a man I'd willingly be yoked to."
> "But," Guy expostulated, "it is ordained in Holy Writ. . . ."
> "Our Lord said nothing of it."
> "Saint Paul commended, 'Wives, submit yourselves unto your own husbands.' "
> "Saint Paul," she stated unanswerably, "was a man."

By the mid-1970s the number of prosecutions of men charged with rape began to increase dramatically, rape crisis centers were being established all over the country to counsel victims, and women were expressing anger at their perceived vulnerability to this special kind of assault. So, too, were many of the heroines in the bodice rippers: "With a feral snarl, she reared up and swung blindly in his direction with the broken goblet. Saber, though he moved with the speed of a striking snake, could not escape unscathed. Her wild slash caught him diagonally on the ribs, down across his stomach and groin, ending on his thigh. It wasn't deep, but blood was seeping from the jagged wound. He backed away from her, but Nicole stalked him like a maddened animal, intent upon destroying that portion of him that had so recently taken her virginity. Saber eyed her warily. That she had every intention of castrating him was obvious—that she would enjoy it was even more apparent" (Shirlee Busbee, *Lady Vixen*, Avon, 1980, 106–7).

In their struggle for equal justice and respect, these heroines fought many a battle for control over their own bodies, not only with lovers or husbands, but also with the Catholic church. In *Skye O'Malley* (Ballantine, 1980), a bestseller by Bertrice Small, the heroine's sister acts as her midwife twice in ten months. When the sister, a nun, tells Skye she must take an herb potion in order to "rest" between pregnancies, Skye protests, " 'But doesn't the church forbid such wicked practices?' " Her sister answers, " 'The church has not seen innocent babies dying of starvation because there are too many mouths in the family to feed. What do the well-fed priests and bishops, snug in their stone houses on this snowy night, know of these poor souls and their endless torments? The innocent and superstitious poor I offer a "tonic" to help them regain their strength. If they knew what I offer them they would not take it because they truly believe the Church's threat of eternal damnation. You, sister, are not so foolish' " (p. 68).

Erotic romance heroines also began to experience multiple orgasms, a uniquely female phenomenon first given credence by Kinsey, as in Elizabeth Bright's *Passion's Heirs* (Richard Gallen/Pocket Books, 1981, 21): "The flames burst inward and upward. She gasped and clutched his arms . . . just before she again erupted, harder and longer than the other times. . . . As long as he remained hard within her and she could move her hips against him, she continued to erupt into flames which lit her inner explosions."

Though the erotic historical romance conflagration burned brightly for only eight short years and by 1981 had burned down to glowing embers, they were years in which readers flexed purses and pens in increasing numbers to let publishers know that they did not like rapist heroes or "unrealistic" virgin heroines whose sexual participation often was physically forced or in some other way beyond their control. Even if this was a sneaky way to get permission to do something society might not approve (Haskell 1976) or, as Beatrice Faust (1980) suggested, to either indulge in sex before marriage or simply enjoy it, romance readers were ready to move on to something else. The result was that by 1981 editors at the first Romance Writers of America conference in Houston were passing the word to authors that "heroines are older and more mature, the hero no longer gets his ultimate thrill from being first, and no more rape!"

In 1979, women's organizations successfully lobbied for a three-year extension of the deadline for ratification of the ERA, and also began talking about equal pay for comparable work. Determined to achieve not only social and sexual equality but the economic independence to make that possible, more and more women were entering the work force. Many of them moved into traditionally male fields, "not because they were envious of his private parts," as Trisha Flynn (1982) pointed out, "but because they envied his paycheck." Some women became auto mechanics, fire fighters, and astronauts, and more women became veterinarians, stock brokers, lawyers, and physicians than ever before. Not many were successful in working their way into senior management positions, but there was a sizable increase (69 percent between 1972 and 1982) in the number of women who decided to go into business for themselves. Though couched within a historical setting, the conversation between the heroine and a female friend in Valerie Vayle's *Seaflame* (Dell, 1980, 203) undoubtedly reflects the sentiments of many of these women.

> "I have ships of my own," Garlanda said. She was no longer a pretty, pleasant hostess, but a businesswoman.
> "Your husband's you mean?"
> "No. My husband has a shipping line, but I have several vessels that are entirely my own. Three of them are in port now, having just been unloaded. I would send them along to back you up, for a percentage we would discuss later. I would also suggest this not be mentioned to the men. They would almost surely have opinions in the matter which we would probably rather not know."

By 1980, 54 percent of all women sixteen years of age or older were in the labor force, but now they were earning fifty-nine cents for every dollar men took home. Four out of ten marriages were ending in divorce, double the rate of a decade before, and one and a half million unwed couples were living together, three times as many as in 1970 ("Census Figures," 1982). In working outside the home women made changes in traditional lifestyles and sex roles possible, and many couples were both marrying and having children at a later age. (The number of women bearing their first child after the age of thirty tripled between 1960 and 1980.) In a 1982 interview with *U.S. News & World Report*, Census Bureau Director Bruce Chapman interpreted the latest census figures to mean that "the expectation of women now is that they will have a career, marry late, have children, stay home for a period and then resume their careers." And it was not long before romance heroines began to echo his words, in the process making it all sound so terribly easy.

> "This is one of the best things the women's movement did for us," Maureen continued. "Freed us to make real choices. Remember back when women were going to have careers and no children?"
> "Right. Then it was career and children simultaneously, no matter who suffered."
> Maureen's dark eyes danced with understanding and humor. "The Superwoman complex. Then there's the New Wave—us—who think sequentially. I want a career, children and then more career." (Barbara Bretton, *No Safe Place*, Harlequin American Romance, 1985, 187)

Until the end of 1980 there were basically two types of popular romance stories on the market—historical romances that were issued as single titles by a number of publishers, most of them with "sensuous" content (the exceptions being gothic and regency romance novels, which by 1978 constituted a very small percentage of a very large market), and the contemporary sweet romance lines published by Harlequin and a few other houses, generically referred to as brand name, series, or category books.[5] Packaged under logo cover illustrations and issued in a given number at the same time each month, these stories are written to publisher guidelines. During the 1970s most of them were 200 pages or less in length and were sold through both retail stores and reader services, which meant that every title was delivered to readers' homes by mail and therefore readers were choosing books by series name rather than individual author or story.

If the novels written in the 1920s and 1930s by Georgette Heyer, Kathleen Norris, Barbara Cartland, Fannie Hurst, Faith Baldwin, and Daphne du Maurier are viewed as a kind of first wave of popular romance in this century, rolling gently and slowly across the entertainment landscape, then the erotic historical romance was a veritable tidal wave that crested in 1979, and, while still near its peak, metamorphosed into an even higher third wave after the sexual element was introduced into series contemporary romances at the beginning of 1981. Promoted as more realistic—in one the hero lost an arm in the Vietnam War and wears a metal prosthesis in its place—the first of this erotic contemporary breed were two short books issued by Dell as a new line, Candlelight Ecstasy Romances. By the end of 1983 a dozen new contemporary erotic romance lines were on the market, together amounting to more than sixty new titles each month.[6]

These new texts contain the erotic element that until 1980 could be found only in the historical romances, but usually without rape or other kinds of violence. Most heroines are older and sexually experienced. They are also career-oriented, with many holding nontraditional jobs which they rarely give up when they marry. In Samantha Hughes's *Diamonds in the Sky* (Dell Ecstasy Supreme, 1984, 220), for instance, the heroine, a thirty-nine-year-old professional photographer, is dismayed at how "David was talking about a very conventional marriage, a ready-made family [his three children by a previous marriage], and homemade bread. And what about her job? Didn't he know her well enough to know that she had never intended to retire to long lunches, afternoons at the museum, or, God forbid, mornings baking loaves for the church bazaar?"

Though it can be argued that the potential for fantasy is greater in a historical setting because most of what happens is beyond the realm of experience for everyone, there apparently is something equally enticing about fantasies that carry the potential for becoming reality. In the sensuous contemporary romance, one woman's reality—becoming a college professor, a computer programmer, a psychiatrist, a sheriff, or managing a ranch—is another's fantasy, and the evolution of the "liberated" woman is chronicled with ever-increasing breadth and bravado, as the heroine takes full control of her body and her destiny. In a novel about a commuter marriage, which both wife and husband find unsatisfactory, the wife comes very close to giving up marriage rather than her job. She decides to stay with her husband only after getting what she believes is a better job in the same city in which he works (Kate Wellington, *A Delicate Balance*, Berkley/Jove To Have and To Hold, 1984).

The heroine in the erotic romance of the eighties decides with whom, when, and how she will be sexually active, often taking the initiative and sharing control, as in Nora Roberts's *A Matter of Choice* (Silhouette Intimate Moments, 1984, 167):

> Before Slade could rise to carry her to the bed, Jessica was pulling him to the floor. . . . She tugged at the buttons on his shirt, impatient to have his flesh against hers while her mouth was already making wild passes over his face and throat. Her aggression both unbalanced and aroused him. . . . Vulnerability was something new to him, but he found himself trapped in a sultry, viscous world where he had no guards, no defense. . . . This strong man, this hard man, was completely powerless under her spell . . . [and] she realized that she loved him more on finding that he could be weak.

It is generally recognized today that most women value compassion and sensitivity in men above physical prowess and domineering behavior, a change in values that has given rise to a number of books about new sex roles for men, one of the more thoughtful being Mark Gerzon's *A Choice of Heroes: The Changing Faces of American Manhood.* Surely it would be difficult to find a more convincing illustration of just how deeply this change has penetrated our society than the results of a questionnaire given to 100 mothers and their young daughters at a weekend conference on "Understanding Human Sexuality," cosponsored by Planned Parenthood and the Girl Scouts (Kelly 1981). Asked to rank the characteristics they considered most important and attractive in males, these two generations of females put "emotionally strong enough to be unafraid to admit vulnerabilities and weaknesses" at the top of the list, along with gentleness, intelligence, and the ability to express feelings. A domineering personality joined genital size at the bottom of the list. In spite of such evidence, however, many self-styled feminists seem out of touch with grassroots women, as evidenced in Kay Mussell's (1984, 23) assertion that "socialization encourages women to desire strong and dominant men."

Romance authors also are beginning to describe the female sexual response with much greater realism, as in Laura Matthews's *Emotional Ties* (Avon, 1984, 67).

> He slid into her before she was ready and, taken by surprise at what had appeared the midpoint of a lengthy build-up, Sarah had to concentrate on the friction, had to marshal her lazily erotic tinglings into a straggling mass in order to achieve her own orgasm before he spent himself. He seemed unaware of her struggle, merely gratified by her evident release. It wasn't the first time Sarah had found herself lagging, and she was never sure whether her body, or a man's timing, was at fault. Perhaps a little of both, she decided. "Sometimes I need a little more preparation than others. I almost didn't catch up with you."
>
> "God, I'm sorry," he apologized . . . "you didn't fake an orgasm, did you?"
>
> "No, I don't do that. But I had to work at it, and it's not as much fun that way."
>
> He looked puzzled. "Work at it? How do you do that?"
>
> "Well, I concentrate," she said, a little embarrassed. "And sometimes I fantasize. Not tonight. Instead of just sort of letting it happen, slowly and surely, I have to think about the sensations, focus them like a magnifying glass on paper, so they'll leap into flames."

By 1984 there was a feast of sexually stimulating (to women) material openly and broadly available in a broad array of retail outlets — drugstores, newsstands, discount chains, and the great American supermarket — and women were free to pick and choose according to their individual needs or fancies. Though without conscious intent or plan, in rejecting rape as sexual fantasy the great majority of romance readers had freed themselves to recognize and embrace the role of erotica in developing their own sexuality, and ultimately a sense of self. And for those who have caught even a glimpse of this elusive self, the idea-reality is a veritable Circe, endlessly beckoning, beguiling, and transforming. The very words "sense of self" seem to puzzle many men, perhaps because they have never been without it. But they also have not been defined for most of their lives in terms of their relationship or lack of it to the opposite sex, nor have they been systematically denied their very humanity. As Gerda Lerner (1982, 14–15) pointed out in her presidential address to the Organization of American Historians, "All women have in common the fact that their history comes to them refracted through the lens of men's observations and refracted again through a male-centered value system. The historic condition unique to women is that, for more than 5,000 years, they have been excluded from constructing history as a cultural tradition and from giving it meaning. Women have not held power over symbols and thus have been truly marginal to one of the essential processes of civilization."

Roberta Gellis is among the authors who have elevated the romance genre into the realm of "literature" with her unfailingly meticulous historical research and unforgettable characters, portrayed in more than fifteen historical romance novels published over two decades. In her first book, *Knight's Honor* (Doubleday and Curtis, 1964, 281), Gellis's heroine ultimately comes to recognize the relationship between her developing sexuality and her sense of self, as well as the effect of both on the quality of her relationship with her partner:

> Her sexual satisfaction, established and repeated so that she had confidence in her ability to give and receive that pleasure at will, removed an immense core of frustration and unhappiness that Elizabeth had not known to exist until its weight was lifted from her soul. Moreover she had discovered that, yielding this, she had gained everything and lost nothing, so that she was sure that the more she gave Roger throughout her life the more he would give her of trust and confidence in return. Most important of all, however, was that she knew she would not need to sit still in fear and ignorance, waiting, waiting.

The primary opposition in the fight for ratification of the ERA during the late 1970s was Phyllis Schlafly's "Eagle Forum," whose members lobbied state legislators with homebaked cookies. One reason Schlafly (1986) and her group oppose the ERA is that "it would eliminate the obligation of a husband to support his wife, a right that women traditionally have had in this country by state law—we think good laws." Another version of this philosophical stance appeared in the books of Marabel Morgan, who asserted that a woman's primary role and happiness were to be found in pleasing the man in her life, in return for which he would take care of her. In one section of *Total Joy* (1978, 97) titled "365 Ways to Fix Hamburger," Morgan assured readers that "a wife has the potential to turn on her husband time after time for a lifetime, but like hamburger, you may have to prepare yourself in a variety of different ways now and then. Like 365, or 183."

In *Only a Housewife*, one of a pioneering series of stories called Love and Life: Women's Stories for Today, published by Ballantine between 1981 and 1983, Stephanie Austin created a heroine-wife who, bored and trying to put more zest into her marriage, joins W.I.F.E. (Womanly Ideal of Feminine Excitement), an organization dedicated to instructing women how to "turn their husbands on." In what must surely be a parody of Morgan's woman-as-hamburger, Austin's heroine resorts to using a bonbon to entice her husband to perform cunnilingus. However, when he discovers a chocolate "in the warm woods between her thighs," he is so turned off he leaves the house muttering darkly about degradation. In the end, the two lovers are reunited, but only after the wife has gone back to school and begins to develop her own interests and life goals.

When the June 1982 deadline arrived, the ERA was three states short of ratification. Almost immediately reintroduced in Congress with more than two hundred sponsors (some of whom later voted against it), the amendment failed to win approval in the House in 1983 by six votes. In 1984 Congress passed legislation requiring states to help mothers who do not receive court-ordered child support whether on welfare or not, and also a pension equity bill that provides pension protection to working women and spouses of workers. A federal court ruled in favor of female state employees seeking equal pay for comparable work, finding that the state of Washington had systematically underpaid female employees, and returned an $800 million judgment against the state ("Michigan Employees," 1984). The FBI reported that the incidence of rape had increased 51 percent since 1973, in part because more rapes were being reported and prosecuted (Mouat 1983), and for the first time a husband was convicted of raping his wife while living with her. By 1985 twenty-three states plus the District of Columbia had new laws or court decisions making marital rape a criminal offense ("Marital Rape," 1985).

In 1984, with 63 percent of all women aged sixteen to sixty-four in the civilian work force, they were carrying home only sixty-two cents for every dollar paid to a man, in spite of the fact that slightly more than half of all college graduates now were women. Economist David Bloom (in Castro 1985, 64) called the growth of women in the work force "probably the single most important change that has ever taken place in the American labor market," and he predicted that "their arrival at high executive levels will be the major development for working women over the next 20 years."

In 1985, after it was reintroduced in Congress yet again, women were still fighting for passage of the ERA with a tenacity echoed in Parris Afton Bonds's *Widow Woman* (Silhouette Intimate Moments, 1984, 131), when the heroine asks the hero, a Mexican-American labor organizer, why so many of his "lieutenants" are women: " 'I've learned that women have something very special, Cass—staying power. With men it's always we *want* it, let's *do* it. We want to finish it up in seconds. But women just keep going. If a man is full of machismo, he can't appreciate what women do. But if he's not . . . well, it's really something beautiful.' "

The nomination of a woman for vice president in 1984 elicited a number of stories in the mass media about the changed roles and status of women. Abigail Trafford (1984a, 50), in a *U.S. News & World Report* cover story titled "She's Come a Long Way—or Has She?" observed that "the new women of the 1980s are slowly showing up in books, films and television shows, appearing as wage earners and family heads instead of as stereotypical bumbling housewives, frustrated man chasers and sexual vamps." Distributed by the millions, the most popular type of paperback romance novels on the market already had begun doing just that a decade earlier, both reflecting and acting as agent of continuing social change. In the process, they were reconstructing history for women, sending the message to women everywhere that the drive for dignity and respect has motivated and united women for centuries.

> "What have you always wanted, from the very beginning, John, even when you were a little boy?" Failing to elicit a response, she provided him with one. "Freedom, dignity, the right to pursue your own destiny, the opportunity to make those decisions that affect and influence your spirit and soul and body." She paused. "We are no different from you, John. Oh, our physiology is different, but that's all. And the difference does nothing to alter our hearts or our minds or our needs. For years, centuries, we've tried to convince each other that it does. But it doesn't, not in any fundamental or profound way." (Marilyn Harris, *Women of Eden*, Ballantine, 1980, 593)

In her monograph on the women novelists she called "new realists" —Jane Austen, Charlotte Brontë, Elizabeth Gaskell, Edith Wharton, and Virginia Woolf—Anthea Zeman (1977, 2) said these writers recognized the "serious women's novel" as a way to report to women on the

110 07110-8-$2.50 Silhouette Intimate Moments

The Male
Chauvinist
Alexandra Sellers

"new freedoms, lost ground, new dangers, new possibilities of emotional tax-evasion, and up-to-date reminders of those bills which still have to be paid." That description also fits the most evolved romance novels today, for whether consciously intended or not, some of the fundamental assumptions and values portrayed in these novels during the past decade and a half match those issuing from the women's movement. One such is Alexandra Sellers's *The Male Chauvinist* (Silhouette Intimate Moments, 1984, 8−9), which opens with the heroine swimming topless at a beach in Greece while mulling over in her mind the arbitrary social constrictions placed on women in American society:

> Why was her freedom being dictated like this by a simple question of geography? . . . For years she had felt hampered by the moral code that dictated the particular parts of her body that must remain covered in her particular society; she had felt it alien to herself. No inner voice had ever told her that certain parts of her body were shameful. . . . So, if [covering those parts of her body] was not instinctive in women . . . what had caused the taboo in the first place? Or who? Well, monotheistic religion, for a start. Judaism, Christianity and Islam all seemed to have gone a little rabid on the subject of female modesty. But of course all the great monotheistic religions had more in common than the One God: they were all also fiercely male-supremacist. . . . [But] while women saw this new trend as establishing ownership over their own bodies, men were simply abandoning the importance they had previously given the area called *breast*, and were satisfied that their ownership was still signified by that one area of the body still left covered.

That the audiences for erotic romance novels have for the most part been different from and much larger than those for today's "serious women novelists" has been crucial in helping to achieve the kind of changes in women's lives that have, as Rena Bartos (1979, 272) observed, "permeated the hearts and minds of all women, whether or not they themselves have gone to work and whether or not they themselves live in traditional life styles."

Notes

1. These figures have been used repeatedly in *Publishers Weekly* and other trade publications. The readership figure has been in use at least since 1981; both Rosemary Guiley (1983, 2) and Eileen Fallon (1984, 60) cited 20 million romance readers, as did *Newsweek* in 1982 (May 10, 82). Guiley also reported 150 new romance titles per month and 450−500 million dollars in sales in

1983, and that romance novels made up nearly 50 percent of the entire paper-back market at that time (p. 2). In 1982, John Gfeller, then president of Silhouette Books, estimated that the romance market was growing at the rate of between 15 and 25 percent a year.

2. It was not until the 1930s, for example, that the female ovarian cycle was understood by American doctors. Diana Scully and Pauline Bart (1973, 287) examined gynecology textbooks used in medical schools over the previous thirty years and found that "in the last two decades at least half of the texts that indexed topics stated that the male sex drive was stronger than the female's; she was interested in sex for procreation more than for recreation. In addition, they said most women were 'frigid' and that vaginal orgasm was the 'mature' response." The women's health movement is reflected in a number of romance plots: for example, Pamela Browning's *Cherished Beginnings* (Harlequin American Romance, 1985), in which the heroine is a nurse-midwife who battles the male medical establishment's control over and treatment of women giving birth. An even stronger, and certainly more eloquent, protest of the way the medical profession has treated women historically is found in Barbara Wood's *Domina* (NAL/Signet, 1984), with a fictional heroine modeled in part on the life of Elizabeth Blackwell, the first American woman to earn a medical degree.

3. Unless noted otherwise, all figures for women in the work force and the earning differential between men and women are from the U.S. Department of Labor bulletin *20 Facts on Women Workers* (1985).

4. It takes anywhere from one to four months to write a short series book and up to two years for a "big book," and generally about one year elapses between manuscript purchase and publication of a romance novel. Thus the narratives excerpted here probably were written one to three years prior to publication.

5. The word "category" is one of the most ambiguous in the romance publishing business, used variously by both editors and agents to mean genre or formula writing (as when a book is said to be "out of category"), as well as to refer to series romances that are written to publisher-specified guidelines, packaged between covers that carry numbers and some kind of logo, all of which are issued together and in a given number at the same time each month. The term "category romance" as used herein is synonymous with romance line or series, sometimes also called brand-name books; one of the latter terms generally is used for purposes of clarity.

6. Single-title erotic historical romance novels continued to be published during this time, though in somewhat diminished numbers, adding another thirty to forty new romance titles to the sixty-five category titles available each month. Within about four years, however, after the category romance market appeared to hit a saturation point and flatten out, the erotic historical romance experienced a resurgence of popularity.

Chapter Two

VIRTUE AND SEXUALITY

IN WOMEN

And Never the Twain Shall Meet?

From an early age, we are alienated from ourselves as
sexual beings by a male society's ambivalent definition
of our sexuality; we are sexy, but we are pure; we are
insatiable, but we are frigid; we have beautiful bodies,
but we must paint and shave and deodorize them. We
are also alienated because we are separated from our
own experience by the prevailing male cultural definition of sex—the male fantasy of active man and
passive woman.

Linda Phelps, "Female Sexual Alienation"

Priests preached so often the lustful nature of women,
who seduced men from the path of virtue, as Eve had
seduced Adam into eating the apple. The suspicion
was always buried somewhere in a man's mind, even
those men who thought they believed implicitly in the
love and virtue of their wives. The preaching had its
effect on women, too. However sure they might be of
their own honesty, they sadly accepted the general
statement.

Roberta Gellis, *Alinor*

*I*n a work that has become a kind
of bible among scholars of formula writing—which he described as "a
combination or synthesis of a number of specific cultural conventions
with a more universal story form or archetype"—John Cawelti (1976,
41) said, "The crucial defining characteristic of the [modern] romance
is not that it stars a female, but that its organizing action is the
development of a love relationship, usually between a man and a
woman. . . . The moral fantasy of the romance is that of love trium-
phant and permanent, overcoming all obstacles and difficulties." What
specific cultural conventions, especially gender attributes, sex-role
portrayals, and power relationships, are thought to characterize the

romance novel? What seem to have been the most tenaciously unchanging, thereby traditional, conventions of popular women's fiction?

A number of scholars take issue with Cawelti's disclaimer about the female "star," arguing that both a female protagonist and a female readership are characteristics so defining as to be responsible for the genre's long history of negative critical treatment and neglect. As Margaret Jensen (1984) pointed out, Cawelti himself lent considerable credence to this view in giving surprisingly short shrift to the romance —one and a half pages—in a 300-page volume titled *Adventure, Mystery and Romance*. Annette Townend (1984) cites critical judgment of the romance as "unserious" literature as early as the end of the sixteenth century, which she believes was the result of the shift from a male to a female protagonist, as well as the transition to a single-sex readership. Romances became, as it were, inferior or weak fiction for the weaker sex.

While many scholars point to Samuel Richardson's *Pamela* and *Clarissa*, both published in the 1740s, and the so-called seduction novel as the precursors of modern popular fiction for women, Nina Baym (1978, 12) instead cites the "women's fiction" that appeared between 1820 and 1870, written by and for American women (called variously "domestic" and "domestic sentimental" by other scholars). Baym argues that these novels are the wellspring of contemporary women's fiction because they are about "the formation and assertion of a feminine ego," about achieving a sense of self-worth as a female rather than remaining a permanent child. Much like Helen Papashvily before her, Baym interprets the essential message carried by these novels as "a moderate, or limited, or pragmatic feminism, which is not in the least covert but quite obvious, needing only to be assessed in mid-nineteenth-century terms rather than those of a later century to be recognized for what it is. That is, it was a feminism constrained by certain other types of beliefs that are less operative today" (p. 18). All of these novels "tell, with variations, a single tale. . . . They chronicle the 'trials and triumph' of a heroine who, beset with hardships, finds within herself the qualities of intelligence, will, resourcefulness, and courage sufficient to overcome them" (p. 22).

Though many of these fictional women achieved no more than an intangible moral victory over the men and circumstances that oppressed them, certainly E. D. E. N. Southworth's Capitola, as Papashvily (1956, 126–27) described her, was a New Heroine: "Spirited, beautiful, independent, unafraid, she flouted her guardian . . . fought a duel with a gentleman who slandered her and shot him full of dried peas; she outwitted [the villain]; she foiled the brigand Black Donald and his henchman sent to kidnap her; she laughed at everyone including herself, thumbed her nose at her enemies, stuffed herself with tarts and 'abhorred sentiment'." An 1859 bestseller, *Capitola* was so popular that "women wore Capitola hats and suits in honor of the heroine. Towns, boats, and hotels appropriated her magic name. Forty dramatic versions were made, and one or more eventually played in almost every city in the United States" (p. 128).

It was during this same half century, according to Baym, that American women became both authors and readers, solidifying the American female-fiction partnership that has continued unabated to the present, when an estimated 70 percent of all fiction readers are female. Reading and writing these novels was, and continues to be, a way for women to rebel against their domestic imprisonment—an interpretation that gains considerable credence through the voices of women readers today, articulated variously as a need to escape, as the need for privacy and "some time to myself," and a way of "staking out my own territory." Indeed, a number of romance readers surveyed in both 1982 and 1985 reported that their husbands often reacted to their reading at two levels: hostility to the activity itself ("Why don't you watch TV with me . . .) and then to what was being read (". . . instead of reading that garbage"). Thus, the very act of reading at times is an assertion of independence.

Strong women though the nineteenth-century heroines might be, acting out of conscience and high moral standards, even becoming activists for political and social reform, they could not experience success in these areas except vicariously, through a man. Their public participation was legally restricted in the societies and times in which they lived, and their primary proving ground was the domestic or private sphere. Baym (1978) makes a distinction between "domestic," meaning descriptive of where events take place, and the "cult of domesticity," meaning fulfillment for women in marriage and motherhood. She argues that this fiction was domestic only in the sphere in which most women operated. Papashvily (1956, xvi) also points out that it was the common woman who was glorified, whose "petty trials and small joys [were] magnified to heroic proportions."

The overriding social context of the late nineteenth century was characterized by what Sheila Rothman (1978) called the "virtuous woman concept." Heroines rarely were allowed to develop as sexual, whole beings, and women authors of the time were, in Baym's (1978, 18) words, "both as Christians and as Victorians, disinclined to acknowledge the body and physical sexuality as elements of self either inherently spiritual or capable of being spiritualized. Especially where sexual politics was concerned . . . , they saw themselves as disadvantaged compared to men. Hence rather than integrating physical sexuality into their adult personalities they tried to transcend it." Women found themselves in the paradoxical situation of being at the same time defined solely in relation to their gender and denied the right to a natural, self-controlled sexuality, which Dorothy Sayers (1947, 142–49) described as "a period when empty head and idle hands were qualities for which a man prized his woman and despised her. . . . When to think about sex was considered indelicate in a woman, and to think about anything else unfeminine. When to 'manage' a husband by lying and the exploitation of sex was held to be honesty and virtue."

Much of the fiction for women, from the time of the medieval romance to the eighteenth-century seduction novel to nineteenth-century women's fiction and continuing even in twentieth-century modern gothics, has been characterized by the schizoid portrayal of the female persona, with supposedly gender-related personality attributes split between two characters: the chaste, self-sacrificing, domestic, tractable heroine and the sexy, impulsive, selfish, and aggressive Other Woman. This pervasive and long-lived portrayal has served not only as parable or morality tale but also to define womanliness for women themselves. In her analysis of domestic sentimental and gothic novels, Kay Mussell (1978, 151) concluded that "women are cast as victims in a man's world, but through demonstration of feminine virtues, the victim proves herself worthy of the love of the hero, who becomes her deliverer from the terrors that beset her." But the feminine virtues associated with becoming a good wife and mother did not include a sexuality that speaks to either self-awareness or self-expression. Sexuality for the heroine, by definition the "good" woman, was covert and generally had meaning only in relation to her reproductive function or her capacity to arouse desire in males.

The domestic novel continued to be popular in both Great Britain and America after the turn of the century (e. g., works by Kathleen Norris, Emilie Loring, Faith Baldwin, and Fanny Hurst), along with domestic-religious parables of the type written by Grace Livingston Hill, which are reprinted even today. The historical romance was gaining in popularity, however, especially the regency romance, a tale of manners and morals that took inspiration from Jane Austen's *Pride and Prejudice*. Set in the period between 1811 and 1820, during which the Prince of Wales served as Prince Regent for an incapacitated King George III, the protagonist of the regency romance is an innocent young woman who is dominated and victimized by a cruel and conniving father/brother/guardian/stepmother. The heroine assumes the role of standardbearer of morality and social conscience, guardian of the family as an institution, and welfare worker among the less fortunate and the oppressed. The hero is a virile, rich, aristocratic rake who spends his time sampling the sensual delights of the beau monde — fine clothes and fine horseflesh, balls and routs, gaming hells and racing curricles, and his pick of the beauties at Almack's. The women who warm his bed are not only sexy but also witty, sophisticated, aggressive, selfish — and expensive (Stevenson 1984).

Georgette Heyer, a British writer of some feminist sensibility and skill whose work first appeared in 1921, was probably the best of the modern regency romance authors and is still considered so by many of today's readers. Heyer's heroines, though young and inexperienced, are far from submissive, tending instead to be quick-witted and witty, independent-minded, enterprising, and articulate. A prolific writer until 1975, in more than one genre, Heyer inspired a number of other writers, among them the also prolific and long-lived Barbara Cartland, who has honed the "poor little Cinderella" plot line to a dull edge.[1]

It is the regency romance, and especially Cartland's variations on the theme and Cartland herself, as a highly publicized personality, dripping with furs, jewelry, and pink prose, that have fueled the most tenaciously held stereotype of the popular romance novel, heroine, and author today.[2] By 1985 (at the age of eighty-four), Cartland had written more than 370 short, ellipses-filled tales of love, all of them based on a plot line that has changed little, if any, in fifty years: a delicate little ingenue with heart-shaped face ultimately is "saved" from her depraved stepmother or the old lecher to whom her father has sold her or from freezing to death in the poorhouse by a worldly duke who has through extensive experience become disenchanted with women. Cartland's heroines operate under the imperative to respect and "honor thy father" — or any other member of her family — even if she is beaten senseless or sold to pay off gambling debts. Secondary female characters are either sexually insatiable, malicious, and exotic, or cruel and greedy mother-in-law stereotypes. The heroine appeals to the hero's protective instincts and restores his faith in women, ultimately transforming him through her own goodness and purity. For example, in *Love Leaves at Midnight* (Bantam, 1978, 138):

> "Tell me—tell me by all that you hold sacred—as if you were in the presence of God Himself, that you have never belonged to another man, that no man has ever touched you."
> "Th-that is . . . true," Xenia whispered again.

Cartland heroines are invariably small, soft, gentle, quiet, and spiritual, exemplifying traditional femininity. They also are inarticulate in the extreme when it comes to expressing feelings or emotion (*Love Is Mine*, Pyramid, 1972/1952, 278): "I am yours . . . yours forever . . . and ever. Do you . . . understand?" Ellipses, another of the author's trademarks, are used both to eat space and underscore the heroine's inexperience and insecurity. For Cartland heroines, marriage means protection, submission, and service to others, and it is their highest ambition in life; for heroes, marriage conveys the right of possession and control—over the heroine's heart, mind, soul, body, and property. After the ceremony he "transports her up to the stars," a euphemism for sexual intercourse.

Quite a different tale stunned the public and stirred the embers of the female erotic imagination in 1921, the same year Georgette Heyer's first romance was published. Soon after the end of World War I and the extension of suffrage to women, and in the midst of an almost unparalleled period of innovation in music, art, and literature, Edith M. Hull took a proper British heroine on an adventure far from the security of the mundane domestic setting. In *The Sheik*, a story so popular it is considered by some to be the first romance of the twentieth century, Hull posited the unlikely pairing of a cold, class-conscious socialite with a hot-blooded Arab sheik who kidnaps and holds her captive in his tent in the desert. Between them develops a love so intense and consuming that it overcomes their apparently vast social and cultural differences, a love unmistakably more physical than spiritual.

In common with most of her predecessors, Hull depicts a hero ultimately obsessed and enslaved by love, the source of the heroine's power, though initially he demands a formidable level of submission from the object of his desire. *The Sheik* broke the pattern of the traditional seduction novel, however, in allowing Lady Diana Mayo to be both seduced and virtuous, a fantasy that had, and to some extent still has, great appeal to women readers. (Transported across the ocean, *The Sheik* became the most popular silent film ever made and transformed its male star, Rudolph Valentino, into a cult figure.) What is even more interesting about *The Sheik*, however, is the twist it puts in the submission tale. Raised by her brother, Diana Mayo is an independent-minded young woman who scorns all things feminine, so has thrown over the social norms of her culture even before she is kidnapped by Sheik Ahmed ben Hassan. Her "masculine" attitudes and behavior are further underscored by her physical form, which is described as boyish, and it is her independent behavior—traveling alone and unprotected—that makes her vulnerable to kidnapping. In requiring her submission, Ahmed (who it turns out is English himself) forces Diana both to conform to her own culture's norms and to discover herself as a woman through what begins as a purely physical relationship.

Though more antiromance than romance, Margaret Mitchell's *Gone with the Wind*, a 1936 bestseller, is still cited as an all-time favorite by many romance readers. Mitchell's heroine is a spoiled, self-centered Southern Belle with many of the Other Woman's attributes, who both rejects traditional domesticity and is in love with the wrong man. The Other Woman is domestic, syrupy sweet, tractable, and self-sacrificing in the extreme—after all, what good wife would deny her husband's pleasure, even if the result (pregnancy) should mean her death? Tara, Scarlett's beloved land, is the center of her life, and in spite of her selfish willfulness, she is a woman who overcomes—to save her home, her family, and all those who are dependent on her—through toughness and ingenuity, attributes generally assigned to males. Though Rhett leaves her in the end, it is Scarlett's indomitable spirit that leaves readers with hope for the future—with or without him—providing a different but nonetheless happy ending of sorts.

Historical novels written by women and with female protagonists became more and more popular in the 1940s, 1950s, and 1960s. Among them were Kathleen Winsor's *Forever Amber* (1944), about a sexy Cinderella who, as the cover blurb describes her, "rose from the teeming streets of London to become the most sought-after woman in Restoration England—and the man she desired was the king of England." Jan Westcott, called the "Queen of Historical Romance" in spite of the fact that some of her stories did not have happy endings, created strong, independent-minded heroines who were "fair and wayward" (*The Border Lord*, 1946) or "beautiful and seductively intelligent" (*Captain for Elizabeth*, 1948). This kind of heroine begins to appear with ever-increasing frequency, in Anya Seton's *Katherine* (1954) and

Jan Cox Speas's *Bride of the McHugh* (1954) and *My Lord Monleigh* (1956), in which the heroine spends a "night of love on the moors" with Scotland's most notorious traitor, who "found in her green eyes a wild spirit to match his own." The first two of Roberta Gellis's historical novels with strong female protagonists appeared in 1964 (*Knight's Honor*) and 1965 (*Bond of Blood*), foreshadowing her later six-volume Roselynde Chronicles set in medieval England (*Roselynde, Alinor, Joanna, Gilliane, Rhiannon,* and *Sybelle*), complete sets of which are now collector's items among romance readers. Gellis's best books excel in character development and historical background, and though she often includes vivid sexual description it is there to enhance the reader's understanding of both the characters and the time in which they lived.[3]

In 1960 the first of what was to become a nine-volume series (which by 1985 had sold a total of fourteen million copies) was published in the United States as a paperback reprint. Written by a French husband-wife team, Serge and Anne Golon (as Sergeanne Golon), and set during the seventeenth century, *Angelique* is notable not only for a transformed heroine but also a new hero. At seventeen Angelique marries the disfigured and crippled Comte Joffrey de Peyrac. Her sexual initiation is described as an experience in self-discovery—"the abrupt revelation she had of her own body overwhelmed her," and "she gave him a smile which possessed a seductiveness of which she was not yet aware, for a new Angelique had been born in a matter of minutes, a free, fulfilled Angelique" (pp. 197–98)—a convention this and many other historical novels share with much of Victorian erotica. Joffrey is an elusive and idealistic hero, an agnostic in a religious age, whose free-thinking ideas and interest in science cause his apparent burning at the stake. Subsequently, he appears infrequently, though his presence is often felt as the mysterious Mediterranean pirate Rescator. He is a strong but gentle man who loves not only their two sons but also Angelique's daughter, conceived during a gang rape.

A romantic adventure that goes far beyond the emotional or geographical scope of *The Sheik*, the Golon stories constitute the saga of a heroine who treks across the world to encounter one lover (subhero) after another, some of whom are antiheroes. Along the way she develops into a mature, strong, self-reliant woman, who above all else learns that when the chips are down there is only one person she can really count on—herself! Angelique is just one of many heroines (including the more recent Skye O'Malley) who disprove the claim that "once a woman's love story has been told, repetition of the experience for her is inappropriate—repetition would, in fact, undermine the entire premise of her story—her life is, for dramatic purposes, over" (Mussell 1984, 6). A host of students of the romance genre, it would appear, could not possibly have met Angelique and still believe that romance is virtually the only adventure that literature allows to females.

Also called romantic suspense, the modern gothic romance reached its peak of popularity in the United States during the 1960s, after paperback reprints of stories by Mary Stewart, Victoria Holt, Nora Lofts, and Dorothy Eden became widely available. This twentieth-century version of the gothic gives as much attention to the developing love relationship as to the mystery; more often than not the two are the same, a plot device exemplified in the title of Joanna Russ's 1973 article, "Somebody's Trying to Kill Me and I Think It's My Husband: The Modern Gothic." The frequently cited prototype of the modern gothic romance is Daphne du Maurier's *Rebecca*, published in 1938 and essentially a retelling of *Jane Eyre;* Victoria Holt's *Mistress of Mellyn* (1960) is an unabashed retelling of *Rebecca*.

Rebecca is the Other Woman, and though she is already dead when the story opens, she is a formidable adversary—sophisticated, self-confident, and beautiful, all the things the plain, naive, awkward, and thoroughly inadequate second Mrs. de Winter is not. The heroine has such a poor opinion of herself, in fact, that she cannot believe the handsome and rich Maximillian de Winter could possibly be in love with her. Why he married her is only one of several questions she cannot bring herself to ask out loud. In the end, it turns out that Max loves her for the very attributes she was so sure made her unlovable: her physical plainness, unassuming goodness, loyalty, her dependency on him, and, of course, her sexual naiveté.

Much of the scholarly criticism of the modern gothic not only vilifies the heroine as dependent, submissive, helpless, frightened, and confused (see Russ 1973; Weibel 1977; Modleski 1982) but interprets her role as domestic in the traditional, or cult of domesticity, sense. Kay Mussell (1975, 88) concluded that "almost all of the contrasts between the conventionally domestic heroines and the passionate women occur in the context of competition between women in male-female relationships, indicating that such rivalry is a basic assumption of gothic novels"; the formula "proves" that if women fail to fulfill traditional roles (motherhood and nurturing others), then the family is in trouble, because women who are interested in sex rather than motherhood cannot hold it together. Radway (1981, 150), too, found that "female sexuality may be combined with active independence only if that independence expresses itself in something other than a woman's sexual behavior." She advocated an elaborate analysis of the narrative, not just the endings, found feminist elements in the developing stories, then based her conclusions only on the endings because despite their pretensions as feminist novels, gothic romances are fundamentally reactionary in asserting that the "feminist goals of individual fulfillment and independence can be achieved through the maintenance of traditional male-female relations" (p. 160).

Josephine Ruggiero and Louise Weston (1977) arrived at quite a different conclusion after developing a classification system that takes into account both psychological and sociological dimensions of sex-role characterizations, which they used to categorize female characters as traditional, mixed, or nontraditional. They found that while heroines and supporting female characters are portrayed differently in the gothic, it is the Other Woman (the negative role model) who is more likely to be the traditional woman: "Heroines, while certainly not liberated in the extreme, are portrayed as rather independent women who have strong convictions and are not overly worried about public opinion. They frequently view their lives as containing a number of options or alternatives and tend to see marriage and motherhood as only one of these possibilities. . . . More often than not, marriage may be a pleasant by-product of the heroine's involvement in career and/or adventure goals" (pp. 294, 296).

Simultaneously with the modern gothic in the United States, domestic fiction for women got a new lease on life when Harlequin, a Canadian paperback reprint house, began distributing British Mills and Boon romances under its own imprint in 1957 (distributed in the United States primarily after 1970, when Pocket Books became Harlequin's American distributor). Basically Barbara Cartland—type stories in modern dress, these Mills and Boon/Harlequin novels have heroines who are "loving people who often care more about others than they do about themselves. The most outstanding character traits of a heroine are her warmth, compassion and generosity. . . . [They] are also honest, sincere, pure and innocent" (Jensen 1984, 84). In a 1984 radio series she produced for the Canadian Broadcasting Company, Claire Harrison described the sexuality of the heroine in pre-1980, British formula Harlequins as covert and repressed: "A young English girl, virginal and orphaned, travelled to an exotic Mediterranean locale and fell in love with the hero, who was dark, brooding, masterful and wealthy. The heroine was either a nurse, governess or secretary, or maybe had no job at all. The conflict between the protagonists that kept the plot moving was a thin disguise for the real issue at hand: his lust versus her virginal resistance. . . . The hottest sexual moment in these books was 'the kiss' " (p. 2).

Anne Snitow (1979, 144) came to a similar conclusion: "Virginity is a given here; sex means marriage, and marriage, promised at the end, means, finally, there can be sex." Though the Harlequin heroine "tries to cover up all signs of sexual feeling, upset, any extreme of emotion," Snitow found in these stories a "sexually-charged atmosphere throughout," and that the heroine "lies constantly to hide her desire, to protect her reputation" (p. 148). Rosemary Guiley (1983, 155) also described the early Harlequins as featuring "young, usually virginal heroines pursued by older, more sophisticated, usually arrogant men. The heroines always won a marriage proposal, usually after their pristine virtue subdued the challenge from a nasty 'other woman.' The books were exceedingly chaste by today's standards — mostly the heroines just got kissed, grabbed, pushed around and sexually threatened by the heroes."

Not a few critics have pointed to the gothic as well as domestic novel elements in these Harlequins, concluding that these purportedly chaste stories are, in fact, neither sweet nor innocuous. Tania Modleski (1980, 439) found that "although the hero of Harlequins is not suspected of being insane or murderous, he *is* more or less brutal," and ultimately "male brutality comes to be seen as a manifestation, not of contempt, but of love," thereby perpetuating the confusion of male sexuality with male violence. "A great deal of our satisfaction in reading these novels comes, I am convinced, from our conviction that the woman is bringing the man to his knees and that all the while he is being so hateful, he is internally groveling, groveling, groveling . . ." (p. 441). Mariam Frenier (1981, 39) went a step further in arguing that "Harlequins tell wives that if they behave like battered women they will obtain and keep a good marriage." [4]

Weibel (1977, 38) described all modern romances (gothic, Harlequin, and historical) as basically alike, the differences between them being so minor "they might not seem worth mentioning fifty years hence." She concluded her analysis of the images of women in popular fiction with a short scenario that suggests the romance is and will forever remain the same old story: "Alone in the world created by her own mind and by the book in her hands — the woman of the fifties (and the sixties and the seventies) returned to the safety of the familiar fantasy. Climbing into the heroine's chaste and barely pretty body, she turned back the clock to her future housewife days, becoming again a passive and sought after young woman—who would be claimed, dominated, even loved just for the price of existing" (pp. 44—45).

Even when all of the varying interpretations are accepted, two of the sturdiest cultural conventions of women's fiction and romance—from the eighteenth-century seduction novels and nineteenth-century women's fiction, through the regency, gothic, and Harlequin Romances of the twentieth century—remain: the "good" woman's role, function, and sphere as primarily domestic and the split female persona that allows the heroine no more than a covert and undeveloped sexuality. Both are reflections of the values and norms that have operated as primary mechanisms for the social control of women in patriarchal society throughout most of the history of Western civilization. Whatever the political, economic, and religious context or rationale used to justify or explain this away, society's prescription of the female persona as schizoid has acted as a powerful reinforcement of patriarchy—because denying the "acceptable" or "approved" female the right to a fully developed sense of self, achieved in part through denying her a fully developed sexuality, has resulted in the defeminization of women, dehumanization, and loss of power.

Notes

1. It is unfortunate that Heyer's reputation often has been maligned through pairing with Cartland. The popularity of both Heyer and Cartland in the United States occurred largely after 1960, when an increasing number of paperback reprints from England became available.

2. Cartland's stories today are as out of fashion with readers as the author is out of step with the majority of women, in spite of the more than 150 million copies of her books in print, accrued over a period of sixty-five years. The consensus among romance readers queried in 1982 was that "her books are for teenagers—childish and unrealistic," or "I've outgrown her." The author received even more than her usual attention in the popular press after Lady Diana, her step-granddaughter, married Prince Charles of England, enhancing Cartland's own opportunities to expound her nineteenth-century views on the "proper" role of women. "Equality with men is rubbish," she proclaimed in a 1983 interview. "It's a mistake for women to take men's jobs; men don't like women over them. My son says that so many working women today have these dreadful, strident voices." Margaria Fichtner (1984) paraphrased Cartland in a way that, not surprisingly, also describes her heroines: "Women —most of whom Cartland doesn't like—are set on this earth to be cosseted

and fussed over. They are not to let their intelligences show. They are not to be aggressive or interfering. And she is convinced women belong in the home, not in the House."

3. Gellis points out that the distinction made today between historical fiction and historical romance is often an artificial one, "devised to induce more women to read books." That many of the historical novels published during the 1950s and 1960s, in both hardcover and paperback, were reissued in paperback during the late 1970s when sales of erotic historical romances were at a peak, and were packaged, distributed, and promoted as romances, underscores Gellis's point. Westcott's novels were reprinted by Bantam in 1976 and 1977, all three of Speas's historical romances by Avon in 1978. Dorothy Dunnett's six-volume Lymond Chronicle (1961–75) assumes a highly literate reader and, in addition, does not really fit the romance formula, but all were reissued and distributed as such during the late 1970s.

4. The use of "Harlequin" as a generic term or even as a descriptor of all romances published by Harlequin (rather than qualified by specific line name) became problematic after 1983, when Harlequin began publishing several romance lines containing not only explicit sexual content but significantly different sex-role portrayals (different, that is, from the Harlequin Romance and Harlequin Presents lines examined by Snitow, Modleski, and Frenier). Though sexual content may vary from more to less in these two lines today, cruelty continues to characterize many of the heroine-hero relationships in both the Romance and Presents titles.

Chapter Three

NEW RELATIONSHIPS

Between Heroines and Heroes,

Readers and Publishers

Editors help direct the creativity of the authors with
editorial guidelines which are market-oriented.
Harlequin Annual Report, 1974

Heroines are older and more mature, the hero no
longer gets his ultimate thrill from being first—and
no more rape!
Romance editor, Romance Writers of
America Conference, 1981

I've gotten fed up with the poor dumb little chit who
lets everyone walk all over her before she starts to wise
up. Women aren't like that, at least not the ones who
might interest the men I want to read about.
Romance reader, 1982

*I*f there was little change between
the covers of the romances published by Harlequin before 1983, what
was new was the way they were marketed. In 1971 the company hired a
new management team headed by Lawrence Heisey, whose expertise
and experience were in marketing (at Proctor and Gamble). In 1972
Harlequin bought controlling interest in Mills and Boon, and in 1973
added six more Mills and Boon romances under the Harlequin Presents imprint. But it was the Heisey team's new marketing scheme
that boosted sales and profits and made Harlequin synonymous with
romance in the public mind, and gave birth to the brand name or
series romance.

Heisey's aim was to build the image of the brand name, not just one
title or author, which would justify a large advertising budget. First,
he initiated consumer research, then had his editors "help guide the
creativity of authors" via editorial guidelines based on the results of
that research. By varying the type size to accommodate small differences in word count, Harlequin was able to print books that were all

46

the same length (192 pages), which they displayed in specially designed racks located "where the women are"—in supermarkets and other mass merchandising outlets. As soon as the brand name was established, the company initiated a reader service, a book club without a return option, which delivered all six Romances and/or six Presents romances directly to readers' homes. Not only were production costs reduced through uniformity and volume, but the reader service guaranteed sales of six or twelve books every month with the full cover price recovered by the publisher, saving the 50 percent discount to book wholesalers, a marketing strategy that proved to be one of the most successful in the history of the publishing business.[1]

Harlequin published at least 144 romance novels per year from 1973 to 1980, the period of greatest growth for the company, and "worldwide" began to accompany its reported sales figures. According to Peter Mann (1974), Harlequin sold thirty million books in English in 1973. In 1976 the company took on its first American author, Janet Dailey, and in 1977 sales reached thirty-five million dollars in the United States alone (Wagner 1979). Today it is difficult to believe that the simplistic stories, cartoonlike covers, and simpering cover blurbs of the 1970s Harlequins were the product of consumer research. But because they were, and because the kind of research Heisey initiated has become an important part of the romance publishing business, they serve as one illustration of how much romance novels, and women, have changed.

Patricia O'Toole (1979, 63) called the mass appeal of romances "starring passive virgins" an anomaly that "flies in the face of two of the most significant trends of our time: increasing sexual freedom and increasing opportunities for women to acquire money, power and status on their own rather than as appendages of men." What O'Toole, Kathryn Weibel, and a host of others were ignoring—as did Harlequin's Heisey, to what must have been his great regret—was the revolution in romance that was going on right next to the gothic, regency, and Harlequin racks, where the fat and lusty bodice rippers were selling like hotcakes, at the rate of about 150 a year, and to a very different group of women.

During the late 1960s Avon, unable to compete with wealthier paperback houses for reprint rights to hardcover bestsellers, began publishing paperback originals in an attempt to create its own bestsellers (Fallon 1984). As a result, the house was actively searching for original fiction when editor Nancy Coffey pulled Kathleen Woodiwiss's *The Flame and the Flower* from a pile of unsolicited manuscripts. Launched in 1972 as an Avon Spectacular, with all the promotion and advertising support usually given to bestseller reprints, *The Flame and the Flower* was distributed through drugstores and other mass merchandising outlets as well as bookstores. Avon's ploy not only proved the commercial viability of paperback originals but also opened the door to a new American publishing enterprise after Woodiwiss's erotic tale of love and adventure—"the bold, tempestuous romance of a kidnapped and ravished aristocratic girl"—caught the imagination of hundreds of thousands of women and launched the erotic historical romance as a mass entertainment phenomenon.

Set in England and America at the beginning of the nineteenth century, *The Flame and the Flower* is the story of Heather Simmons, an ill-treated and overworked orphan (not unlike the typical Cartland heroine) who mistakenly believes she has accidentally killed her would-be rapist. While running away from the miserable home provided by her aunt, in which the attempted rape occurred, Heather gets lost near the London docks and is mistaken for a "woman of the streets." Hauled aboard a newly arrived ship to assuage the American captain's "needs" after a long sea voyage, Heather's resistance counts for little since he believes she is "in the business." Brandon Birmingham forces himself on the young girl, discovering too late that she is a virgin. Woodiwiss makes no attempt to confuse rape with seduction here: "It seemed with each movement now she would be split asunder and tears came to her eyes" (p. 34). Heather escapes the ship the next morning, feeling both fear and hate for her ravisher, but soon finds herself trapped by pregnancy and a forced marriage to Brandon, followed by a voyage across the ocean to a foreign land. His courtship of Heather takes place after this unfortunate beginning, after physical intimacy and marriage, and a tender tale it is in spite of the initial "mistake." Though *The Flame and the Flower* could be classified a domestic romance with gothic overtones (murder and blackmail), in her telling of a young girl's awakening to both herself and to love, Woodiwiss casts her magic spell via a veritable pall of sensuality that is both pervasive and constant, amounting to 350 pages of sexual foreplay.

The book drew thousands of fan letters from readers, and two years later Avon followed with another Woodiwiss title, *The Wolf and the Dove*, plus two by Rosemary Rogers, *Sweet Savage Love* and *The Wildest Heart*. Rogers's *Dark Fires* sold two million copies within three months of issue in 1975, and later that year *Publishers Weekly* reported more than eight million copies of the first six Avon original

KATHLEEN E. WOODIWISS

By the author of A ROSE IN WINTER

THE FLAME AND THE FLOWER

AVON/82750/$3.95

AVON

THE FLAME AND THE FLOWER
KATHLEEN E. WOODIWISS

82750·6·395
0·380-00525·5

Printed in U.S.A.

HEATHER AND BRANDON

In an age of great turmoil,
the breathtaking romance of Heather Simmons
and Captain Brandon Birmingham
spans oceans and continents!
Their stormy saga reaches the limits
of human passion as we follow
Heather's tumultuous journey from poverty...
to her kidnapping at a squalid London dockside...
to the splendor of Harthaven, the Carolina
plantation where Brandon finally probes the depths
of Heather's full womanhood!

OVER THREE MILLION COPIES IN PRINT!

ISBN 0-380-00525-5

00525

0   71001 00395

paperback romances had been sold "so far." Editor Coffey said "the fans are insatiable for more." She described this "new genre in women's fiction" as replete with "history, travel, romance, titillation, a passionate brooding male plus . . . a strong, female lead. The heroine may be hung up on a man but she is not dependent on him" (in "Trade News," 1975). Instead of simplistic stories and insipid heroines, the erotic historical romances mixed love with adventure, in plots and characters that were complex and well developed—especially the heroines, who experienced life firsthand. By 1976 the gothic romance was all but dead, swamped by a rising tide of raging rapture, defiant desire, proud passion, and wild wickedness, after Ballantine, Dell, Fawcett, Jove, Playboy, Warner, Pinnacle, Popular Libary, and Pocket Books all began competing with Avon for a share of this highly lucrative market.

Woodiwiss's books focus unremittingly on the developing physical and emotional relationship between heroine and hero, while Rogers's stories "travel"—from England, France, Spain, and Tripoli to Texas, Louisiana, and Mexico—with the heroine experiencing a variety of adventures and men, leaving the reader near exhaustion (as if all of Angelique's nine "adventures" had been compressed between the covers of just one). Rogers articulated her heroine's development as an individual in Sweet Savage Love (Avon, 1972, 578) in this way: "during the short time they spent together he had learned that she was no longer the green girl he had first possessed. The very strength that she had gained from all the degrading experiences she had been subjected to, and the fact that she had somehow managed not only to rise above them but to win her own brand of independence against tremendous odds, annoyed him more than he could ever admit to her." In addition, Rogers's sexual passages are much more explicit and adventuresome: "She felt him drag her thighs apart and lift her legs over his shoulders and gave a muffled scream of outrage. He held her with his hands on her breasts, fingers torturing her nipples, and then his mouth found her. She heard her own wild sobbing, her moans of shame that were mixed, humiliatingly, with desire as his tongue drove deeply into her softness" (p. 221).

Perhaps more than any other attribute, however, it is the mixing of pain with pleasure and cruelty with love that is the hallmark of Rogers's work—"Without any warning she felt his teeth sink savagely into the soft flesh of her shoulder and she shrieked; digging her nails into his back, only to find that just as suddenly he had begun to kiss, very tenderly and gently, the aching wound that he had just inflicted on her" (*Sweet Savage Love*, 1972, 577)—which gave rise to "sweet savagery" as a generic label. Exploitative and often sadistic, the Rogers hero is not only unfaithful but often flaunts his sexual escapades with other women (including the heroine's stepmother in *Sweet Savage Love*) simply to punish the heroine. When Rogers translated these characteristics into contemporary settings, she quite thoroughly turned off romance readers, at least those surveyed in 1982 and 1985, who point to these titles (*The Crowd Pleasers*, 1978; *The Insiders*, 1979; and *Love Play*, 1981) as examples of "perfectly awful" books.[2] Woodiwiss remains by far the all-time favorite romance author among readers, even though they are not very enthusiastic about her more recent titles.

The *Flame and the Flower* and *Sweet Savage Love*, along with *Angelique* and *The Sheik*, served as models for much of what followed during the 1970s. As with television and other mass media, success tended to beget more of the same rather than innovation and variety, in spite of the increased number of competing publishers. Settings, plots, and characters, as well as titles and cover illustrations, were sometimes so similar that readers soon began to suspect "I've read this one before." Patricia Phillips's *Anise* (Jove, 1978) and Lynn Bartlett's *Courtly Love* (Warner Books, 1979), for instance, are interesting variations on the theme played by Woodiwiss in *The Wolf and the Dove*, all set against the backdrop of the Norman Conquest, while Johanna Lindsey's *Captive Bride* (Avon, 1978) updates *The Sheik* in little more than packaging. An exception is *The Kadin* (Avon, 1978), in which Bertrice Small embarks on a flight of fancy suggestive of the real Aimée Dubucq de Rivery, cousin to Napoleon's Josephine.[3] Small lets the reader in on what life in a harem was like for a beautiful, smart, feisty, and determined woman—right down to the most intimate details. At the same time the author involves her heroine in a political power play in which the stakes are life or death, and this intertwining of political intrigue with sexual adventure has become a Small trademark. Her heroines operate at two levels, both personal and societal, in their struggle for power and autonomy.

Though the popularity of the erotic historical romance was still running at fever pitch during the late seventies, readers had gradually become not only fans but critics, and they objected more and more to rape and violence, to the long separations the lovers were subjected to during their wide-ranging adventures, and to passive-teenage-virgin heroines. Other seeds of change were germinating as well, for at about this time Harlequin decided to take over its own marketing in the United States, which left Pocket Books (the paperback division of Simon and Schuster) with a well-developed distribution system for series romance but no product to sell. It was more than predictable that they would create one. Though other Harlequin imitations were already on the market in the United States (e.g., Dell's Candlelight Romances), none constituted a significant threat to Harlequin's estimated 80–90 percent share of the series romance market, until May 1980 when Simon and Schuster's first Silhouette Romance appeared in the stores, backed by a huge advertising and promotion budget.

The 1980 version of the Silhouette Romance tip sheet for authors confirms their similarity to the Harlequin model, not only in length (192 pages, averaging 55,000 words) and appearance, but in a number of by now tired clichés:

> [The heroine] is always young (19 to 27). She is not beautiful in the high fashion sense, is basically an ingenue and wears modest make-up and clothes. . . . In spite of her fragile appearance, she is independent, high-spirited and not too subservient. . . . Though she wants to work, and plans to after marriage, her home and children will always come first. She is almost always a virgin. Her reactions to the amorous advances of the hero mirror the conflict between her desire for him and her strong belief in romantic love. She never truly believes the hero loves her until the final chapter of the novel . . . and she is usually without parents or a "protective" relationship.
>
> [The hero is] self-assured, masterful, hot-tempered, capable of violence, passion and tenderness. He is often mysteriously moody. . . . Always older than the heroine, usually in his early or late 30's, he is rich and successful in the vocation of his choice. . . . He is usually dark, although we have seen some great Nordic types, and recently, a gorgeous redhead. . . . He is never married to anyone but our heroine, but may be widowed, and even divorced, provided it is made clear that his ex-wife sought the divorce.
>
> [It is all right for these two characters to] go to bed together, although they should not make love before they are married. Bringing them to the brink of consummation and then forcing them to retreat either because of an interruption or because one or both of the lovers suffer from doubt or shame is an appropriate Silhouette device.

Within only a few months of the Silhouette "launch," however, the so-called sensuous or erotic contemporary series romance appeared on the market—Dell's Candlelight Ecstasy Romance line in December 1980 and Richard Gallen/Pocket Books' contemporary romances in April 1981, both issuing two titles each month—which quickly turned the entire romance market upside-down. Incorporating the erotic element found previously only in the single-title erotic historical romances, these new sensuous series romances also started a massive migration of heroines into the public sphere, putting any domestic thoughts they might have on a parallel track with career aspirations that go far beyond the secretarial pool, nurse's station, or classroom. It turned out to be a winning combination, attracting not only women who were already reading series romances but also readers of the fat erotic historicals, who for the first time began to cross over to the brand name "quick reads." After only a few months the ecstasy diet was increased to six titles each month.

Dell promised more realistic heroines and heroes, and more sensuous stories, and one of its first ecstasies, Jayne Castle's *Gentle Pirate*, featured a twenty-nine-year-old heroine and a thirty-eight-year-old hero who put off making love, with the usual number of teasers or near misses along the way, until the night before their marriage (p. 178 in a 187-page book). When it did happen, however, Dell did not close the door on the scene. Echoes of Rosemary Rogers as well as the Harlequin Romances of the 1970s resonate through the pages of *Gentle Pirate*, from an angry and punishing hero (who believes all women are bitches and/or whores, which, of course, he learned from the example his mother set) to people as property—in the heroine's words, " 'I consider you as much my property as you consider me yours' " (p. 180), and the hero's confession that " 'I knew you were fully capable of going through life alone and the knowledge hurt' " (p. 175). Punishing the heroine takes a new twist when the hero uses sex to extort what he wants from her, in what might be called the "Uncle, Uncle" plot device—a contemporary contribution to the old standbys such as the Forced Marriage and the Mystery Baby.

> "How shall I touch you, Sweetheart?" he murmured against her lips. "Like this?" He took a nipple between thumb and forefinger and tugged with infinite gentleness. Kirsten gasped and clung more closely. . . . "Simon, I don't think I can stand it!" she wailed, a shudder going through her.
>
> "Do you want me, sweetheart?" His mouth moved to her throat and she gave a small cry of joy.
>
> "Yes, Simon. Please!" Was this really her? Kirsten wondered, amazed.
>
> "I'm all yours, honey," he promised soothingly. "But there's a price tag attached," he added. . . .
>
> "What—what price?" she asked fearfully, a foreboding feeling beginning to push aside the passion of a moment earlier.
>
> "You must surrender to me completely first," he said, his words thick and

rough against her throat. "I won't allow you to taunt me with other men, honey. You can't lie with me tonight and then see another man this weekend." (pp. 86–87)

Because now the female can be enslaved by her uncontrollable sexual urges, the hero "stirs the flames," physically arousing her until she is beyond rational control, and then backs off, withholding what she craves until she cries "uncle." This type of hero is the signature of Jayne Krentz, who writes under her own name for Harlequin Temptation and Worldwide, as Jayne Castle for Dell, and as Stephanie James for Silhouette Desire and Intimate Moments.[4] A somewhat more benign and common variation on the theme appears in Kristin James's *The Golden Sky* (1981, 251), one of the first contemporary romances produced by Richard Gallen for Pocket Books.

> "Oh, Brant," Alexis groaned softly. "Please don't."
> "Don't what?" He took her other nipple in his mouth and began to tease it while he slid one hand over her stomach and inside her panties, exploring, probing, awakening, but not fulfilling. . . . He toyed with her, withholding until she quivered with passion.
> "Do you want me now, Alexis?" he murmured.
> A ragged sob escaped her throat. "Please, Brant."
> "Please what?" He moved over her, his erect, hard shaft poised between her inviting legs. "Tell me, Alexis. I want to hear you say it. Say you want me."
> "I want you."

Gallen had been producing historical romances for Pocket Books since 1979, but in 1981 the books began to carry his RG logo in the lower right-hand corner of the cover, though many readers never realized they were buying a series or category romance. Cover art and paper stock were reminiscent of quality magazine illustrations rather than the Sunday comics, à la Harlequin. And while Gallen editors also used written guidelines for authors, it was a much less rigid formula. Stories were more complex, almost twice as long (averaging 100,000 words) as Harlequin and Ecstasy titles, and heroines were more mature as individuals and already well established in their chosen careers (e.g., lawyer Alexis Stone in *The Golden Sky*).

> [The heroine] is a spirited, intelligent, involved and caring person, who often initiates the story's action rather than simply reacting to it. . . . In the contemporaries she need not be a virgin, but she is never promiscuous, and former love relationships should be kept at a distance. She should be actively involved in a glamorous career or life style, though this should not

overshadow her romantic involvement. The author must be able to speak authoritatively on the profession or industry so that the reader gets a sense of an inside view.

[The hero], too, is a dynamic person—strong, passionate and physically attractive—and we must meet him early in the book. . . . he may be mysterious or even distant to the heroine in the beginning, but we should know what he's really thinking and feeling, and he should remain a fairly constant presence throughout the story. He should never physically abuse the heroine, and "love at first rape" is expressly forbidden!

[Love/sex scenes] should occur with some frequency, but obviously padded or artificially contrived sequences will not do. Sexual tension between the two main characters should be immediate and powerful. When they consummate their passion, the reader should be more than ready for it. The sex should be pleasurable—not painful—with some emphasis on mutuality and caring. These scenes should be rather long; we want a lot of foreplay, during play and afterplay. All sexual description should be imaginative and lyrical—not graphic, clinical or mechanical. Euphemisms should be used in referring to genitalia. We want one woman/one man stories, with the emphasis on emotions and eventual commitment. . . . Whether these scenes are gentle or more urgently dynamic, the distinction between seduction and rape must always be maintained. Though a woman's fantasy may sometimes be to lose control, being carried away on a tide of emotion or sensation is a far cry from experiencing the results of the violent motivation for rape that exists in reality.

Though "real" rape did occur in *The Golden Sky*—a kind of historical hangover—such scenes quickly disappeared from the line. Gallen editors were right on target with readers in 1981, in spite of the fact that their market research consisted largely of surveying booksellers and brief questionnaires bound into their books. Though the Dell line hit the shelves a few months ahead of them, the Gallen romances were by far the more explorative, portraying women as they had rarely been portrayed before—and never in the series, or brand name, romance. The Gallen books drew the attention of women who were not regular romance readers, as well as those who were (mostly erotic historical romance readers initially), thereby enlarging the universe of romance buyers; Dell's Ecstasy Romance drew largely from the already existing readership for series romance, which in turn began a shift in market share among series publishers. The result was a rapid proliferation of erotic romance lines and more and more titles on the market every month, as other publishers hurried to tap this new vein of "realistic" gold.

In June 1981 Jove introduced its Second Chance at Love line, featuring mature heroines (initially twenty to twenty-nine, now twenty-six to forty), who are divorced, widowed, or simply had an unsatisfactory relationship the first time around. "And none of them can be in the typing pool," said former editor Carolyn Nichols (in Rudolph 1982, 51). Pocket Books quickly realized it no longer needed the Gallen arrangement, which called for an even split of both costs and profits, and in 1982 the Gallen contemporaries metamorphosed into a new Silhouette line called Special Editions, which then President John Gfeller said provided readers "explicit sexuality with good taste" (in Jennings 1984, 51). Later the same year, the Gallen historicals were similarly transformed into a new two-per-month historical line at Pocket Books, named Tapestry (not part of the Silhouette operation, which was limited to contemporary series romance). Silhouette then launched still another erotic line, the Desire Romance, with a half-million-dollar television and print advertising campaign to inform women that "Desire's greatest appeal is to an audience distinctly different from our other Silhouette lines." The short Desire Romance was designed to compete with Dell's Ecstasy Romance, which by now had become very popular indeed. By the end of 1982 there were fifty new series romance titles appearing on the market each month, at least thirty of which were erotic romances, most of them with contemporary settings.

In July 1982, into a sea of redundancy that was rushing headlong toward market and reader saturation, Ballantine, a house with a long-standing reputation for innovation, thrust a series called Love and Life—Romantic Novels for Today, later changed to Women's Stories for Today. These 185-page novels were an attempt to expand the boundaries of sex-role portrayals even further than the new erotic romances had up to this time. With emphasis on "psychological realism," the Love and Life line chronicled the pivotal period in one woman's life during which she consciously emerges as an individual true to herself, despite the demands of society, of marriage or children or career. In the process, she sheds the man who is unwilling to allow her to grow and change and encounters the New Man, sometimes younger and sometimes older, who does not need to dominate and control her in order to elevate himself. With an ego and masculinity secure enough to seek a relationship based on equality and sharing, the New Man is sensitive and vulnerable—and he always plays fair.

Love and Life was an inspired editorial concept that lasted little more than one year before silently slipping into oblivion without most of its likely target audience knowing the stories even existed. Set

Searching, © 1982 by Jessie Ford Osborne. Reproduced by permission of Ballantine Books, a division of Random House.

All She Can Be, © 1983 by Fern Michaels. Reproduced by permission of Ballantine Books, a division of Random House.

in among the rows and racks of Harlequins, Ecstasies, and Desires, the Love and Life novels were laid waste by a self-destructing marketing strategy. Though built around the predictable romance fantasy of a happy ending, these "different" stories were expected to attract an audience consisting of the most nontraditional romance consumers, who generally do not buy series books, as well as an amorphous group of women interested in novels that focus on contemporary women's issues and concerns, many of whom not only do not buy series books but purposefully avoid the romance display racks. In addition, the Love and Life books carried photographic covers which pictured women and men in their thirties and forties, close up and sharply focused, which turned potential women readers off at first glance. Even when they did look further, readers still could not escape the face staring out from the cover, to which the protagonist in the story was irrevocably tied, a fatal mistake for a product whose popularity rests largely on its ability to call into play the reader's imagination. Though potential readers themselves might be forty years old, the pictures in their heads would *never* match those on the covers. Cover photos were quickly softened in both focus and distance, but it was already too little and too late to override the initial impression in consumers' minds.

Though Harlequin had introduced its new SuperRomance line in June 1980, claiming it was "a new type of love story . . . in keeping with today's lifestyles," it in fact carried on Harlequin's sadistic hero tradition with a vengeance. The message inside the cover of the first of the lot, Abra Taylor's *End of Innocence*, invites readers to "sit back and enjoy a passionately beautiful love story," then "treats" them to a hero who rapes his wife on their wedding night, an act done deliberately, in cold anger and with the clear intent to punish: " 'If I'd had a real sword to work with tonight I probably would have driven it into the bull in the heat of the fight,' " he tells her. " 'And now I want that moment I've been robbed of—the moment of drawing blood' " (p. 338). Not only brutal but emotionally flawed, this hero is capable of articulating only the most minimal civilities throughout, usually with barely controlled rage. True to the old-style Harlequins, the heroine suffers in silence: "It is said that the bull feels little at that moment when the sword plunges to the hilt, and bullfighter and bull seem almost to become one. It was not so with Liona, perhaps because he had taken no time to prepare her body for his onslaught" (p. 340). With only a few exceptions (see Meg Hudson, *Love's Sound in Silence*,

1982), it was not until former Gallen editor Star Helmer took over in 1983 that the character of content in this line began to change.

In spite of stories like *End of Innocence,* and while one American publisher after another was entering the erotic contemporary romance arena, Harlequin executive Fred Kerner said, "We have no overt sex in any of our books. . . . we publish happy stories" (in Dahlin 1981a, 35). The whiz kids of marketing seemed to be sticking fast to the sweet-sadistic domestic romance formula, apparently convinced that changes being wrought by an increasingly worldwide women's movement and a host of other social forces either did not exist or were not going to touch their bedrock conservative-traditional readers.[5] But Lawrence Heisey and his management team were dead wrong, which they soon realized as profits dropped and returns shot up to a reported 60 percent. (Five years earlier Harlequin was routinely printing 500,000 copies of each new title, of which less than 25 percent were returned. See Berman 1978.) The result was that in just two years Harlequin lost half its share of the American market for series romance, and the company's operating profits in 1983 were down 55 percent from 1982 ("Harlequin Operating Profit Down," 1984). Harlequin scurried to try to recoup, launching the American Romance line in 1983 ("sensuous and emotional love stories — contemporary, engrossing and uniquely American") with a five-million-dollar initial advertising and promotion budget. The company followed with the Temptation line in 1984 ("compelling stories of passionate romance for today's woman") to compete with Dell Ecstasy and Silhouette Desire. (Within four years of launch, Silhouette Books was neck and neck with Harlequin in romance market share.)

Bantam, too, made an expensive mistake during this period of market turbulence with a new sweet romance series called Circle of Love. Admitting that their research had gone out of date while the line was in preparation, Bantam quickly folded its new-old tent in favor of a new line of erotic contemporary romances called Loveswept, with a cover so loaded with phallic symbolism that it was an instant visual clue as to what readers could expect to find inside. Loveswept aimed at what Stuart Applebaum, then director of publicity for Bantam, called "the hardcore romance reader," the woman who reads at least one romance novel a day (in Maryles and Symons 1983, 55). The line uses the author's real name and includes a photo and short biographical sketch inside the front cover, has garnered a reputation for including humor in the stories, and by 1985 was leading the pack in domestic store sales. Among romance readers surveyed in 1985, Loveswept, Silhouette Intimate Moments, and Silhouette Desire were the top three favorite lines, in that order—at a time when there were eighty new series romance titles being published every month (see Table 1).

It is somewhat paradoxical that it was to the most constrained form of genre writing, the series or category romance, with its publisher-specified guidelines for authors, that the wand of evolutionary change and development passed in the early 1980s. Because the majority of series romance authors were forced to at least minimal conformity to guidelines specifying character attributes and overall content, the written guidelines functioned to reinforce the kinds of changes that took place during this time, in stories about characters and relationships that were repeated over and over again, in hundreds of stories written by hundreds of authors, printed by at least 100,000 copies each.[6]

Certainly there is continuity aplenty in the romance genre, especially in the fantasy of the woman as transcendentally powerful—the most powerful attraction of the romance as a literary form among women readers in modern times. In the traditional romance the hero is all-powerful in the public world (intellectual or instrumental), though ultimately he is enslaved by emotion, which is the private world where the heroine reigns supreme and over which the hero has little if any control. But all romance novels today are not the same, nor have all of them changed in fundamental ways. In those that have, however, which as a type continue to be more popular than those that have not, power in the public world is shared by the hero and the heroine.

To simply say that formula conventions develop and change through audience selection somehow fails to convey the complex and dynamic character of the relationship between product and consumer when it comes to today's popular romances. Audience feedback can take multiple forms, including selection in the marketplace, fan mail, and various kinds of consumer research. It also can create market conditions that operate as a secondary force to speed up or dampen change. In the case of paperback romance novels, for example, the popularity of a specific kind of story—at two different moments in time—brought a huge flood of more of the same into the marketplace, which in turn changed the selection process itself. In the resulting highly competitive market, publishers either took heuristic risks or resorted to more and more consumer research in an effort to design the product to fit their constantly changing female consumers and to enlarge the universe of romance consumers, at times even identifying new markets in

Table 1.   Paperback Romance Publishing Calendar (1957 through 1985)

	Date	1985 titles/month
Harlequin Romance/Mills and Boon paperback reprints **introduced** (sweet)	1957	6
Mistress of Mellyn by Victoria Holt (Fawcett)—nominal beginning of period during which modern gothic romance was most popular in U.S.	1960	
Angelique by Sergeanne Golon (Bantam)	1960	
The Flame and the Flower by Kathleen Woodiwiss (Avon)	1972	
Harlequin Presents line **introduced**	1973	8
Sweet Savage Love by Rosemary Rogers	1974	
Gothic romance market bottoms out; editors rejecting manuscripts with gothic elements	1976	
Harlequin/Pocket Books U.S. distribution arrangement	1976	
Peak of popularity of single-title erotic historical romances published by Avon, Ballantine, Dell, Fawcett, Jove, Playboy, Leisure, Ace, Signet, Warner, Pinnacle, Popular Library, and Pocket Books	1978–80	
Richard Gallen/Pocket Books historical romances (erotic) **introduced**; RG logo on both historical and contemporary beginning Apr. 1981	1979	
Silhouette Romance line **introduced** (sweet)	May 1980	6
Harlequin SuperRomance line **introduced** under Worldwide imprint	June 1980	4

Table 1.   Paperback Romance Publishing Calendar (1957 through 1985) —
Continued

	Date	1985 titles/month
Candlelight Ecstasy Romance line **introduced** by Dell (erotic)	Dec. 1980	8
Second Chance at Love line **introduced** by Jove (erotic)	June 1981	6
Most regency romance lines ceased publication	end of 1981	
Silhouette Special Edition romance line **introduced** (erotic)	Feb. 1982	6
Circle of Love line **introduced** by Bantam (sweet)	Mar. 1982	
Silhouette Desire Romance line **introduced** (erotic)	June 1982	6
Love and Life line **introduced** by Ballantine (erotic)	July 1982	
Pocket Books/Tapestry historical romance line **introduced** (erotic)[a]	Oct. 1982	2
Finding Mr. Right line **introduced** by Avon (erotic)	Oct. 1982	
Richard Gallen romances **dropped** by Pocket Books	Nov. 1982	
Harlequin loses half of its American market	1981−83	
Rapture Romance line **introduced** by NAL (erotic)	Jan. 1983	
Harlequin American Romance line **introduced** (erotic)	Apr. 1983	4
Silhouette Intimate Moments line **introduced** (erotic)	May 1983	4
Circle of Love line **dropped** by Bantam	1983	
Loveswept line **introduced** by Bantam (erotic)	May 1983	4

Table 1. Paperback Romance Publishing Calendar (1957 through 1985) —
Continued

	Date	1985 titles/month
Dell Ecstasy Supreme line **introduced** (erotic)	Aug. 1983	4
Serenade line **introduced** by Zondervan (sweet-inspirational)	Aug. 1983	4
Finding Mr. Right line **dropped** by Avon	Fall 1983	
Scarlet Ribbons historical romances **introduced** by NAL/Signet (erotic)	Fall 1983	
To Have and To Hold line **introduced** by Berkley/Jove (erotic)	Oct. 1983	
Love and Life line **dropped** by Ballantine	Jan. 1984	
Silhouette Inspirations line **introduced** (sweet-inspirational)	Feb. 1984	
Harlequin Temptation line **introduced** (erotic)	Mar. 1984	4
Harlequin buys Silhouette Books from Simon and Schuster	July 1984	
Velvet Glove line **introduced** by Avon (erotic-suspense)	July 1984	
Harlequin Intrigue line **introduced** (erotic-suspense)	Aug. 1984	2
Scarlet Ribbons line **dropped** by NAL	1984	
Promises (name changed from Cherish) line **introduced** by Thomas Nelson (sweet)[a]	1984	2
Popularity of erotic historical romances on the rise again	mid-1984	
To Have and To Hold line **dropped** by Berkley/Jove	Jan. 1985	
Rapture Romance line **dropped** by NAL	Feb. 1985	

Table 1.   Paperback Romance Publishing Calendar (1957 through 1985)—
Continued

	Date	1985 titles/month
Silhouette Inspirations line **dropped**	June 1985	
Old regency romance lines reappear (Fawcett, NAL/Signet) along with two new "sexy" regency romance lines (Warner and Zebra)	1985	
Velvet Glove line **dropped** by Avon	Dec. 1985	

ªDropped in 1986

the process. When market research in the early 1980s showed that teenagers were reading Harlequin Romances and Barbara Cartland stories, publishers quickly created young adult romance lines for this newly identified and very large audience. By 1984, young adult romances (around a hundred new titles per year, including Dell's Young Love, Silhouette's First Love, and Bantam's Sweet Dreams) reportedly constituted half the entire young adult market.

According to John Cawelti (1976, 35), the formula story functions "to enable its audiences to explore in fantasy the boundary between the permitted and the forbidden and to experience in a carefully controlled way the possibility of stepping across this boundary." In the case of the paperback romance, at least during the 1970s and the first half of the 1980s, it was in large measure the audiences—the composition of which was changing, as were the individuals themselves—who determined what territory was being explored and what was to be permitted or forbidden. Whether or to what extent readers actually stepped across one boundary after another in actions, attitudes, or both, the erotic romance has been an important voice in the social dialogue responsible for raising the consciousness of millions of women during this period.

Notes

1. A rarely mentioned additional savings accrues to the company from reduced royalty payments as well, since authors' royalty rates are significantly lower on book club sales than on retail store sales, even when the book club is

owned by the publisher to whom the author is under contract. Today a number of publishers have initiated this type of reader service.

2. Most romance review publications either panned or refused to review Rogers's *The Wanton* (1985), and today many booksellers say her work does not sell either new or used to romance readers. By mid-1985 Avon was no longer Rogers's publisher. In 1985, Avon reported that twenty-five million copies of the first five Woodiwiss titles were in print, and that trade-size editions of her books have a less than 15 percent return rate (*Romantic Times*, no. 25, 1985, 5).

3. Aimée was on her way home to Martinique on the eve of the French Revolution when she was captured by corsairs and given by the Dey of Algiers to the Sultan of Turkey (see Brand 1983). Believed by some to have been the mother of Sultan Mahmoud I, though little is actually known about her life, she has inspired a number of fictional accounts, most recently Margo Bode's *Jasmine Splendor* (Gallen/Pocket Books, 1981) and *Sultana* (Avon, 1983) by Prince Michael of Greece.

4. Though it is widely assumed that many paperback romance authors write under pseudonyms because, like authors of pornography, they do not wish to openly admit to what they do for a living, most of them do so out of the exigencies of contractual arrangements with more than one publisher. When one publishing house holds an option on the author's next book under a given name and the author wants multiple exposure or more work, he or she contracts with the second house under a different name. Thus, Sandra Brown was Laura Jordan for Richard Gallen romances, is Rachel Ryan for Dell Ecstasy and Erin St. Clair for Silhouette Desire, and writes under her real name for the Bantam Loveswept and Jove Second Chance at Love lines. In a few cases a pseudonym is owned by the publisher and may be used as a generic name under which several authors write, as is the case with Kristin Michaels and the Mack Bolan series for men. Male authors of romance with few exceptions use female pseudonyms because many readers say they do not like the way men write romance, particularly the love scenes, and will not buy their books. Though she did not use pseudonyms, an earlier parallel is Laura Jean Libbey, whose "working-girl" novels were popular during the late 1800s, when she was under contract to six publishers at the same time and enjoyed a yearly income of $75,000 (see Nye 1970, 28).

5. To date there has been no adequate public explanation for this failure to "read" the market correctly. In April 1984, Brian Hickey, Harlequin president for North America, said the Toronto management had research data indicating what was happening, but that editorial control was in the London office. That such a disparity would not be corrected by the company that originated the practice of "helping to guide the creativity of authors" to fit the market is hardly credible.

6. Samples of publisher tip sheets are in the Appendix.

Chapter Four

SWEET SAVAGERY
AND FLAMING FEMINISM

Another Perspective on the
Erotic Historical Romance

"What," men have asked distractedly from the beginning of time, "what on earth do women want?" I do
not know that women as women want anything in
particular, but as human beings they want, my good
men, exactly what you want yourselves: interesting
occupation, reasonable freedom for your pleasures,
and a sufficient emotional outlet.

   Dorothy Sayers, "Are Women Human?"

What do you see when you look at me? Do you see a
human being who thinks and feels much as you do?
Or do you see only a female—a body to be used how
and when you wish?

   Lynn Bartlett, *Courtly Love*

*T*he erotic historical romance as
an identifiable entity is widely considered to have appeared on the
American scene with the 1972 publication of Kathleen Woodiwiss's
The Flame and the Flower. Two years later Avon again struck gold
with Rosemary Rogers's *Sweet Savage Love* (a manuscript she is reputed to have addressed to "The Editor of *The Flame and the Flower*"),
setting off an avalanche of feisty heroines, high adventure, and sex
that sounded the death knell for the suddenly tame gothic and regency
romances. So popular did the bodice rippers become, in fact, that in
1980 Stephen Grover, writing in the *Wall Street Journal*, called them
"publishing's answer to the Big Mac: They are juicy, cheap, predictable and devoured in stupifying quantities by legions of loyal fans."
Romance editors later admitted that in 1978 and 1979 they were buying
every (erotic) historical manuscript they could get their hands on.

 Arriving just when more and more women were beginning to out-
grow the submissive and childlike heroine of the regency and domestic

romances, these stories and others like them caught the imagination of readers with their obstreperous and rebellious women, all fighting for equal respect, fair treatment, and some measure of independence, no matter how "upstream" all that might be for the time in which they lived. Long before Sally Ride and Kathryn Sullivan circled the earth aboard the space shuttle Discovery, historical romance heroines were becoming pirates, highway(wo)men, or whatever else it took in the battle to become mistresses of their own fate, in settings ranging from harems in the Middle East to revolutions in England, France, and the United States, from the Battle of Hastings to the California Gold Rush. The result was a mass migration of readers that proved to be a one-way street, for no matter the variations in time, place, or story that have appeared since, the strong, independent-minded heroine—a woman bent on being a full-fledged human—has become as essential to the romance as a happy ending.

Describing what she called "passionate paperbacks" for *New York* magazine in 1978, Alice Turner said, "Above all, the New Woman of the new romance is resilient. She has to be. Brutalized, degraded, mistress to many, she retains her spirit and her love for the one man with whom her destiny is linked. She is, needless to say, beautiful, voluptuous, adaptable, opinionated, and not terribly introspective" (p. 47). Heroes, according to Turner, remained unchanged—"dark, dashing, rakish, powerful, scoundrelly, passionate, often a bastard, and always with 'a hint of cruelty' lurking around his hard blue eyes or his hard sensuous mouth" (p. 47). The indictment is both broad and broadly accepted, sometimes accompanied by an idle reference to romances as an "anti–women's liberation fad" or a rhetorical question as to what these fantasies say about the mental health of the women who read them.

Asked to summarize the advances made by the women's movement during the seventies, the same decade during which the erotic historical romance reached its peak of popularity, Gloria Steinem said, "We've come to understand that it is the power to choose that is important, not what we choose." This same understanding and a thirst for personal freedom, respect, and dignity are expressed far more eloquently in Megan Castell's *Queen of a Lonely Country* (Pocket Books, 1980, 181). The truly heroic figure in this haunting story set in fifteenth-century Wales is a secondary character named Cerridwen, a woman who is kind and compassionate but who does what needs to be done and what is "right," whether it is appropriate for a woman or not.

"Till now there has not been an hour in all these passing years, Cerri, when I would not have gladly made you my wife and mistress of Heriot. You know that very well!"

"As I know there has not been one moment when you would have left me my own person."

"Yes," he said, mocking. "You must be queen. Even if it is a lonely country where beasts and birds are your subjects along with those who serve you — that mad fish-man Dai, your convict farmer, ill-favored Meg."

Cerridwen stood quiet and straight, unmoved by his attack. "Sir Rhys, my old friend-enemy, you have forgotten the loneliest country of all."

"What?" he challenged.

"The country of the self." She smiled and watched him with her sea-variable eyes until he scowled and looked away. "And there I will rule. If the price of that is living lonely, then I will live alone."

"Rubbish!"

"There have always been women who ruled themselves," she returned equably. "Men forced them to be goddesses, saints, or witches, or they took refuge on islands or in nunneries. Men have never known whether to worship or destroy them, and so have done both." She laughed and turned to Gillian. "But I have hope, my dear. Perhaps you, or at least your daughters, can love a man and be yourselves, too. Perhaps you won't have to rule to keep from being devoured or broken."

"It is not in nature," Rhys growled.

"Nor is it in nature — except in man's — to clip the wings of swans to bind them to earth and your territory."

Written in a lyrical prose that transcends the genre, Castell's 239-page gem is admittedly not the average bodice ripper in either conception or quality of writing, and it would be more accurate to call it what it is — a historical novel. But it was marketed in exactly the same way as *Tender Torment* and *Savage Surrender* — that is, as an original paperback, this one with a cover price of $2.50, of the type sold all across the country in supermarkets, discount stores, and newsstands. The cover illustration shows a woman with generous breasts in a precariously low-cut dress with a handsome man hovering over her, in what the romance publishing business calls the "near-kiss." Though it may not be as lurid as some, this cover was intended to send a similar and recognizable signal to potential consumers. That the signal was misleading or inaccurate in this case is not in itself unique.

Sometimes the heroine's craving for individual dignity is fulfilled and sometimes not, but similar sentiments also are to be found in more typical stories, such as *The Captain's Doxy* (Lafayette Hammett,

Leisure Books, 1980, 471): "As your wife I feel I have rights of my own. Not the least of these is the right of respect and trust, not only from those considered by some to be beneath me, but by you also, my husband."

"Not terribly introspective," Alice Turner called these heroines, yet in Jocelyn Carew's *Golden Sovereigns* (Avon, 1976, 293, 310) we find two passages that are just that—one of which echoes Anya Seton's *Katherine* (1954), who makes a similar vow:

> None of the men she knew—from her father on down to Howard Vickery —had looked at her as a person, as an individual with wants and desires of her own, with thoughts that were valuable, that were prized because they were hers and no one else in the world could have just the same combination of thoughts, ideas, of personality. . . .
>
> But she was not yet conquered. And by him, she never would be, she vowed. He could treat her body as he chose—he had the legal right. But he could never touch the glow inside that was the essence of Carmody. That frail flame was her own, to give or withhold, her own individuality that she would cherish and nurse in secret.

Much of the feminist criticism of paperback romance novels lumps them all together, primarily because no substantive changes in the conventions and assumptions of the classical romance formula are admitted; behavioral changes are superficial, and the relationship between men and women—the power structure—remains fundamentally unchanged. It generally is argued that the romance novel continues to reaffirm the domestic, subservient role of women in a patriarchal society. In her thought-provoking book on *Women, Sex and Pornography*, however, Beatrice Faust (1980, 154) pointed out that the emphasis in the bodice rippers is on adventure, not domesticity. Though "marriage remains the ideal goal . . . it is no longer a union of unequals—a traditionally masculine man and a traditionally feminine woman. The men have acquired tenderness and the girls have matured into strong, independent, capable women who are also very sexy. The balance of power has changed." Faust called "sweet savagery" an example of "the genuine pornography of women," but her treatment of pornography in general and the insights she presented as to how these erotic novels may function for readers set her poles apart from others who have written about the implicit-explicit sexual aspect of the romance (e.g., Robinson 1978; Snitow 1979; Douglas 1980).

Data gathered in a quantitative and qualitative content analysis of fifty-six erotic historical romance novels published between 1972 and 1981, along with readers' perceptions of heroes and heroines in this type of romance, form the core of information presented in this chapter. Taken together, the findings support both Faust's conclusion and Ruggiero and Weston's (1977) evolutionary perspective (placing the modern gothic romances in the context of sociopolitical transition), and suggest that fundamental change was indeed underway in the assumptions and conventions of the centuries-old romance "formula."

Content Analysis

All of the novels in the sample[1] were written by well-known authors of more than one paperback romance title, the majority with a million and more copies of their books in print. These novels were read by six female coders who completed identical content questionnaires within a nine-month period. Intercoder reliability, calculated using O. R. Holsti's (1969, 137) formula for multiple coders, was 90.6 percent. (Some of the findings presented here were reported in Thurston and Doscher 1982 and Thurston 1985.)

A number of these romances would perhaps be more accurately labeled as historical fiction, in which a sexual relationship may be described fully and in fairly explicit terms. Other classification breakdowns, as between stories in which the heroine has multiple sexual partners (sweet savagery or bodice rippers) and those in which the hero is her one and only sexual partner (sensual or romantic historicals), were not considered useful. It is not so much whether sexual intercourse occurs with one man or with several that marks the difference in the types of erotic historical romances, as some observers suggest (e.g., Falk and Kolb 1981), as it is the matter of force versus choice. The character of the sexual act itself is more important in terms of classification, since it is in the quality of this interaction that significant change in the way female sexuality is portrayed is most evident. (Even though the legal definition of rape is forced intercourse, because at times in these stories the word is used to describe acts or behavior that are clearly attempts to persuade or seduce, rape was defined for coding purposes as forced sexual intercourse without the consent of and with no pleasure to the woman.)

The titles included in the sample are considered as one type because (1) all were marketed in the same way; (2) they carried at least the suggestion of explicit sexual content, conveyed through the title, front or back cover illustrations, and inside blurbs; and (3) all variations within the broad classification of erotic historical romance were being read by virtually the same readers.

Most heroines in the erotic historical romances examined are independent-minded and strong-willed women determined to overcome the injustices that beset them, even as they refuse to comply with the submissive behavior expected of their sex. Gentleness and concern for others are characteristic of admirable males, while roughness, cruelty, and selfishness are attributes of undesirable males in nearly two-thirds of the stories. Heroes have a desire to control events, as do heroines, but a sense of fairness, sexual security, and understanding usually allows them to compromise. While the macho male dominates cover illustrations and blurbs, only 40 percent of heroes start out that way, and most of them are transformed during the course of the story into caring and compassionate lovers. By the late 1970s the macho stud patterned after Rosemary Rogers's Steve Morgan—inarticulate and unknowable, demanding, cruel, even sadistic—had begun to fall out of favor, and by 1980 he was more often than not the villain of the piece. After reading Rogers's *Lost Love, Last Love* (1980), a sequel to her 1974 books, one reader commented that "it's so disappointing to have waited all this time, only to discover that Ginny and Steve still haven't matured."

An unexpected number of heroes in the erotic historical romances are androgynous types who are tender, caring, and adaptive enough to understand the strivings of the strong heroines, whom they admire above all others. (Androgyny is used here in the sense of exhibiting both what traditionally have been considered feminine and masculine personality traits, though the use of the term has been questioned in recent gender theory and research.) Prized as sexual partners, as friends, and even as business partners, whether it be in privateering, cattle ranching, or managing a medieval keep, these obstreperous female protagonists are far more appealing than the submissive wimps the heroes may have initially tried to force them to be.

He had an imagination, however seldom it stirred, and he wondered how it would be to be born a woman, condemned to a lifetime of subservience, the pains and perils of childbearing, household cares and the bringing up of children. Most women seemed to accept their fate; they married the men their parents chose for them and laboured with them to live. For the girl bound to a brutal husband there was no escape in this world but widowhood, and he wondered uneasily how many obedient wives secretly cherished that hope. A rare girl like this one, of courage and spirit and temper that few husbands would tolerate, had reason to rebel. (Grace Ingram, *Gilded Spurs*, Fawcett, 1978, 108)

Illustration by Tony D'Adamo for *Newsday* (the Long Island, New York, daily newspaper).

Economic independence is a problem for most of these romance heroines, limited as they are by the need for historical authenticity. Nearly a quarter of the stories state or imply that the only means of support available to a woman, outside of a wealthy family or marriage, is to either "sell her body" or do the kind of work generally assigned to servants. In nearly half of the stories it is considered proper for a husband to "own" his wife, in the sense that he assumes control of any money and property belonging to her at the time of their marriage; she is thereafter expected to do as he dictates and desires, a situation all heroines deplore. But most of these women are exceptions to existing social norms, yearning and striving for what they rightfully see as fundamental to real freedom of choice—economic independence. One likely reason for the popularity of stories set in the Middle Ages, particularly in England, is that women had both effective power and some measure of equality during this period of history, deriving from their control of industries that everyone depended on, such as spinning, weaving, baking, brewing, preserving, and ministering to the sick and injured. In *Roselynde* (Playboy Press, 1978, 298), the heroine's husband-to-be recognizes that Alinor, the matriarch of Roberta Gellis's Roselynde Chronicles, is a woman whose "body was warm and eager for love, but her body was not central to her existence as with most women. She was really more interested in the fishing trade and how the politics òf the Low Countries would influence the price of fleece." Alinor and Simon manage to wrest royal approval of a marriage contract that allows her to keep control of her lands, an arrangement that is carried forward into Alinor's second marriage and subsequently to her female descendants, who are the protagonists of the other titles in this six-volume chronicle.

Though choices and opportunities were limited, women on the American frontier also yearned for the freedom that economic independence would bring. In Lynn Erickson's *The Silver Kiss* (Pocket, 1981, 96), the heroine vows that "she would not rest until she had everything money could buy. She would never again be at anyone's mercy, especially not a man's. . . . She would never have to marry anyone." And Patricia Matthews, author of a dozen bestselling titles with fifteen million copies in print by 1981, made this wry comment on a woman's attempt to gain economic independence in such an environment—and a man's response to how she does it:

> "This is not the proper place for a lady such as yourself to be operating."
> "You mean because gambling is a sin?"

"Well—Yes." He shifted his feet uncomfortably. "The Bible speaks against it."

"What does the Bible suggest that a woman alone, in a strange country, and after being used most foully, should do to earn a livelihood?" (*Love's Wildest Promise*, Pinnacle, 1977, 468–69)

Some demographic characteristics of heroes and heroines in erotic historical romances document predictable and well-worn clichés: most heroines are between sixteen and twenty-one years old while heroes are about thirty; she is beautiful and he is handsome/striking/rugged; and one or both have beautiful hair, described as sexually stimulating, and eyes of some unusual color (silver or violet, for instance). In most titles (92 percent), the hero and heroine marry or their marriage is imminent as the story ends; and the heroine marries more than once in a third of the stories. Homosexual males appear in 24 percent of the stories, and in more than two-thirds of these they are portrayed as immoral or undesirable (there was no mention of homosexual women in any of the stories). It comes as no surprise, either, that most heroes have had extensive sexual experience, while most heroines are virgins.

The significant departure from the traditional romance, however, is that heroines do not remain virgins for long, and their sexual experiences underscore Beatrice Faust's (1980, 153) observation that erotic romance novels "legitimize a wide range of sexual experience for women. . . . the heroines are entitled to their sex lives just as the heroes are." Sexual acts are explicitly described in nearly 90 percent of the books examined. Heroines feel sexual needs of a physical nature as strongly as their lovers (overtly expressed in 96 percent of the books) and are not ashamed to seek satisfaction of those needs. As in Jude Deveraux's *Velvet Promise* (Richard Gallen/Pocket Books, 1981, 254), "They were hungry for each other. . . . Never had she been so aggressive. Her bare breasts pushed against him. Her hand moved over his body, delighting in the smooth skin, the thick mat of hair on his chest. Then it moved lower and lower." Afterward the hero realizes "that's what he loved about making love to her—one time quiet and sensual, the next aggressive and demanding. Other times laughing and teasing, another acrobatic, experimental" (p. 278).

By story's end well over two-thirds of the heroines in these romances have had sexual intercourse without benefit of marriage, in two-thirds of these with more than one man (the range was two to seven). Half of the heroines find sexual satisfaction only with a man they love, while 87 percent of the heroes experience greater satisfaction with the heroine than with any other woman. In 37 percent she becomes pregnant before marriage, and in one out of five she is sexually enterprising outside of her marriage; 17 percent of heroes and 9 percent of heroines have sex with another partner while married to each other. Oral sex was depicted in 43 percent of the books. One of the classic folktales about males, the physical impossibility of abstaining from sexual intercourse for more than a short time or at least acceptance of the fact that a man may "take" a woman simply to "service his needs," appears in almost two-thirds of the stories examined.[2] But now the heroines have begun to speak out about their own needs. When her estranged husband accuses her of taking a lover, for instance, the heroine of a story set during the American Civil War responds,

> "How dare you accuse me of wrongdoing, when you are sleeping with my brother's wife? When you brought a prostitute into our own house to service you?"
> "Damn it, I am a man, not a statue. I need release."
> "Release! What about me? . . . It has been over three years since you deigned to grace my bed. What about my needs? Do you think I have no passion?" (Lisa Gregory, *Analise*, Jove, 1981, 291)

Certainly all this sexual activity sounds more like contemporary society than eighteenth- or nineteenth-century America and Europe. Not unexpectedly, the historical setting does not impede the imposition of contemporary social values and mores, especially those associated with changing sex roles, many of which indicate that behavioral norms for both the heroine and the hero (who are read as role models for desirable attributes and aspirations) are coming together. When a hero urges a wife or lover to be honest rather than using "feminine wiles" and "veiled ploys" to get him into her bed (Donna Comeaux Zide, *Lost Splendor*, Warner, 1981), we are seeing a change in the traditional meaning of feminine, which once excused all manner of devious behavior on the basis that it was in the nature of the beast — the female.

Another example appears in Grace Ingram's *Gilded Spurs* (Fawcett, 1978, 246), when the heroine apologizes because she has never "learned to please men." The hero responds, " 'Don't. You please me as you are. . . . You don't fear I'd think any ill of your lovely honesty, my heart?' " In Cynthia Wright's *Silver Storm* (Ballantine, 1979, 314), the hero tells the heroine, " 'You are as priceless as the most brilliant diamond. Very nearly a miracle — a beautiful, brave, intelligent, witty female who is totally without guile.' " And the heroine in one of Roberta Gellis's novels set in twelfth-century England is admired for attributes overtly characterized as male:

> "You want a helpless, mindless thing as a wife, or no wife at all. If I could be that for you, I would, so much do I love you, but I cannot be other than I am. . . ."
>
> "I would not have you other than you are. . . . You are the only woman I have ever known whose heart, mind, and spirit I can admire. You are the only woman I have ever known that is deserving of the kind of love a man gives to a man." (*The Sword and the Swan*, Playboy Press, 1977, 381–82)

Further evidence of contemporary social mores is that in 80 percent of the books the heroine possesses more education than was common to women of her time, and she is especially admired by the hero for her intellect and interest in public affairs. In *The Frost and the Flame*, for example (Drusilla Campbell, Pocket Books, 1980, 69), appears a hero who "appreciated women who cared enough about their world to have opinions. . . . All his adult life, Alexei had sought women who combined both beauty and intelligence. And spirit." Reciprocal sexual satisfaction is portrayed as important to both hero and heroine in 87 percent, and heroes shed tears in nearly 40 percent. In one-third of the stories the heroine either poses as a man or boy (such as squire to a knight, binding her breasts in order to conceal her gender) or assumes a male role even though she is known to be female—often as a pirate, as did one of the two heroines in Valerie Vayle's *Seaflame* (Dell, 1980). Rather than a denial of her femininity, these episodes read as the acting out of an equal-to-men fantasy, in which the heroine becomes player rather than spectator.

Attempts to find a successful method of contraception appear fairly frequently in these stories, even within the historical context—special herbs known to harem women in the Middle East, for instance, and sponges used by brothel ladies in the Old American West, who pass on the information to rebellious heroines. Contraceptives are almost always used without her partner's knowledge, causing him to wonder why she does not conceive, which he believes will seal his control over her in a more permanent way, and virtually all are attempts to escape domination by men. Nonetheless, with a lot of sexual activity and no reliable or widely known methods of contraception available, child-bearing occurs with considerable frequency. This does not mean, of course, that heroines are always reluctant mothers. In *Skye O'Malley*, for instance, Bertrice Small created a heroic heroine who fearlessly engages in psychological and physical warfare with the Queen of

England, among others, has four different husbands (including the Whoremonger of Algiers, who, it turns out, is a gentle and loving man), and bears six children—and then four years later came a sequel! That Skye stretched the credibility of many of Small's admiring fans is evident in the comment of one that "I enjoy Bertrice Small when she isn't putting poor Skye O'Malley through her four-hundredth adventure." Another found it "a little hard to believe that Skye had a body that drove men insane after bearing ten or eleven children."

In a 1976 piece for *Ms.* magazine, Molly Haskell argued that "one of the few instances in which society seems able to condone sensuality in a woman is when she is 'taken' and overwhelmed by the male. It is under these circumstances, in which the male assumes total responsibility for the figurative rape, that a woman can shed her guilts about enjoying sex." In the sample of books examined here, the heroine is raped in more than half (54 percent), giving considerable credence to the "rape saga" tag. In only 18.5 percent of the stories is rape portrayed as a sexual act—the "rape fantasy"—an act of seduction in which the heroine ultimately finds pleasure and even reaches orgasm, thus "getting permission," as Beatrice Faust described it, or absolving herself of guilt for enjoying sex, according to Haskell's interpretation. A less contrived explanation of this curious phenomenon that seems more consistent with contemporary reality, however, is Star Helmer's observation that "for a lot of women it's very difficult to reach a climax, and in the rape fantasy she is forced to have one" (in Harrison, 1984, 17). Judging by what many sex therapists report about female clients, Helmer might well have added "during intercourse with her partner."

Whatever the interpretation, the distinction between rape and seduction is one that most readers appreciate. Typical of many readers surveyed in 1985 was the one who questioned, "But is it really rape?" when asked to agree or disagree with the statement "Romance novels in which the hero forces the heroine to have sex against her will (rape) are exciting, sexually stimulating fantasies." Another added the comment, "There's a vast difference between seduction and rape. The heroine usually ends up loving [rape] in the books—not the same as in real life!" A little more than 60 percent disagreed with the statement, while 8 percent were undecided.

In nearly three-quarters of the stories examined in which rape actually occurs, the hero expresses the belief that the victim suffered a physical and psychological assault that was not her fault—a decidedly contemporary point of view. The rebellion and rage many women feel today at their perceived vulnerability to this special kind of assault

and social control is echoed repeatedly in the experiences and responses of the heroines who live in these historical novels. As Faust
(1980, 153) observed, "Even sexual insults are not entirely negative;
although the heroines are often victims, they are no longer passive,
spineless or vapid." Turning the tables on the stereotypical male-
dominance scene in which so many historical romance heroines find
themselves, Janine, who is captain of her own pirate ship, accedes to a
captured captain's plea for mercy by demanding that he satisfy her
sexually or take his chances with her crew, and then she carries
through on her decision. He finds some difficulty in "performing"
under these unusual (for him) conditions:

> His face became bathed in perspiration, and trickles rolled down his
> neck. "The—the circumstances make it difficult for me. The atmosphere
> isn't—well, it isn't right for making love. Please be reasonable."
> Janine looked him up and down slowly, making him even more con-
> scious of his nudity. "I assume you've been intimate with a number of
> women on many occasions over the years. Am I correct?" He had no idea
> where her question might lead, but was forced to nod in agreement. "Surely
> you never stopped to wonder whether the circumstances were appropriate
> for the lady. You were interested only in your own pleasure and didn't think
> of her."
> "But that was different—."
> "Nonsense," she declared, her voice sharp. "A man has such vanity that
> he believes a woman will be receptive to him at any time and under any
> circumstances. Now you begin to know better." (Michelle de Winter, *Janine*,
> Fawcett, 1979, 249)

No matter whether accomplished through rape, seduction, or her
timidly eager cooperation, the heroine's first experience with sexual
intercourse usually opens the door to her dormant sexuality, and force
is rarely present in subsequent sexual episodes, some of which the
heroine initiates herself. Losing her virginity is a rite of passage, the
dawn of a self-awareness that ultimately becomes a fully developed
sense of herself as an individual, not defined by sex, marriage, or
family lineage.

Rape is just one of many misfortunes that befall women in the
bodice rippers or erotic historical romances, however. Heroines are
sometimes forced into marriage (28 percent) and even prostitution (11
percent), which at times amount to very nearly the same thing. They
may be indentured, kidnapped by savage Indians, or exiled across the
ocean to a strange new world without benefit of family, friends, or
finances. They may even be sold into slavery, destined for service in

some powerful sheik's harem, all of which is reminiscent of Nina Baym's (1978, 22) description of the characteristic hardship plot of nineteenth-century women's fiction, except that these heroines have broken out of the domestic arena.

To simply call them victims would be to miss the crucial point, however, because hardship is the device used to set the stage for what readers prize almost as much as the developing love relationship—the heroine as a woman of indomitable spirit and wit, a fighter who "gives as good as she gets" and overcomes by "holding her own ground," as readers often describe her. Erotic historical romance heroines are an extremely strong and determined lot, bent on throwing off the yoke of self-sacrificing subservience imposed on them by the society and time in which they are imprisoned. One such is Scotswoman Janet Leslie, who (after half a lifetime of being subject to the command of others) agrees to be mistress to the man she loves but refuses to sacrifice her newfound freedom by marrying him: "She started to laugh. 'Oh, Colly! Don't ye understand? My whole life has been controlled by men. This is the first time I've ever been in control of my own destiny. Neither Adam nor Charles [her sons] would dare to interfere wi' me, and I am wealthy in my own right. I like it! If I married ye, then ye would hae the right to control both me and my money. I should never be free again.' " (Bertrice Small, *The Kadin*, Avon, 1978, 398)

How Readers See Heroines and Heroes

A number of personality and sex-typing tests developed over the years have been based on an either/or concept, which meant that the "healthiest" male was one who achieved the highest "masculinity" score, while the female with the highest "femininity" score was deemed the "healthiest" female. The Adjective Check List (Gough and Heilbrun 1965), for instance, used traits categorized as feminine (including fickle, weak, high-strung, emotional, submissive, meek, talkative, and prudish) and masculine (aggressive, steady, stern, unemotional, and courageous). In the 1970s, in part due to the influence of women's liberation advocates, the concepts of androgyny (exhibiting both masculine and feminine characteristics) and psychological health began to come together. Sandra Bem (1976) proposed that weak rather than strong sex-role identity is associated with better mental health, and that gender identity is not bound to traditional concepts of masculine and feminine personality, though the "healthy androgyne" needs "a secure sense of one's maleness or femaleness" (p. 60). The Bem Sex-

Illustration by Bob McGinnis for Avon Books paperback edition of *The Kadin*, © 1978.

Role Inventory (1974) treats masculinity and femininity as two separate dimensions and assigns a score for each; subjects who score high
on both dimensions are considered psychologically androgynous.
Among the feminine traits in the BSRI are gentle, yielding, faithful,
and forgiving, while masculine traits include dominant, independent,
and competitive. Using a similar scale of their own, the Personal
Attributes Questionnaire, Janet Spence, Robert Helmreich, and Joy
Stapp (1974; Spence and Helmreich 1978) found that, though women
usually score higher on the feminine dimension and men on the
masculine dimension, individuals with the highest levels of both feminine and masculine personality traits have higher levels of self-esteem
and are exceptionally well-adjusted.

Over time, the BSRI and PAQ, the concept of masculinity-
femininity as it relates to sex roles and attitudes, and the validity of the
construct of androgyny as realized in these scales, have been vigorously
questioned and debated (e.g., Henley 1985); so, too, has the appro-
priateness of labels adopted by various researchers to describe the relationship between sex roles, gender identity, personality traits, and attitudes. Janet Spence, for instance, points out that the personality *traits*
comprising the BSRI have no demonstrated relationship to sex *roles*,
and what were formerly called feminine traits are now referred to as
"expressive" while the so-called masculine traits have become "instrumental."[3] Bem (1981) has modified her theoretical approach, moving
from gender-related self concepts to cognitive structures that organize
perceptions of both the self and others, which she calls "gender schema
theory." Spence and Sawin (1985, 59) have proposed throwing out the
old concepts of masculinity-femininity, gender-role identity, and gender schema and replacing them with a more global concept of gender
identity—the "basic, existential conviction that one is [psychologi-
cally] male or female."

In spite of these unresolved issues, the expressive and instrumental
traits used in both the BSRI and PAQ are deemed useful in the context
of assessing readers' perceptions of the primary characters portrayed
in popular romance novels.[4] What is of particular interest here is to
discover what expressive and instrumental characteristics are exhibited
by both sexes and how these character profiles conform to our most
cherished notions of masculinity and femininity, especially when it
comes to romance heroines and heroes. Rather than interpreting
characters who exhibit both expressive and instrumental traits as androgynous, we can describe them as less sex-typed.

A set of twenty-eight adjective scales was selected from the BSRI, the Spence-Helmreich scale, and others for the purpose of describing some personality traits of romance heroines and heroes. These (semantic differential) scales were pretested and then presented to seventy-five romance readers who were asked to "describe" the heroine and hero in a historical romance novel they had just finished reading by placing a mark in one of six response spaces between the opposing adjectives. (This was not a statistically random sample, since the forms were distributed through two new/used/exchange bookstores in Austin, Texas.) The three spaces closest to each adjective were interpreted to mean "very," "fairly," and "slightly," which allowed readers to decide, for example, just how dominating or how submissive each character was. Scores for each pair of adjectives were averaged and are graphically displayed in Figure 1.

While all except five of the mean values for personality characteristics of heroines and heroes are significantly different (passionate-cold, high spirited-docile, brave-fearful, interesting-uninteresting, wise-foolish, and handsome/beautiful-plain), both heroines and heroes display varying degrees of both expressive and instrumental traits. Heroes are more mysterious, rigid, serious, stubborn, aggressive, and independent than heroines (both domineering and stubborn are socially undesirable instrumental traits on the PAQ). That readers probably did not get to know heroes as well as heroines is suggested by the fact that about one-third of the mean values for male characters fell near the midpoint of the scale, between 3 and 4. Heroines are more kind, just, moral, outspoken, warm, generous, faithful, gentle, forgiving, open, impulsive, fragile, flexible, trustful, and submissive than heroes — which does not mean that they are submissive, any more than it means that heroes are immoral or selfish. While both characters score higher on the traits generally ascribed to their gender (as did the subjects tested by Spence, for instance), they can nonetheless be described as less sex-typed than the traditional stereotypes. For heroines and heroes, the mean values lie on the independent and aggressive side of the midpoint, both of which are masculine, or instrumental, traits, as opposed to the dependent and timid side.

Factor analysis of readers' responses to characters, a statistical technique used to determine what types of attributes, behavior, or attitudes tend to occur together, resulted in two strong groupings, one labeled temperament traits and the other sociability traits. As shown in Table 2, nine temperament traits and six sociability traits tend to occur together for both characters.

Since most of these romance novels are written from the heroine's

HISTORICAL CHARACTERS

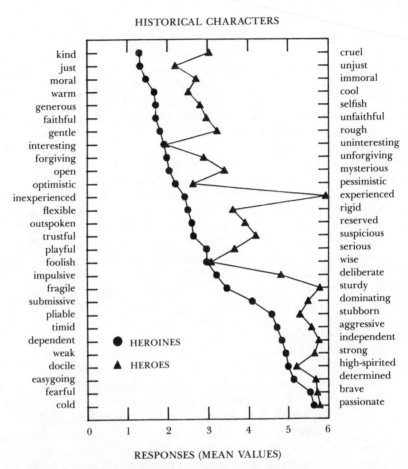

Figure 1. Reader responses (N = 75) to adjective scales used to describe heroines and heroes in erotic historical romance novels, 1981. Traits were ordered to visually clarify the differences between male and female characters.

Table 2.   Personality traits that tend to occur together in heroines and heroes of erotic historical romances, based on factor analysis of reader responses (1981) to adjective scales (four-factor oblique rotation resolution[a]). Attributes that do not group together for both sexes appear in bold type.

HEROINES	HEROES
Temperament	
high spirited/docile	high spirited/docile
determined/easy going	determined/easy going
independent/dependent	independent/dependent
playful/serious	playful/serious
stubborn/pliable	stubborn/pliable
optimistic/pessimistic	optimistic/pessimistic
passionate/cold	passionate/cold
deliberate/impulsive	deliberate/impulsive
dominating/submissive	**interesting/uninteresting**
aggressive/timid	**brave/fearful**
reserved/outspoken	**strong/weak**
Sociability	
kind/cruel	kind/cruel
generous/selfish	generous/selfish
just/unjust	just/unjust
gentle/rough	gentle/rough
trustful/suspicious	trustful/suspicious
flexible/rigid	flexible/rigid
	moral/immoral
	faithful/unfaithful
	forgiving/unforgiving
	stubborn/pliable
	open/mysterious
	dominating/submissive

[a]Only traits that loaded above .4 are included in this listing. Retaining four factors, these two clusters of traits account for 78.7 percent of the variation in the responses to heroes, and 74.8 percent of the variation in the responses to heroines.

point of view, and even in the case of a mixed point of view she is usually the leading character, the impression readers get of heroes is filtered through her. In addition, most of the novels examined are written by women, and all the readers responding to the adjective scales were women. Taken in this light, some of the differences (the dominating-submissive trait clustering among temperament traits for female characters but among sociability traits for males, for instance) may say more about how women interpret certain traits in men than about hero traits per se.

Evolution and Change

The majority of titles examined in this study conform to the generalized definition of a courtship–love story, focusing on the male-female relationship and portraying the love of the hero as the most important motivation in the heroine's life (as the love of the heroine also comes to be in the hero's life). However, the fundamental power relationship between men and women has begun to change, or at least to be challenged. It is not a simple case of love overcoming all problems and obstacles, as John Cawelti (1976, 41) described the moral fantasy of the romance, but a specific kind of love, one that frees respect and the right of self-determination from gender. Indeed, contrary to Cawelti's view that the female protagonist is not a "crucial defining characteristic" of the modern romance, the new heroine is inextricably bound up with the overcoming itself. In these stories, the heroine's ability to overcome hardship is a metaphor for her struggle and eventual emergence as an individual capable of the kind of love that overcomes all problems and obstacles. Because of the changes that followed it in the contemporary romances of the 1980s, the erotic historical romance of the 1970s now can be seen as perhaps the most significant *evolutionary* generation in the history of the romance novel.

Certainly the romance convention of yore, the split female persona, is well and truly dead here, which is, in fact, the major reason why readers migrated to these stories en masse. The heroine—by definition the paragon of virtue—cares about herself, about her own wants, needs, and goals in life, yet she is never depicted as selfish. For her, the virtues now include self-awareness, in both the emotional and physical sense, and the giving and receiving of sexual pleasure. Taken together, the heroine's fight for at least some measure of independence, and her desire for the sexual satisfaction and individual respect and dignity accorded males, amount to the driving force in her life.[5] The result is that the customary happy ending now is possible only through the heroine's emergence as an autonomous individual, no longer defined solely in terms of her relationship to a man.

The men with whom these women fall in love are strong-willed but not invincible, physically or emotionally. They are sensitive and capable of showing emotions—exhibiting the very traits they admire in women—if not in the beginning then through learning, loving, and understanding. Heroes also like women to share in taking the initiative, in bed and out, interpreting such behavior as expressions of caring and love. Though these heroines may seem bothersome and prickly at first, heroes ultimately come to find less-determined and outspoken women both uninteresting and unattractive—even to simply "service their needs."

During its first decade the erotic historical romance served as a kind of testing ground for women readers struggling to find new ways of seeing and thinking about themselves and their place in the world. Comparing content analysis data from the books published during the first half of the seventies with those published in the latter half confirms that the stories themselves were in transition as well, and there is a great deal of evidence suggesting that both consumer feedback and market forces interacted to bring about these changes. The Other Woman (the competition-over-a-man plot device) is seen less and less as the decade progressed, and is almost completely gone in the contemporary series romances published during the first half of the eighties. Heroines were becoming more and more overtly rebellious as the decade progressed, too, which often created an authenticity problem in the historical context. Both changes were due largely to reader complaints about story elements they found "boring," "contrived," "unrealistic," and "childish."

In the main, the erotic historical romance heroine of this period emerges from the data as superwoman—lover, mother, activist, partner, competitor—a description that fit most of them for at least a decade before those words, applied to "The New American Woman," appeared on the cover of *Esquire* magazine in 1984. Though her career aspirations do not match those of contemporary women, she nonetheless sounds very much like the kind of woman Betty Friedan (1981) described as the natural end product of changes wrought by the "first stage" of the women's movement. The fact that so many contemporary social values are reflected in these books is consistent with the view that popular culture and the mass media reflect existing social norms. But because the popularity of these novels coincided with a period of rapid social change, they also acted for many women as agents of change.

Certainly the portrait of female sexuality drawn in the titles examined is far more complex and feminist than most critics of the genre indicate. Though erotic romance heroines are with few exceptions still decidedly beautiful, these books do what Ellen Morgan (1973, 185–86) claimed for neofeminist historical novels—they give women back their history in a new form. "Emphasis is given to their ingenuity and courage. . . . the focus reflects neo-feminist consciousness that power, beauty, fame are not the wellsprings or housing of dignity and worth, that dignity and value of a person are to be found in the degree of inner growth achieved, in compassion, in the affirmation and acting out of humanistic values over and against the specifics of one's condition."

The erotic historical romance novels of this period go beyond Morgan's neofeminist historical novels, however, for in reflecting specific contemporary women's concerns within the historical setting, they project a powerful sense of shared experience and unity among women, one that transcends both time and place and is often explicitly articulated, as some of the excerpts presented here demonstrate. In addition, they mark the first appearance of a large and coherent body of sexual literature for women, providing the opportunity to learn to use sexual fantasy and to explore an aspect of their identities that patriarchal society has long denied women. Easily and widely accessible, these erotic novels carried the tacit stamp of approval of all mass culture—and by the end of the 1970s they were being read at an average rate of four or more per month by at least one out of every six American women over the age of fifteen.

Notes

1. No gothic, regency, or category romances were included in the sample since these types did not contain explicit erotic content during the period of time under study. It was not until after an apparent upsurge in the market for historical romance in late 1984 that some houses began publishing what editors called "sexy" gothics and regencies. The content analysis sample consisted of the following titles, 68 percent of which were published from 1978 through 1981 and 32 percent from 1972 through 1977 (given names of authors who write under pseudonyms are included in the fiction bibliography):

Jane Archer, *Tender Torment*, Ace, 1978
Clare Barroll, *The Iron Crown*, Ballantine, 1975
Lynn Bartlett, *Courtly Love*, Warner, 1979
Jennifer Blake, *The Storm and the Splendor*, Fawcett, 1979
Stephanie Blake, *Secret Sins*, Playboy Press, 1980
Parris Afton Bonds, *Sweet Golden Sun*, Popular Library, 1978
Shirlee Busbee, *Gypsy Lady*, Avon, 1977; *Lady Vixen*, Avon, 1980
Drusilla Campbell, *The Frost and the Flame*, Pocket Books, 1980
Jocelyn Carew, *The Golden Sovereigns*, Avon, 1976
Megan Castell, *Queen of a Lonely Country*, Pocket Books, 1980

Jude Deveraux, *The Black Lyon*, Avon, 1980; *The Velvet Promise*, Richard Gallen/Pocket Books, 1981

Michelle de Winter, *Janine*, Fawcett, 1979

Lynn Erickson, *The Silver Kiss*, Pocket Books, 1981

Julia Fitzgerald, *Royal Slave*, Ballantine, 1978

Chloe Gartner, *The Image and the Dream*, Dell, 1980

Roberta Gellis, *Roselynde*, Playboy Press, 1976; *The Sword and the Swan*, Playboy Press, 1977

Constance Gluyas, *The House on Twyford Street*, Signet, 1976

Lisa Gregory, *Analise*, Jove, 1981

Julia Grice, *Lovefire*, Avon, 1977

Lafayette Hammette, *The Captain's Doxy*, Leisure Books, 1980

Flora Hiller, *Love's Fiery Dagger*, Popular Library, 1978

Grace Ingram, *Gilded Spurs*, Fawcett, 1978

Lydia Lancaster, *Her Heart's Honor*, Warner, 1980

Andrea Layton, *So Wild a Rapture*, Playboy Press, 1978

Susannah Leigh, *Glynda*, Signet, 1979

Johanna Lindsey, *Captive Bride*, Avon, 1977; *Fires of Winter*, Avon, 1980

Patricia Matthews, *Love's Avenging Heart*, Pinnacle, 1976; *Love's Wildest Promise*, Pinnacle, 1977

Laurie McBain, *Devil's Desire*, Avon, 1975; *Chance the Winds of Fortune*, Avon, 1980

Fern Michaels, *Captive Passions*, Ballantine, 1977; *Captive Splendors*, Ballantine, 1980

Saliee O'Brien, *Captain's Woman*, Pocket Books, 1979

Laura Parker, *Silks and Sabers*, Dell, 1980

Natasha Peters, *Savage Surrender*, Ace, 1977

Patricia Phillips, *Anise*, Jove, 1978

Janette Radcliffe, *Stormy Surrender*, Dell, 1978

Barbara Riefe, *So Wicked the Heart*, Playboy Press, 1980

Rosemary Rogers, *Sweet Savage Love*, Avon, 1974; *The Wildest Heart*, Avon, 1974

Christina Savage, *Dawn Wind*, Dell, 1980

Bertrice Small, *The Kadin*, Avon, 1978; *Skye O'Malley*, Ballantine, 1980

Jan Cox Speas, *My Lord Monleigh*, Avon, 1978 (original hardcover published in 1956)

Diane Summers, *Wild Is the Heart*, Playboy Press, 1978

Valerie Vayle, *Seaflame*, Dell, 1980

Jennifer Wilde, *Love's Tender Fury*, Warner, 1976

Claudette Williams, *Blades of Passion*, Fawcett Crest, 1978

Kathleen Woodiwiss, *The Flame and the Flower*, Avon, 1972; *The Wolf and the Dove*, Avon, 1974

Cynthia Wright, *The Silver Storm*, Ballantine, 1979

Donna Comeaux Zide, *Caress and Conquer*, Warner, 1979

2. Not long ago, according to Bernard Starr and Marcella Weiner (1981, 67–68), the prevailing view was that men had "orgasmic urgency" and if aroused needed immediate release because men could get "blue balls," a "painful condition that demanded they turn to 'bad girls' or prostitutes to ease their suffering. Every respectable woman prior to the 1960s tolerantly accepted this. But who ever heard of 'blue clit,' even though there is a medical condition, called Taylor's syndrome, in which high levels of excitement in the female results in vasocongestion that can lead to pain and physical complications if orgasm does not occur."

3. Where formerly subjects were categorized according to their scores on the PAQ as androgynous, masculine, feminine, or undifferentiated, Janet Spence and Linda Sawin (1985) labeled them as high expressive and instrumental, instrumental, expressive, or low expressive and instrumental.

4. Looking at sex-role portrayals in magazines, M. Dwayne Smith and Marc Matre (1975) found that women in romance magazines (short stories aimed at low socioeconomic status female readers) were portrayed as domestic, weak, passive, emotional, and dependent, while men were strong, masterful, confident, aggressive, and protective. At the same time, women in adventure magazines aimed at male readers were more aggressive, both sexually and otherwise, and "made things happen, although they did not ultimately supplant males as being the more dominant and masterful of the sexes" (p. 314).

5. In a fuzzily reported study that provides no indication as to how many novels were examined, Josephine Ruggiero and Louise Weston (1983, 19) state that two types of novels have dominated the romance field over the past twenty years—the modern gothics and the historical romance. Exactly where they place the multimillions of Harlequins sold during the 1970s is not clear. Their piece is riddled with small errors: for example, Ace Books has never produced a line of "numbered romance novels," either successfully or otherwise; the implication that Silhouettes, like Harlequin Romances and Candlelight Regencies, enjoyed increasing popularity during the 1970s, when in fact the first Silhouette did not appear until May 1980; the statement that Harlequin was releasing six romances each month, when the company had been publishing at least twelve per month since 1973, including Harlequin Presents romances, which Ruggiero and Weston indicate were initiated in the 1980s; and that Ricardo Montalban advertised Harlequins on TV, when in fact he spoke for Silhouette. They conclude about the historical romance heroine that "little is revealed about her attitudes and convictions," and they indicate that one of the "cultural stereotypes about women" encountered in historical romances is that "they want to be raped" (p. 24). That neither of these assertions is true of the large sample examined here is evident from both the content analysis and the excerpts presented.

Chapter Five

THE REALITY FANTASY

Challenging the Power Structure in the

Sensuous Contemporary Romance

Traditionally, a man's life is his work; a woman's life is
her man. That a woman's life might have connections
with her work is a revolutionary idea in that it might
—indeed, must—lead her to examine and question her
place as a woman in the social order. The idea may be
especially revolutionary when it is not simply in the
head of a Wollstonecraft, a Fuller, a de Beauvoir, but
an idea in all our heads.
  Florence Howe, "Feminism and Literature"

"You and I will do a lot of loving just for ourselves,"
Sy promised, taking her hand. "We'll take our time to
find out just what direction our life together will take.
I see the magic in your eyes when you want me, but
I've also seen the same magic in your eyes when you
talk about your work."
  Christina Crockett, *A Moment of Magic*

*M*any sociologists, anthropol-
ogists, and psychologists agree that sex roles are shaped largely by
economic issues, and that different sets of responsibilities for men and
women resulted in men having greater status and power (see, e.g.,
Chafe 1972), a "power structure" enforced and bolstered by law and
custom in most societies throughout the centuries of human history.
Ernestine Friedl (1975), for instance, argues that even in agrarian
societies it is the right to distribute and exchange valued goods and
services to those outside a person's domestic unit that historically has
conferred power and prestige. The redefinition of sex roles that has
taken place in the United States during the past two decades is seen
largely as the result of the redistribution of women into "more important positions" as well as the redistribution of rewards, both of which
promote sex-role crossover (similar lifestyles for men and women),
which ultimately will create a value system characterized by comple-

mentarity and interdependence rather than priority and social hierarchy (Giele 1978).

The erotic contemporary series romances which began appearing in 1981 reflect many of the ways sex roles have been redefined during this time, and the ways American women have begun to challenge the power structure of patriarchal society, both economically and sexually. They are for the most part stories about women who attempt to expand the possibilities and opportunities for their own growth, development, and fulfillment, and to change the way society perceives and values them as individuals. And these popular romances have done so precisely because the "creativity of authors" has been tightly controlled by market-oriented editorial guidelines.

During the 1970s readers began to demand characters who were more realistic, who they could identify with more closely, displacing the submissive ingenues as well as the glamorous jet-set crowd. Heroines not only aged but became more mature and more sexually experienced. Editor Tara Hughes advised aspiring romance authors attending a 1985 Silhouette-sponsored workshop that "nothing turns a reader off more than a heroine who continually sets herself up for abuse." She warned them to "steer clear of traditionally feminine jobs. Pick something unique, such as a judge, probation officer or sheriff." The *Wall Street Journal* (Morris 1984) headlined an article about Silhouette's success, "If the Damsel Is in Distress, Be Sure It's Career-Related."

Heroines blazed new trails in their attempts to become economically autonomous—as chemists, cartoonists, caterers, and construction workers, as lawyers, psychiatrists, and government agents—a reflection of the interest among readers in widening career opportunities for women. Today the series romance heroine might be a speech therapist or a veterinarian, president of a trucking firm or a newspaper editor, but she is almost always involved in some kind of work outside the home that does more than simply pay the rent. Her dedication to a career is borne out not only by content analysis of sixty-five erotic series romance titles published between 1982 and mid-1985,[1] which found that 97 percent of heroines had careers, but also by publishers' tip sheets for authors:

> Aged 26–40 . . . she should have either a profession, a great interest (sports, the arts, etc.), or a demanding job in or out of business. She should not be a typing-pool secretary, but executive/administrative assistant positions are definitely acceptable. (Berkley/Jove Second Chance at Love)

Generally 23–32, she is intelligent and mature. . . . Independent and accomplished, she supports herself successfully in her chosen profession and is never clinging or weepy. (Silhouette Special Edition)

The heroine is a capable, mature American woman in her twenties or thirties, established in an interesting career. (Harlequin Temptation)

Most Ecstasy heroines are between the ages of 25 and 35, most are established in an interesting career. (Dell Candlelight Ecstasy)

Heroine [is] to be 28 to 45 years old. . . . Generally a good portrait of the heroine's career/job, at which she should work hard and be fairly successful. (Ballantine Love and Life)

Certainly these women do not fit the stereotype drawn largely from 1970s-style Harlequin heroines, who were "teachers, nurses and nurserymaids" (Snitow 1979), or "marginal workers with little commitment to the labour force, who work for 'pin money' rather than for necessities" (Jensen 1984, 97). What a different picture is painted in Möeth Allison's *Love Everlasting* (Silhouette Intimate Moments, 1983), in which the heroine earns $400,000 a year as a chemist who runs her own cosmetics company! Though she obtains outside financial help from the hero to expand her business, this thirty-year-old woman quite obviously is not working for pin money, and her necessities include a great deal more than food on the table and a roof over her head. She has worked hard and with considerable personal sacrifice to develop her company, as well as her skill and knowledge, and she refuses to allow the hero to dominate her business decisions.

> "You've got to sell. Are you so stupid, so wrapped up in your own ego, that you can't see that elementary fact?" He took a deep breath and tried to gauge her reaction. Was he getting through? . . . "Who the hell do you think you are—Superwoman? You're killing yourself trying to pull a rabbit out of the hat and you don't know enough to stop. You're behaving hysterically. . . . After the sale goes through, you'll be a rich woman . . . you can stop worrying about stockholders and cash flow. My own suggestion would be that you try becoming a three-dimensional woman for a change. Marry me and find out what the rest of life is all about." . . .
>
> "I don't have time for all this oratory right now," she said in a strangled voice. "Why don't you find some other soapbox." She turned and ran up the stairs, leaving him drained and speechless. . . . Anger had clotted her throat and tightened her muscles. It was still there now, like a throttling hand on her neck. How dare he call her hysterical! How dare he imply she wasn't a whole woman if she didn't marry him. It was an insulting proposal that sounded as if she were some poor stupid slob who'd made a hash of things and needed a man to take care of her. (pp. 222–23)

After she goes against his advice and brings off a roaring success for herself and her stockholders, she tries to explain to this "traditional" man that she wanted to "prove I was a three-dimensional woman on my own first." When she asks if his offer of marriage is still open, he responds, " 'I had a wife in mind, not a one-woman cartel. You've got a corporate achievement chart where your heart's supposed to be.' " She denies it. He dares her to prove it.

> "Eastern Chemicals still wants the corporation. Go for the merger, resign from the board, and make a new career out of being my wife."
> Knowing how much of her life she had poured into Drieser Industries, he was calmly demanding she get rid of it, not out of necessity now, but just to satisfy his whim. . . . He was mad because she'd proved him wrong, that's what all this was about. She had done the unpardonable—ignored his sacred advice and succeeded. He couldn't handle it. . . . Now her own anger was pumping molten steel through her veins. Suddenly she was on her feet and shaking with rage as she headed for the door. "You insecure, small-minded bastard! You don't need a wife," she said, her voice strong and clear. "You need a lame duck to make you feel superior." (pp. 236–37)

Is it possible that we are hearing the sentiments of Virginia Woolf on the lips of a romance heroine? In *A Room of One's Own* (1981/ 1929, 35), Woolf talked about looking-glass vision: "half of the people . . . say to themselves as they go into the room, I am superior to half the people here, and it is thus that they speak with that self-confidence, that self-assurance which have had such profound consequences in public life and lead to such curious notes in the margin of the private mind. . . . That is why Napoleon and Mussolini both insisted so emphatically upon the inferiority of women, for if they were not inferior, they would cease to enlarge." Though Woolf may have made her point more elegantly, certainly no reader could fail to understand Allison's message, sent via a "pulp" romance novel—one of that breed so often contemptuously referred to as the opiate of the female masses—a story that very likely was read by some half-million women, not only in the United States and England, but all around the world. Cassie Miles broadcast similar sentiments in *Tongue-Tied* (Harlequin Temptation, 1984, 143), when her speech therapist-heroine wonders, "What did he want from her? A political wife? Someone to sit beside him on the podium and laugh at his jokes and applaud his brilliance? He must know by now that that was a person she could never be. She hated that identity, considered it a total waste of time. 'And talent,' she said aloud. 'I'm a skilled person, one of the best in my field. I can't be happy as an adoring bystander.' "

Most romance heroines reflect the sentiments of the work-directed and undomesticated New Woman Margaret Edwards described in 1985: "If a woman calls a new tune because she's earned enough to pay the piper, it doesn't mean she has to dance unpartnered" (p. 55). Both Roper (1980) and Gallup polls (in "Women's Ideal Lifestyle," 1980) found that three-quarters of American women favor marriage as a way of life, but that marriage has been redefined as sharing the responsibilities for earned income, homemaking, and child-rearing. Today it makes about as much sense to call women who desire marriage and children "traditional" as it does to apply that label to a woman with a vagina.

Marriage may be the end point of most erotic contemporary romances, though some begin with that state already established, but few heroines intend to give up their work when married. The plot conflict thus often centers on the marriage versus career question, and heroines wrestle with the dilemma so many women face today. K. C. Coles (1982, 9) observed that "if most women I know resent being defined in terms of narrow philosophies, it's because their lives are so often steered by pure pragmatism. They pursue traditionally male careers primarily because it beats earning half the salary at traditionally female jobs. They prize their independence because they know what happens to women who depend on someone else for a lifetime of support. But that doesn't mean they're ready to give up their boyfriends or husbands, their children or their rice casseroles."

The heroine's relationship with the hero is not the be-all and end-all of her existence, however, as illustrated by what the heroine of Jessie Ford's *Searching* (Ballantine Love and Life, 1982, 155) comes to understand: "From the very beginning a major obstacle to ever getting on the right track was her belief that the secret to happiness was having a man at the center of her life and wanting him to make her feel like a complete person. In effect she was asking someone else to take responsibility for her very existence. She realized now, becoming and discovering she was a complete and independent person was essential before she could ever have a successful or lasting relationship with a man."

More and more heroines explain the importance of their work in terms of self-definition, as in Carla Neggers's *Heart on a String* (Bantam Loveswept, 1983, 102): "I'm a dedicated puppeteer. I can't and I won't sacrifice my work, who I *am*. I won't change to make your life more convenient. I—it took me long enough to find out who I am." In the end it is the hero in this tale who must convince the heroine that a lasting relationship is possible without either of them having to give up what they want and need as individuals. He offers to move his medical practice from Philadelphia to Boston, where her puppet workshop is located—just as the cartoonist hero relocates to suit the career needs of the psychiatrist heroine in Carol Katz's *Then Came Laughter* (Harlequin SuperRomance, 1985). And when the hero in Tate McKenna's *Enduring Love* (Dell Ecstasy, 1983), who lives in Arizona, asks the heroine to marry him, she protests, " 'I don't see how you can ask me to give up everything I've worked for all these years. My career, my personal goals, my home. It isn't fair to me.' " Her career-personal life conflict is solved by the hero's suggestion that she keep her Washington office and condo, and his offer to "fly you across the country to keep up with your eastern clients. . . . You can have it all, *mi amor*. Anything you want."

Like McKenna's heroine, 31 percent of the heroines in the titles included in the content analysis of erotic contemporary series romances are self-employed, and most of them are superwomen who want it all—economic self-sufficiency and a sense of autonomy, along with an intimate relationship with a man in which love and respect mutually are shared, as are the responsibilities associated with a home and family. A member of an Air Force missile launch crew, the heroine in Mary Ruth Myers's *An Officer and a Lady* (Ballantine, 1984, 9) resents "the logic that said because she could stand on her own if need be, she didn't need love." She has male as well as female friends, which the hero at first finds difficult to accept or understand. A computer fraud investigator who can work from any location, he ultimately decides to follow wherever her career takes her.

Certainly the New Heroine's career activities shift the emphasis away from the domestic role, the theme of the traditional romance. And some romance texts carry still another overt strike to the very heart of domesticity—the kitchen. After spending the night together, marketing consultant Ryan Hastings asks his fashion designer—employer Laura Renati, " 'Where are the wheat cakes you promised?' " She laughs and says, " 'You're fantasizing again.' " Later, munching on a piece of toast, he mutters, " 'I can't believe the only thing you can cook is toast.' " She tosses back, " 'I never had time to learn' " (Kathryn Kent, *Silk and Steel*, NAL Rapture, 1984, 108). One heroine, a mystery writer, is hard to pin down about marriage. In Kay Hooper's *Something Different* (Bantam Loveswept, 1984, 84), when the hero says, " 'I'm playing for keeps,' " she has to fight back "a sudden unease," then suggests, " 'Can we talk about that tomorrow?' " She continues to "drag her feet," protesting, " 'I can't cook and I'm not a housekeeper,' " until he responds, " 'How you do harp on that. . . . Do you think I give a damn. . . . So what? I couldn't write a book if you took me through it sentence by sentence' " (p. 129).

Sometimes the question of continuing her career after marriage is resolved through another man, which has become a common way to portray the differences between unacceptable males and the New Hero. In a story by Maureen Bronson (*Tender Verdict*, Harlequin Super-Romance, 1985, 27), the reader learns early on how the lawyer-judge heroine feels about her work through a flashback conversation with her former fiancé:

> "Let's be the first husband-and-wife team [in the building], with offices next door to each other."
> "Don't be silly. You won't have time. . . . You'll be too busy raising our family to even consider becoming a judge. I'd pictured you having a small practice in the suburbs."
> With a quivering voice, she said, "I have no intention of staying home to raise a family and letting all these years of hard work go to waste. . . . I want to carve out a niche for myself in criminal law. The field is financially and mentally rewarding. I've worked too hard to settle for less."

Heroines may still be beauties but now they are also high achievers, and many are introspective enough to realize that they do not conform to traditional sex-role expectations—nor do they have any intention of doing so—and will very likely never find a compatible male partner as a result. This, too, reflects the view held by many women that men in general still hold to traditional (reactionary) attitudes, expectations, and behavior. Again from *Tender Verdict* and a heroine with strong family ties to her Russian immigrant parents and retarded brother: "Anna Provo thought of her limitations. She believed she was inadequate outside of anything but law. Who wanted a woman who wouldn't have children? Who could deal with her hot temper, her single-mindedness about her family and career? It was unreasonable to expect anyone to tolerate her lack of maternal instincts, her busy schedule. What man would put up with being wedged into her busy life?" (p. 77). Who, indeed, but the New Hero? "If there was one flaw he could name that had consistently made him reject a lady, it was a clinging dependent nature. He could never accuse Anna Provo of hanging on him. He was lucky if she even gave a damn if he existed or not" (p. 69).

This particular hero is not unique. In Myers's *An Officer and a*

Lady the hero tells the heroine, " 'You say you like working, like being successful—well, I like it, too. In you, I mean. I'm not looking to make you into some kind of squaw who shuffles behind in her moccasins' " (p. 105). Another hero goes even farther with sex-role crossover when he hires on as housekeeper for a divorced advertising account executive with two young sons. Though she doesn't know it, the real reason he has taken the job is to research a magazine article he's writing about what it's like to be a "house husband." In the end, however, he discovers that he likes the arrangement. It fits his work scheduling needs while giving him more time with her boys, whom he has come to love (Linda Randall Wisdom, *Caution: Man at Work*, Dell Ecstasy Supreme, 1984).

Both the heroine and a secondary female character in Katz's *Then Came Laughter* illustrate how far sex-role reversal can go for women in these stories. The divorced heroine takes her former husband shopping and buys him not only a new suit in preparation for a job interview but also a hairpiece, hoping it will make him look more youthful and enhance his chances of getting the job, thereby getting him "off her back" both financially and emotionally. Her friend and colleague, also a psychiatrist, earns more than her art professor husband, who carries most of the responsibility for housework and child care. She tries to buy his happiness with a larger house and new studio, when all he really wants is more of her time and attention. The hero in this story is a syndicated cartoonist who goes the extra mile for the heroine, offering to "move lock, stock and barrel to the Midwest because it's more convenient for you." He finds himself "at last on the brink of a new beginning—a home, a family and the woman he loved above anyone else in the world" (p. 301), mirroring the feelings of one of the most traditional heroines encountered in the sample, who in the end "had what she wanted . . . a home, a husband who loved her, a baby. She felt whole and it made her strong" (Jackie Weger, *Winter Song*, Harlequin Temptation, 1984, 220).

The New Heroine generally is experienced, confident, self-sufficient, assertive, and even daring—all traits traditionally assigned to men— which means she no longer needs the male guardian, the rake, or the sugar daddy. What *does* she require in a man? Still a strong-willed character (he must be if he is to be her equal), the New Hero also exhibits many traits traditionally assigned to females—openness, flexibility, sensitivity, softness, and vulnerability—transforming him from invincible superman into fallible human being. Thus androgyny has burst into full bloom in the erotic series romance, in characters who "combine both masculine and feminine virtues—who combine both rationality and intuitiveness, humility and self-assertion, depending on the demands of the situation" (Warren 1980, 18).

As the eighties progressed another of the most rigid romance conventions was breached—the story written entirely from the heroine's point of view. Not surprisingly, this change, too, was wrought largely by consumer demand: 71 percent of readers surveyed in 1982 expressed a desire to see "a well-developed hero point of view," and by 1985 "mixed heroine-hero point of view" was at the top of the list of the five most-wanted story attributes. Readers are no longer satisfied with seeing only how the New Hero responds, they now want to look inside his head to discover what and how he thinks, why he responds as he does, what his motivations and problems are, and what he is feeling. In their headlong rush for something new, some publishers have gone overboard, as did New American Library in instituting a one-a-month romance "from his point of view" as part of its Rapture Romance line. In *Wolfe's Prey* (JoAnn Robb 1985), the hero "screams" when the heroine's cat jumps into his lap and startles him, suggesting nothing so much as a heroine-point-of-view story with transposed pronouns.

That readers also perceive heroines and heroes in contemporary series romances as quite minimally sex-typed or sex-differentiated, in the sense that they exhibit similar expressive and instrumental traits, is evident in their responses to the opposing adjective scales (Figure 2). An adjective scale form was included with questionnaires sent to readers surveyed by mail in 1985, and they were asked to complete it using "any romance title published during the past year." The mean values shown in Figure 2 represent only those readers who chose to describe characters in a contemporary series romance novel. (About half the adjective scales are different from those used in 1981, as presented in chapter 4.)

While all but five of the mean values for personality characteristics of heroines and heroes in the erotic historical romances were significantly different, almost the reverse is true for heroines and heroes in post-1981 erotic contemporary romances. Not only is there less spread between the mean values of responses to the two characters, but now only six traits show a (statistically) significant difference: complex-simple, kind-cruel, flexible-unbending, impulsive-deliberate, submissive-dominating, and powerful-powerless—a very strong indication that both heroines and heroes exhibit similar personality traits. To paraphrase Gloria Steinem's observation that we have become the

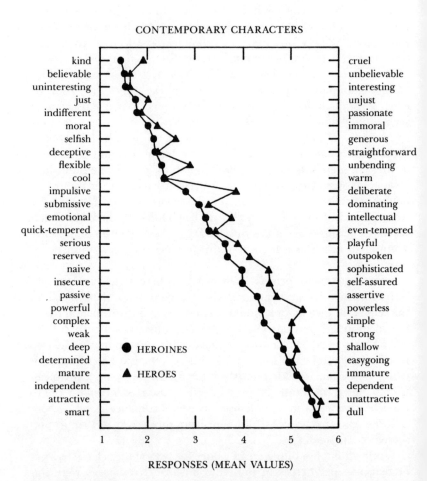

CONTEMPORARY CHARACTERS

RESPONSES (MEAN VALUES)

Figure 2. Reader responses (N = 128) to adjective scales used to describe heroines and heroes in erotic contemporary series romance novels, 1985. Traits were ordered to visually clarify the differences between female and male characters.

men we want to marry, romance readers appear to have created their fantasy heroes in their own image.

In order to look at the differences in responses to characters due to both time and type of romance, the mean scores for heroines and heroes in erotic historical romances were compared with those in series contemporary stories for the fifteen traits that are identical on both scales (see Figure 3). That contemporary heroines are at the same time more independent and more submissive is curious (and perhaps in some way associated with the fact that they are less playful and outspoken), though the score is still slightly past the midpoint toward the dominating side of the scale. Heroines are more serious, reserved, and cool, while heroes have become less assertive and more outspoken, impulsive, and flexible. Changes in heroes are at least in part a reflection of change in the women who read romances, since the hero—presumably the ideal of what women like in a man—is no longer the same "traditional" male. Some of the changes appear to be traits that readers have admired for some time (e.g., humor, playfulness) but only in recent years were able to persuade publishers to include in the stories.

Only three of the heroines in the titles included in the content analysis were virgins when the story opened (one was a former nun), but none remained in that state for long; heroines were sexually experienced in nearly 97 percent of the titles, with 19 percent of heroines and 12 percent of heroes either divorced, widowed, or married to a person who is not the heroine or hero (one of the latter is an MIA, another is brain damaged and in an institution). In nearly 10 percent of the stories the hero and heroine were already married when the story opens (half of these were To Have and To Hold titles, a series about married couples), and in the remaining 90 percent sexual intercourse takes place between the heroine and hero before marriage.

A consummated sexual relationship between the heroine and hero is a predictable convention in the erotic contemporary series romance, again because it was prescribed in written guidelines used during this period, which were based on what publishers tried to determine their customers wanted:

> The writing should be extremely sensuous, providing vivid, evocative descriptions of lovemaking and concentrating on the characters' reactions to each other and the sexual tension between them. . . . Sexual encounters—which may include nudity and lovemaking even when the protagonists are not married—should concentrate on the highly erotic sensations aroused

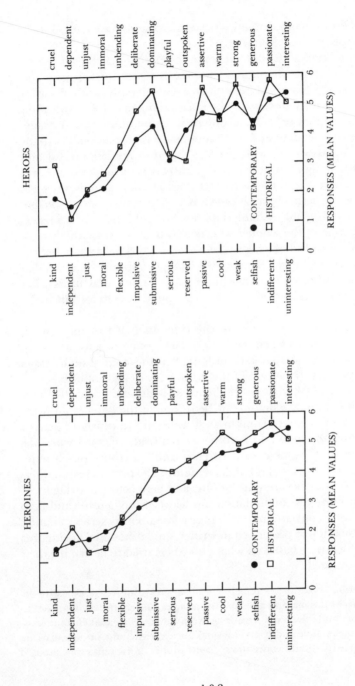

Figure 3. A comparison of reader responses to heroes and heroines in erotic historical romances (1981) with those in erotic contemporary series romances (1985).

by the hero's kisses and caresses rather than the mechanics of sex. (Silhouette Desire)

[The heroine] has already experienced and accepted her own sexuality. . . . Because this series mirrors the lives of contemporary women, realistic descriptions of love scenes should be included, provided they are tastefully handled. . . . [Heroine and hero] should definitely consummate their relationship before the end of the story, at whatever point it fits naturally into the plot. The love scenes should be frequent, but not overwhelming, and should never be gratuitously included. (Harlequin Temptation)

The hero and heroine do make love even when unmarried, and with plenty of sensuous description. No clinical terms . . . [and] no adultery. . . . Mild lovemaking should be introduced as early in the story as is convincingly possible and should gradually build in intensity until the couple actually makes love, by about half-way through the story. They should make love at least once more in the second half of the book. Actual lovemaking should be described in considerable length—in several pages rather than several paragraphs—and with plenty of sensual detail. (Berkley/Jove Second Chance at Love)

Yes, we want smoldering love scenes . . . but we also want to see our hero and heroine finding their way to each other through emotional and intellectual encounters as well. In other words, we want to see the emergence of a convincing, full-dimensional and *mature* love affair. (Dell Ecstasy)

Sex [is] pretty important, when needed for the plot/characters. Grown-ups go to bed with the men they love and even some they do not. (Ballantine Love and Life)

Sexual satisfaction for both parties is guaranteed in most of the "realistic" contemporary stories examined, and in almost 90 percent of them the heroines initiate, take control, and/or share equally in orchestrating the sex act. Stories vary more in the degree of explicitness with which sex acts are described than with whether, how often, or with whom they occur. Once the hero and heroine meet, even the thought of any relationship with another partner, no matter how brief or superficial, was quickly eliminated by a groundswell of negative reader response. (Avon's Finding Mr. Right, a line built around a plot in which the heroine is faced with making a choice between two potential heroes, sometimes between two lovers, failed in part for this reason.)

While the economically autonomous heroine brought the demise of several traditional plots, such as the Forced Marriage and the Protective Guardian, acceptance of a new norm for female sexual capacity and responsiveness has given rise to at least two new plot devices in the contemporary romance. In one, the now sexually experienced superwoman who is divorced-widowed-long separated from a former lover, thereby being deprived of what her body has learned to need, is a walking Time Bomb, ready to explode into nearly uncontrollable flames at the mere touch of the unsuspecting hero. In addition, the heroine's body is at times as uncontrollably reflexive as the male's, making it possible for the Russian dissident hero in Alexandra Sellers's *Captive of Desire* (Harlequin SuperRomance, 1982) to threaten to force the heroine's "traitorous" body to submit to him unless she stops writing articles about him. The Married Virgin is another variation on the sexual theme, in which the sexually experienced woman is still a sort-of virgin because she has never experienced orgasm. The heroine in Barbara Delinsky's *Bronze Mystique* (Harlequin Temptation, 1984, 157) tells the hero, " 'He [her former husband] was little more than a rutting animal. When he felt the urge, I was his receptacle. [He never] tried to arouse me. My pleasure wasn't part of his definition of the act. He was only concerned with relieving himself. . . . When I was dry—which I always was—he seemed to take pleasure in my cries. It was his way of exerting his authority over me, I suppose.' "

Traditional attitudes or viewpoints are still present in a number of stories, of course, as Weger's *Winter Song* illustrates, and also Judith McNaught's *Double Standards* (Harlequin Temptation, 1984)—a cliché-ridden tale that takes top prize in the forked-tongue category, at the same time arguing for and against the double standard, though there is absolutely no doubt which side the author comes down on in the end. First the hero (still another man "done wrong" by his mother) chides the twenty-three-year-old virgin heroine for her reservations about sleeping with him. " 'About what?' he mocked tolerantly. 'About stealing something that belongs to your future husband? Don't be ridiculous. He won't expect you to be a virgin; men don't prize virginity any more. We don't want or expect a woman to be inexperienced. We're liberated too, you know. You have the same physical desires I do, Lauren, and you have the right to satisfy them with whomever you wish' " (p. 87).

It turns out that talk is cheap, however. McNaught's hero begins to change his tune after the "green devil" nibbles away his purported liberation. Eventually he admits he believed what he was saying at the time because it was convenient and " 'I wasn't in love with you then' " (p. 176), allowing the old double standard to blossom forth in all its regressive glory. The heroine worries needlessly: She wanted "to please him always, and in all ways, but what if she failed tonight? Nick was so alarmingly virile and blatantly experienced that her virginity and inexperience might seem like a nuisance to him" (p. 82). When he discovers he is the only lover she has ever had, "the relief Nick experienced was so intense that he hardly knew how to cope with it." He looks at her, standing in the center of the room, "an angel in seductive black velvet. . . . There was a fineness about her, a quiet pride in herself that had prevented her from becoming a convenient receptacle for the passions of boys and men" (p. 178). Nary a word is mentioned, of course, about the stud service *he* has provided for literally dozens of girls and women.

Opportunities to protest variations on the double standard abound in the context of the heroine's work experience — another device used to differentiate the New Hero — as in Maura Seger's *Silver Zephyr* (Silhouette Intimate Moments, 1984, 89–90): " 'There's no denying I've got a heavy dose of [ambition]. . . . I'll never understand why a trait that's so admirable in a man receives so much condemnation when it shows up in a woman,' " Allegra complains. " 'Because it makes men feel insecure,' " Simon answers. " 'Some men.' " And in a story in which the hero and heroine both are FBI agents, another kind of double standard is set aside as fear for the other is expressed as a two-way street:

> "You think you have the right to ask me to transfer into a job that I don't like as much because you love me and want me to be safe. And I guess you have that right. But what about me, Roger? Surely you know that it tears me up to see you hurt and in pain."
> . . . Roger nodded. "I do. Of course you have the right to ask me to get out of danger. It's not chauvinism with me, although I know you've always thought it was. It's a mutual thing. I'm asking you to go into something a lot less dangerous because I love you, and I'm going into something a lot less dangerous because you love me." (Emily Elliott, *A Dangerous Attraction*, Dell Ecstasy Supreme, 1984, 282)

In one of the more unusual stories in the lot, *Lightning That Lingers* (Tom and Sharon Curtis, Bantam Loveswept, 1983, 171), the heroine asks the hero to give up his job as a male stripper, even though he is doing it for a cause they both feel is important (to pay the taxes on land he operates as an animal refuge). He protests that his body is just "tissue and bones," and what he does for money has nothing to do with their relationship or the way he feels about her. " 'Would you mind if I slept with another man?' " she asks. " 'I'm just tissue and bones too.' " When he replies that he is not sure nude dancing can be compared with making love, she says, " 'How convenient it must be, not to be sure. It lets you skip off toward the blue horizon, leaving me alone with the guilt.' "

These stories carry mixed messages when it comes to what love really means, from the enlightened to the ludicrous. Some project the basic premise put forward by anthropologists Nena and George O'Neill in *Open Marriage* (1972)—widely misinterpreted because of its title—that the creation of strong separate identities is the only way to maintain a happy and lasting union in contemporary society, that only honest partnership brings true intimacy. The heroine in Samantha Hughes's *Diamonds in the Sky* (Dell Ecstasy Supreme, 1984, 240), for instance, realizes in the end that "once she might have seen his reaction to her new assignment [in London] as a threat," indicative of his not caring enough. "Now she knew better. He was freeing her, letting her go," telling her that "love could exist unbounded." Christina Crockett's heroine in *A Moment of Magic* (Harlequin Super-Romance, 1984, 169) acknowledges that "she could trust this man who held her within his strong arms yet didn't demand to possess her." But love in a great many of these stories still carries the burden of possession and ownership, even though it may be described as a two-way street, as in Jackie Black's *Payment in Full* (Dell Ecstasy Supreme, 1984, 55), in which the hero says to the heroine, " 'I want to own you again, Sophie.' " Sophie dissembles—" 'I suppose I should resent the way you put that. . . . Is that how you thought of it?' " He asks, " 'Isn't that the way it was? I know you owned me. And I know I'm looking forward to having you hold me in bondage again.' "

The contemporary series romance heroine has an illegitimate child or becomes pregnant outside of marriage in 11 percent of the examined titles. In some the heroines gave up their babies for adoption because they were unable to care for them adequately at the time of birth, usually some years before the story opens. In only one (Rita Clay's *Wise Folly*, Silhouette Desire, 1982) is the child the result of a rape, which also happened years before the story opens and is the only instance of rape in the entire sample. Contraception is completely ignored in more than three-quarters of these love stories, though it is frequently mentioned in some very explicit ways, at times even providing the central focus of the plot line. In the Curtises' *Lightning That Lingers*, for instance, the heroine is an illegitimate child who is fearful of reproducing her own experience, and the lack of contraception prevents sexual intercourse from taking place on several occasions. The heroine in Neggers's *Heart on a String* resists making love, finally confessing to the hero that she is not "prepared." When the heart surgeon—hero expresses relief at the reason for her reluctance, she protests that " 'it's not a trivial problem.' "

> "You are assuming, Joanna," he said lightly, "that I drove all the way up here for the express purpose of seducing you and lacked the foresight—not to mention the sense of responsibility—to come prepared. I felt rather like a college kid, but—"
> "What!"
> "You might not be prepared, my darling," he said, grinning, "but I am." (p. 90)

Equally often, however, the possibility of pregnancy is recognized and accepted without either potential parent being ready or capable of caring for a child, because many a heroine still assigns to a baby the greatest signification of love and many a hero still sees a child as the ultimate proof of his virility. As a result, the exceptions stand out like brilliant gems against a background of dull pebbles. In Crockett's *A Moment of Magic*, for instance, the more traditional "guardian" hero is recast in the context of contemporary social problems:

> "I will never let myself or any other person go through that trapped feeling that comes when a child is conceived and unwanted. Sex is not like playing Russian roulette. A kid has a right to be conceived on purpose— not by chance. When I make love to you, we'll both know what we're doing. The experience is complicated enough without adding the risk of an unwanted pregnancy. We'll be making love, Susie. We won't be making a mistake. . . . I want you to wake up the next morning feeling good and feeling free, not worried or trapped. I care too much about us to take chances with your body or your mind." (pp. 200, 205)

It is in the area of childbearing and how it functions in the context of sexual and social relationships that the contemporary romance most often is murky. The Abortion Misunderstanding, another new-comer to romance plot devices, appears when the mother-to-be suffers a miscarriage which the father-to-be believes is an intentionally induced abortion. In every case in which the subject comes up in the content analysis sample, the man considers abortion an indefensible act, even though he may have deserted the woman carrying his child. In the end the truth comes out accompanied by the heroine's protest that " 'I told you I miscarried, aborted naturally. I wouldn't have an abortion. *Couldn't!* Surely you realize that' " (Tate McKenna, *Enduring Love*, Dell Ecstasy, 1983, 71). The same tune is played in Jacqueline Ashley's *Love's Revenge* (Harlequin American Romance, 1983), which certainly taxes the reader's ability to suspend disbelief. Ashley's unmarried heroine contracts German measles during the early months of her pregnancy and on the advice of her physician has an abortion, though she suffers a great deal of anguish and guilt about it. When the hero discovers what she has done he forces her to marry him—because she "owes" him a child. After he learns the truth, including that the fetus was indeed defective, he magnanimously releases her from their bargain.

Though these examples beg the question, they are not such overtly articulated anti-choice statements as Billie Green's *The Last Hero* (Bantam Loveswept, 1984). Consistent with Green's trademark, a flawed heroine, the psychologically fragile young girl in this story is shocked when she finds herself three months' pregnant, especially since she was not even aware that she had suffered a loss of memory one night while under the influence of a tranquilizing drug prescribed by her psychiatrist. She quickly and righteously decides "abortion was out. She had read all the literature on the subject—the pros and cons. She agreed that she owned her body. But she owned her car, too. That didn't give her the right to drive it into a river if there was a passenger inside. Maybe it wasn't convenient, but should life be looked at in terms of convenience?" (p. 13). Green's tale of a heroine who was sexually abused as a child is both pro-life and preachy, and comparing a human being to a car and ignoring the realities many females face with an unplanned and unwanted pregnancy is flagrantly insensitive.

Though flawed by another stock hero who distrusts all women (his mother is responsible, of course), Leigh Roberts's *Love Circuits* (Harlequin Temptation, 1984) at least attempts to present two sides to the abortion issue, though her example is not likely to engender much sympathy. When the hero reveals that his mother had an abortion in Mexico without telling his father, the heroine tries to help him see the situation from the mother's point of view.

> Frankie felt her heart go out to Jules's mother. "It was a difficult choice to make, certainly."
> "Difficult? . . . There isn't any choice in such a situation. At that time it was legally wrong. Besides, my dad deserved at least a chance to make his own preferences known. That should have kept her from doing it."
> . . . "You've said your mother was very bad at mothering," she pointed out. . . . "Surely she knew she was no good at it. Why should she want to bring another child into the world to make miserable? . . . Try to look at it

from her point view—that of a woman for whom children are a burden and a source of pain. . . . What if you, right now, had to go through a pregnancy, have your body endure an uncomfortable and sometimes fatal experience, and be saddled with the responsibility of a baby at the end of it? Would you stop your work to care for the child?" (pp. 119–20)

It is abundantly clear that publishers, editors, and authors generally have opted for the traditional and the conservative in treating one of the most controversial issues of our time, a path they perceive to be the safest—in spite of the fact that 73 percent of the readers polled in 1985 were pro-choice when it came to reproductive rights. In a popular medium sought for its fantasy and entertainment value, the questions that keep everyone in the romance publishing business on edge are not only what the "moving target" wants but what kind and how much reality the "reality fantasy" can stand.

Not surprisingly, the most popular authors generally constitute the major source of stories and characters who break down the fences erected by romance editors and publishers' guidelines. Janet Dailey, for instance, successfully pairs a hero so homely that he expects overt rejection and cannot believe any woman can love him, with an adoptee searching for her natural mother (*Leftover Love*, Silhouette Special Edition, 1984). LaVyrle Spencer introduces readers of *The Hellion* (Harlequin SuperRomance, 1984) to a middle-aged, overweight hero with three failed marriages, who in an effort to win the heroine starts jogging and dieting, and stops smoking and throwing beer cans out of his car window.

A variety of other social problems are addressed, sometimes as commentaries that are inconsequential to the basic story line, at other times as the centerpiece of the book. In *Love's Sound in Silence* (Harlequin SuperRomance, 1982), Meg Hudson evokes empathy for the physically handicapped by letting the reader in on the thoughts and feelings of a hero who suffers a serious hearing loss as the result of an explosion. His sense of both isolation and loss, his dawning awareness that he will never again be treated as an ordinary human being, his fear that he will be a burden to others, the noise and stress associated with using hearing aids, and the way he seeks relief—all are examined with unique insight and sensitivity. Heroines often speak with sadness and disappointment of the discrepancy between their "traditional" parents and their own goals in life. " 'They just don't understand why I wanted [a career] so much, instead of the things they thought I should care about,' " Maura Seger's heroine tells the hero in *Silver*

Zepher. " 'Like a husband and children?' " he asks. " 'Yes. . . . they've always put family first.' " Her parents may not understand what drives her or what she is seeking, but sooner or later the New Hero does, and he agrees " 'you had to find yourself before you could think of finding someone else' " (pp. 128–29).

The effort to satisfy readers' insatiable appetite for variety and the constant search for something fresh (which had become a buzzword among editors by 1985) at times lets the absurd, if not the irrepressibly nutty, sneak through the gate. Such is the case with Alice Morgan's *Impetuous Surrogate* (Dell Ecstasy, 1982), the story of a wealthy man who wants a child but does not trust women, this time not only because of his mother but also his stepmother. The latter, it seems, took her stepson and a number of other men as lovers, though the reader is never quite sure whether the hero hates her for cuckolding his father or because of the other men. He intends to find a surrogate and use artificial insemination to obtain an heir, but when he falls in love with the woman who has volunteered to act as surrogate, he decides to make her his mistress (believing that is a better way to ensure her fidelity!) and to search for another surrogate to give birth to his heir. Meanwhile, the reader must somehow reconcile the two personalities of the heroine, the one willing to act as a surrogate mother for the hero and the other who refuses to sleep with him until after they are married.

Changing lifestyles, whether the result of economic hardship or new opportunities, demonstrate both the desirability and the need for compromise and cooperation between husband and wife, yet many female members of this partnership today find themselves almost entirely responsible for the cleaning, cooking, and child care in addition to the jobs they hold outside the home. Women also still bear most of the cost of childbearing and rearing, whether to their lifetime earning capacity, their physical and emotional well being, or their autonomy. At least some of the failure of the romance to deal more realistically with the problems women face today, however, is due to the reality that the appeal of this entertainment medium lies largely in its ability to provide relaxation and escape from the stress of everyday life. Readers themselves provide plenty of evidence that they have no trouble recognizing the difference between real life and fantasy; what they do *not* provide is any behaviorial or articulated indication that idealized female stereotypes, new or old, condition consumers to seek satisfaction in fantasies rather than to work for social change.

To suggest that heterosexual bonding is in itself inherently conservative and inimical to women, as some feminists have done, is to both deny human needs and turn a blind eye to where grassroots social change has and is taking place. It is the power arrangement within the bonding relationship that is the focal point of change in most of the erotic series romances examined here—stories that have been written to publisher-specified, market-oriented guidelines. If a large dose of autonomy, equality, cooperation, and compromise, as well as love and respect, are now integrated into the ideal male-female relationships portrayed in these stories, it is largely because readers have demanded it. And even if some or all of that is still a fantasy in their own lives rather than a reality, it is indicative of their aspirations.

Notes

1. Titles included in the content analysis:

Möeth Allison, *Love Everlasting*, Silhouette Intimate Moments, 1983
Jennifer Allyn, *Forgiveness*, Ballantine Love and Life, 1983
Monica Barrie, *Island Heritage*, Silhouette Intimate Moments, 1983
Mary Lynn Baxter, *Tears of Yesterday*, Silhouette Special Edition, 1982
Jackie Black, *Payment in Full*, Dell Ecstasy Supreme, 1984
Parris Afton Bonds, *Widow Woman*, Silhouette Intimate Moments, 1984
Barbara Boswell, *Sensuous Perception*, Bantam Loveswept, 1985
Joan Bramsch, *The Sophisticated Mountain Gal*, Bantam Loveswept, 1984
Joanne Bremer, *Flirting with Danger*, Dell Ecstasy Supreme, 1985
Barbara Bretton, *No Safe Place*, Harlequin American, 1985
Maureen Bronson, *Tender Verdict*, Harlequin SuperRomance, 1985
Sandra Brown, *Tomorrow's Promise*, Harlequin American, 1983; *Relentless Desire*, Berkley/Jove Second Chance at Love, 1983
Pamela Browning, *Cherished Beginnings*, Harlequin American, 1985
Suzanne Carey, *Kiss and Tell*, Silhouette Desire, 1982
Rita Clay, *Wise Folly*, Silhouette Desire, 1982
Nina Coombs, *Love So Fearful*, NAL Rapture, 1983
Christina Crockett, *A Moment of Magic*, Harlequin SuperRomance, 1984
Tom and Sharon Curtis, *Lightning That Lingers*, Bantam Loveswept, 1983
Janet Dailey, *Leftover Love*, Silhouette Special Edition, 1984; *Foxfire Light*, Silhouette Special Edition, 1982
Barbara Delinsky, *Bronze Mystique*, Harlequin Temptation, 1984
Carole Nelson Douglas, *Her Own Decision*, Ballantine Love and Life, 1982
Bonnie Drake, *The Silver Fox*, Dell Ecstasy, 1983
Emily Elliott, *A Dangerous Attraction*, Dell Ecstasy, 1984
Jessie Ford, *Searching*, Ballantine Love and Life, 1982
Heather Graham, *Night, Sea and Stars*, Dell Ecstasy Supreme, 1983

Katherine Granger, *Private Lessons*, Berkley/Jove To Have and To Hold, 1984

Billie Green, *The Last Hero*, Bantam Loveswept, 1984

Jocelyn Haley, *Shadows in the Sun*, Harlequin SuperRomance, 1984

Kay Hooper, *Something Different*, Bantam Loveswept, 1984

Meg Hudson, *Love's Sound in Silence*, Harlequin SuperRomance, 1982

Cally Hughes, *A Lasting Treasure*, Berkley/Jove Second Chance at Love, 1983

Samantha Hughes, *Diamonds in the Sky*, Dell Ecstasy Supreme, 1984

B. J. James, *More Than Friends*, Bantam Loveswept, 1984

Robin James, *The Testimony*, Berkley/Jove To Have and To Hold, 1983

Iris Johansen, *The Golden Valkyrie*, Bantam Loveswept, 1984

Carol Katz, *Then Came Laughter*, Harlequin SuperRomance, 1985

Kathryn Kent, *Silk and Steel*, NAL Rapture, 1984

Tate McKenna, *Enduring Love*, Dell Ecstasy, 1983

Judith McNaught, *Double Standards*, Harlequin Temptation, 1984

Cassie Miles, *Tongue-Tied*, Harlequin Temptation, 1984

Linda Lael Miller, *Snowflakes on the Sea*, Silhouette Intimate Moments, 1984

Alice Morgan, *Impetuous Surrogate*, Dell Ecstasy, 1982

Mary Ruth Myers, *An Officer and a Lady*, Ballantine Love and Life, 1984

Carla Neggers, *Heart on a String*, Bantam Loveswept, 1983

Joan Elliott Pickart, *Look for the Seagulls*, Bantam Loveswept, 1985

JoAnn Robb, *Wolfe's Prey*, NAL Rapture, 1985

Leigh Roberts, *Love Circuits*, Harlequin Temptation, 1984

Nora Roberts, *A Matter of Choice*, Silhouette Intimate Moments, 1984

Erin St. Clair, *Not Even for Love*, Silhouette Desire, 1982

Maura Seger, *Silver Zephyr*, Silhouette Intimate Moments, 1984

Alexandra Sellers, *Captive of Desire*, Harlequin SuperRomance, 1982

Linda Shaw, *Way of the Willow*, Silhouette Special Edition, 1983

Alice Simms, *Of Passion Born*, Silhouette Desire, 1982

Carol Sturm Smith, *The Right Time*, Ballantine Love and Life, 1982

LaVyrle Spencer, *The Hellion*, Harlequin SuperRomance, 1984; *A Promise to Cherish*, Berkley/Jove Second Chance at Love, 1983

Anne Stuart, *Catspaw*, Harlequin Intrigue, 1985

Pat Wallace, *Sweetheart Contract*, Silhouette Intimate Moments, 1983

Jackie Weger, *Winter Song*, Harlequin Temptation, 1984

Kate Wellington, *A Delicate Balance*, Berkley/Jove To Have and To Hold, 1984

Karen Whittenburg, *A Distant Summer*, Dell Ecstasy, 1985

Linda Randall Wisdom, *Caution: Man at Work*, Dell Ecstasy Supreme, 1984

Chapter Six

ROMANCING WOMEN READERS
Who's Running This Revolution?

Why don't they move from *The Flame and the Flower* to
Pride and Prejudice, from *Shanna* to *Jane Eyre*, from
Kathleen E. Woodiwiss and Celeste de Blasis to Brontë
and Lawrence?
Sandra Gilbert, "Feisty Femme"

Those old stories are about as exciting as a mild laxa-
tive in today's fast moving and ever-changing world.
Romance reader, 1985

*I*n a wry little magazine piece
about a local bookstore doing a big business in paperback romances,
Sara Bird (1983, 72) described the stereotyped image of the romance
reader as "that lady who's always ahead of you in the Safeway line, the
one in the polyester pull-on pants pushing a cart loaded with Buck-
horn beer for Buford and a few epics whose covers feature a flinty-eyed
rake pouncing on a heaving *décolleté* morsel, the goal being to keep
said shopping-cart lady occupied while Boof watches the game." By
spending just one afternoon in the store Bird discovered that, "yes, it *is*
the lady from the Safeway, but it's also a whole lot of others you'd
never expect." With one out of every four adult women in the United
States reading paperback romance novels by 1984, it should not be
surprising that the pluralistic nature of the romance readership Bird
alludes to has been its primary characteristic for at least a decade —
which means that attempts to draw a single profile or to single out an
average reader are apt to be misleading, if not actually inaccurate.

One is tempted to answer Sandra Gilbert's question (in the epigraph) with still another question — Why *assume* that readers of paperback romances have not read Austen, Brontë, and Lawrence? Though
she was writing primarily about one small, nonrepresentative group
of readers, Gilbert (1984) generalized her comments to the entire
readership when she asked, "What hooks housewife-readers on these
endlessly repetitive fairy tales of desire?" Her questions serve to illustrate the most common (and erroneous) assumptions made about con-

sumers of romance: that they constitute a homogeneous population of women, usually assigned the generic "housewife" label, who have neither the educational experience nor the intellectual motivation to read the likes of *Pride and Prejudice, Jane Eyre,* or *Lady Chatterly's Lover.*

How we satisfy our needs for relaxation and entertainment varies not only from person to person but also from time to time, with few of us at the individual level behaving consistently as to what we require to assuage those needs. Yet when it comes to romance readers the tendency has been to adopt a different frame of reference. It rarely occurs to us, for instance, to ask about people who watch football on television why they don't move to a documentary on ancient Roman games. That many romance consumers derive considerable gratification from this particular form of entertainment is attested to by the fact that in 1982, two out of every five romance "fans" were reading at least one romance novel every two days, and one out of five was reading one a day—and this in spite of the fact that only 17 percent limited their book reading to romances.[1] That the two extremes of romance reading behavior had changed by 1985—those reading the fewest titles per month had increased while those reading the most decreased, and even the maximum number of titles was down dramatically—also suggests that many readers either were receiving less gratification in 1985 or had less need for the particular kind of gratification they derive from this source.

Typical of the "expert" commentary romance readers have grown used to hearing is the indictment issued by Tom Henighan (in Harrison 1984, 3), a professor of English at Carleton University, who told a Canadian radio audience that he pictured "the Harlequin reader [as] a woman in a very nice house, a suburban house, fairly bored, doesn't have a job, wants to get away from the very efficiency with which she's surrounded. . . . [And] I thought that if I became dictator, God forbid, maybe the first thing I would do would be to ban Harlequin romances and burn down the factory that makes them, and society would be much better thereby, because women would have to go out and face reality instead of reading these fantasies." Henighan also regaled listeners with the results of "a little experiment" he conducted: "I took some women that I know, quite well educated women, and I asked them whether they preferred love—that is, let's say sexuality—with fantasy or without fantasy. In other words, to what extent was their conception of sexuality wrapped up with fantasy, that is, with romantic trappings, with being in love, with being wooed, and so on. And I found that almost uniformly, for whatever reason, it seems that most women prefer to see sexuality in a context of, well, romance" (p. 3). Indeed, though Henighan himself presumably is quite well educated, his experiment, that is, his patriarchal tunnel vision, for whatever reason, reveals a sadly impoverished experience of love—that is, let's say sexuality. This bored-uneducated-unemployed housewife picture may still fit the readers of *True Confessions*, but it is not consistent with the reality of the readership for popular romance novels surveyed in 1982 and 1985.

Who Reads Romance?

In his 1973 survey of British readers of Mills and Boon romances (issued as Harlequin Romances and Presents in North America), Peter Mann (1974) found that only one-third were full-time "housewives," and he went so far as to suggest that they were sufficiently representative of the British population to call them "Everywoman." Mann found that 60 percent of Mills and Boon readers were married, compared with 63 percent of the adult female population; nearly half were between the ages of twenty-five and forty-five, compared with a third of the entire female population over the age of fifteen; 30 percent were housewives with full- or part-time jobs; and 22 percent were single and employed.

Two mail surveys of a national sample[2] of 600 American romance readers show that 35 percent were full-time homemakers in 1982, dropping to 33 percent in 1985, and that they were fairly representative of the general population in terms of most other demographic characteristics. Among these readers is a thirty-year-old single woman with a master's degree "plus thirty hours" who swaps romances with her colleagues, does not read series romances, likes strong female protagonists, watches an occasional movie on television, visits museums, and travels to Europe, the Caribbean, or South America every summer. There is also a mother who lives in a trailer with her husband and four children, who says reading romances "keeps me from bouncing off the walls." A Wisconsin grandmother "managed a retail clothing store for six years, invested my money and now I use the interest to buy books. I am politically active and twice have been president of the county Republican Women." Another reader with three grown children "needs a break" because she spends her days "reading medical books to compile mortality statistics." Still another is an operating room nurse with three children under the age of ten waiting for her when she gets home.

There is also a young mother who is pro-ERA and pro-abortion rights for women, who feels "very tied to [her four children] both by love and a strong feeling of responsibility, or what I owe to them. Consequently I have little time to realize my own ambitions." Another wife and mother reads mystery and romance novels to relax from "the heavy reading I have to do as a full-time college student." And a single graduate student employed full-time while working on her Ph. D. says she needs to "balance the research and statistical data with light reading for entertainment that requires no mental evaluation."

Among these romance readers is a married university professor who says "a good historical romance conjures up pictures of a world we know so little about except in books. I suppose one of the reasons I've always liked fiction is that I never could find any description at all in history books of those things which indicate the imaginative life of people at a certain time." There is also a forty-nine-year-old janitor who earns $11,000 per year and is president of her labor union, as well as a high school graduate earning $200 per week for the eleven-hour days she puts in as a laundress. "Maybe it's a cop-out," she says, "but while I'm reading I'm usually making supper, cleaning or a hundred other things in between. My husband thinks I'm crazy to 'waste' all that time reading."

Are these the bored "housewives" Henighan would like to see "go out and face reality"? Why, one wonders, are full-time homemakers always assumed to be idle and mindless, rather than hardworking and under stress? Do these women sound like those Janice Radway (Harrison 1984, 15) says "want to believe that they are intelligent women, that they are learning, that they haven't languished at home as housewives"? Is to simply be married, as 70.7 percent of these romance readers are (compared with 60.8 percent of the entire adult female population in 1984[3]), synonymous with being a "housewife," with all the implicitly derogative baggage appended thereto?

The survey data stand this old stereotype on its head, showing that full-time homemakers are a minority among readers, since in 1982, when the U.S. Labor Department reported about 60 percent of all women eighteen or older were in the work force ("How Their Lives Are Changing," 1982), 56 percent of romance readers were employed outside the home either full-time (40 percent) or part-time (16.3 percent). By 1985 employed readers had risen to 59 percent, with just one-third working full-time at "housewifery."

Rena Bartos (1979, 28) points to several reasons why the "house-wife" label can be both inaccurate and misleading, among them the often overlooked fact that four out of five employed women also keep house. The fact that a number of readers polled in 1985 (the same sample surveyed in 1982) claimed both full-time homemaker *and* full-time employment as occupations underscores her point. More useful in terms of differentiating between traditional and nontraditional attitudes in women, Bartos argues, is the *reason* women work outside the home or plan to become employed in the near future. The most significant change occurring among women during the 1970s, she believes, was "the heightened perception that work connotes independence. . . . The yearning for an identity beyond that of their traditional family roles is so deeply intertwined with the economic motivations for going to work that they cannot be separated" (p. 28). Bartos points out, too, that "the greatest proportion of working wives are found among families with total household incomes of $25,000 to $50,000 a year [and] there is a good deal of evidence that it is the wife's earnings that have moved the family up the economic ladder" (p. 23). She cites a Newspaper Advertising Bureau study conducted in 1971 and again in 1979 which found that six out of ten working women [4] would prefer to work even if money was not an issue. A *New York Times* poll conducted in 1983 showed that even if they could afford it, 58 percent of working women and 31 percent of nonworking women would rather work than stay at home (Dowd 1983). When it first asked the question in 1971, the Yankelovich organization discovered that 30 percent of employed women saw their work as a career, while 70 percent considered it "just a job." By 1980 those figures had changed to 39 and 61 percent, respectively—and Bartos's studies revealed specific behavioral traits associated with these differing responses. By 1985, according to a Roper poll, nearly two-thirds of all American women wanted to combine marriage and children with a career.

Among romance readers employed full- or part-time in 1985, nearly 39 percent said they considered their work a career rather than "just a job," the same percentage reported by Yankelovich. A little more than half said they would prefer to continue working rather than stay home even if they could receive the same income either way. One-third of the full-time homemakers said they plan to work in the future. From 1973 to 1979 the major growth sectors of the economy were retail trade and services, accounting for 40 percent of all new jobs and the primary source of employment for married women (Eisenstein 1985). More than 36 percent of employed romance readers hold pink-collar jobs (i.e., clerical, retail, and service), occupations characterized by a high level of demand and a low level of control, in which workers have been found to suffer the most stress. Only 6 percent were blue-collar workers, while 12 percent held managerial positions, including government civil service jobs. Slightly more than 28 percent held jobs classified as professional, including medical, technical, and educational fields (no physicians appeared among respondents, but the "professional" figure does include nurses and medical technicians, which in some reports are classified as service jobs). Most readers work in "two economies"—the home *and* the labor market.

That economic necessity is not the only reason for working outside the home is, among romance readers as among women in general, most closely correlated with higher education levels. A number of studies have found correlations between women's presence in the work force and education level (e.g., Thornton and Freedman 1979), and an opinion poll of women carried out by the Roper Organization in 1980 found that "education is the chief factor which differentiates between non-working women who intend to find jobs in the future and non-working women who prefer to remain at home" (p. 5). According to figures from the U.S. Department of Labor Women's Bureau (*20 Facts on Women Workers*, 1985), however, education does not pay off very handsomely for women, since in 1983 a woman with four or more years of college earned only about $2,500 more than men who had one to three years of high school.

A little more than 31 percent of the romance readers surveyed in 1982 had one to three years of college, and 16.3 percent held a university degree (see Table 3), both figures an almost identical match with those for the population as a whole at the time (32 and 16.2 percent respectively). Among romance readers with degrees, however, more than a third (36.3 percent) held a graduate degree.[5]

This is not to say there are no anomalies in the sample, such as the personnel specialist with a bachelor's degree who earns $35,000 per year yet considers her work "just a job" and would rather stay at home if given the choice. She also reads *Good Housekeeping* and *Soap Opera Digest* and says she does not pay much attention to authors' names when selecting books to read. Another is a full-time homemaker who completed high school, married at age seventeen and now wishes she

Table 3. Frequency distribution of romance readers by education, 1982

Level	Percentage
Some high school	4.7
High school diploma	34.4
1–3 years of college	32.2

University degree
    bachelor's 57.5
    master's 33.8
    doctorate (Ph.D.) 2.5
	16.3

Vocational school	12.2
Other	.2

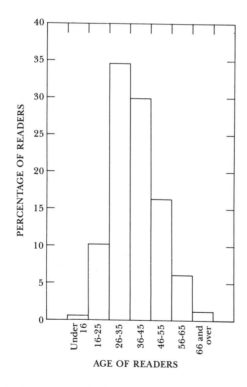

Figure 4. Frequency distribution of romance readers by age, 1982.

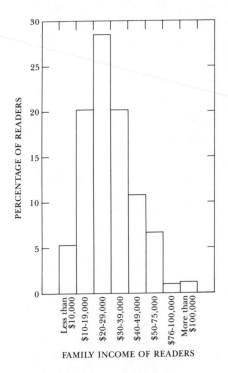

Figure 5.   Frequency distribution of romance readers by family income, 1982.

had gone to college, watches "Nova" and "Masterpiece Theatre" on television, and plans to work in the near future.

The readers surveyed are for the most part solidly in the middle class in terms of family income, with 54 percent earning under $30,000 a year in 1982, and 40 percent earning $30,000 or more (see Figure 4). One out of five had family incomes under $20,000, while slightly less than two out of five had incomes between $40,000 and $75,000 per year. In the 1985 poll (which probably is somewhat age-biased), 54 percent of the readers surveyed reported family incomes of $30,000 and over, at a time when the U.S. Commerce Department was reporting that one out of every five households had an income of at least $40,000.

The age of readers surveyed also is represented by a normal curve (see Figure 5), with 64 percent between the ages of twenty-six and forty-five. They lived in every state in the union, in large (26 percent) and medium-size (30 percent) cities, in small towns (25.5 percent), and in rural areas (17 percent). Almost two-thirds owned their own apartments or houses. Nearly one-quarter had no children, and 64 percent had between one and three children. Ninety-one percent of readers were white (compared to 85 percent of all American females in 1982). More than half were Protestant, 29 percent were Catholic, 2 percent were Jewish, and 8 percent checked "other" religious preferences, including one Druid. When it comes to political affiliation, 45 percent were Democrats, 27 percent were Republicans, and 13 percent were independents (18 percent did not answer the question, the highest number of no responses to any item on the questionnaire). Seventy-two percent of those surveyed reported voting in the 1980 presidential election, in which only 59 percent of all eligible voters participated; 81 percent voted in the 1984 election.

One-third of readers watched television an average of two hours or less a day in 1982, and 70 percent watched four hours or less a day (at a time when, according to A. C. Nielsen, the average viewing time per household was only a few minutes under seven hours a day). The most-watched programs were movies, news, news magazines, and comedy and drama series (such as "Hill Street Blues"), in that order. Fewer than one-third watched daytime soap operas, a fairly predictable figure in view of the number employed outside the home, but only one-third also watched nighttime soaps (such as "Dynasty" and "Dallas"). Seventy percent were regular readers of a daily newspaper.

Attitudes — Traditional or Egalitarian?

In a long-term study of more than 1,000 women, Arland Thornton and Deborah Freedman (1979, 841) observed shifts of "tremendous" proportions toward more egalitarian sex-role attitudes between 1962 and 1977 and concluded that "the events of the past fifteen years have been of such magnitude and importance that they have affected all groups of women irrespective of their experiences and characteristics." Rena Bartos (1979, 3) labels the surge of women entering the work force during the past twenty-five years the "Quiet Revolution," a symptom of the fundamental and irreversible changes that have taken place in women's self-perceptions. The significance of this surge, she believes, lies largely in the fact that it has been due to the increase of married women in the work force—two-thirds of wives were in the work force in 1983 and more than half of mothers with children under six years of age (20 Facts on Women Workers, 1984). Even among the happiest of wives and mothers there is a yearning for a sense of self-identity that goes beyond their family role, Bartos says, which amounts to a strong motivation "that has drawn some women into the work force, other women to pursue mid-life education, and still others to encourage their daughters to seek goals different from the ones they themselves held in their formative years" (p. 4). Zillah Eisenstein (1985, 17) concurs, adding that "the New Right's attack is directed so forcefully against married wage-earning women and working mothers because it is these women who have the potential to transform society. . . . it is they who begin to voice feminist demands for affirmative action programs, equal pay, pregnancy disability payments, and abortion rights."

A number of national polls lend support to these assertions of widespread fundamental change among women. Karen Mason and Barry Bumpass (1975), in a survey of sex-role attitudes and reactions to the women's movement, found level of education and, to a lesser extent, employment among women the most powerful variables predicting egalitarian attitudes toward women's roles at home and toward equal opportunities in areas such as employment. Two major attitude changes that have appeared along with the Quiet Revolution are reflected in a 1980 Roper poll showing that nine out of ten women now approve of a couple deciding not to have children, and that more than half approve of men and women living together without marriage if they care for each other. Ira Reiss (1980, 177), in a study of the American family, concluded that the traditional double standard (premarital sex is okay for men but not for women) was being displaced by "permissiveness with affection," a relationship in which love or strong affection is present.[6] In 1983, three and a half times as many unmarried men and women were living together than in 1970 ("Marriage, Young-American Style," 1984).

A 1984 survey of nearly 120,000 readers of *Woman's Day* magazine —with more than 8 million readers the largest-circulation magazine in the United States—conducted by the Wellesley College Center for Research on Women, described respondents as "mainstream American women" who were neither liberal nor conservative, though the demographic composition leaned somewhat toward traditionally conservative characteristics (Lear 1984). Yet 68 percent of these mainstream women supported the ERA, 79 percent agreed that women should have the right to choose whether or not to have an abortion, 90 percent thought it acceptable for mothers with preschool children to work outside the home (41 percent if it was necessary and 49 percent if they chose to do so), and more than half favored federally subsidized day-care programs.

How do romance readers as a group compare with these women when it comes to some of these vital social, political, and economic issues associated with the realignment of power between males and females, issues that are changing our traditional concepts of femininity and masculinity? Are romance readers primarily traditional or egalitarian in their sex-role orientations? In the resurvey of readers conducted in 1985, respondents were asked to express their own feelings or opinions by indicating whether they agreed or disagreed with fifteen statements representing varying positions in respect to such issues. On the whole, as shown in Table 4, the romance readers surveyed are egalitarian in attitude—not traditional.

Especially when considered in conjunction with results of the *Woman's Day* poll, these responses indicate that the perfusion of most so-called egalitarian attitudes is now so extensive that no specific demographic characteristics (age, education, income, or religion) are correlated with or are predictors of so-called egalitarian attitudes—whether, for example, a woman is anti- or pro-choice on reproductive rights. A case in point is the twenty-seven-year-old full-time homemaker from Texas who completed the eleventh grade, has one child, has a family income between $30,000 and $39,000 per year, is Catholic, feels that truly feminine women are never aggressive, disagrees with the concept of equal pay for comparable work, approves of sex without marriage, supports the ERA, and is pro-choice.

These results not only confirm Thornton and Freedman's conclusion but bring it full circle, precisely because so few statistically significant correlations appear between demographic characteristics of respondents and the attitudes they expressed. Indeed, the changing attitudes these researchers observed, which were newly associated with specific demographic characteristics, are now so widespread as to once again be unrelated to these characteristics. Thus the attitudes that researchers have been characterizing as egalitarian for at least a decade now appear to represent such a large majority of women that they constitute the norm.

That fewer romance readers (58 percent) than *Woman's Day* respondents support the ERA seems odd in view of the fact that 73 percent of them were pro-choice and 71 percent were in favor of equal pay for comparable work, and in view of the other highly egalitarian attitudes exhibited. The reason may be (at least in part) a guilt-by-association phenomenon, with the ERA seen as having effected other legislation which in turn has had dire economic effects on many women, such as no-fault divorces. One romance reader commented (in the margin of the attitude survey) that "my rights as a wife and mother have been taken away by the ERA." Lenore Weitzman (1985) has pointed out that no-fault divorce laws resulted in a 73 percent decline in the standard of living of women with minor children during the first year after a divorce, while men experienced an average increase of 42 percent in the same period.

Table 4. Reader responses to attitude statements, 1985

	Percent		
	Agree	Undecided	Disagree
1. Women should be considered as seriously as men for jobs as executives, politicians, and even as president (egalitarian, from Mason and Bumpass 1975).	87	5	7
2. There is no provocation of any kind, either behavior or appearance, that excuses or justifies rape (feminist, derived from Brownmiller 1975, and others).	86	5	9
3. Women should worry less about their rights or about themselves as individuals and more about being good wives and mothers (traditional, from the Spence and Helmreich Attitude Toward Women Scale, 1978; also conservative, from Marabel Morgan and Phyllis Schlafly).	30	4	65
4. It is all right for a couple to have sexual intercourse without being married if they love each other (Yankelovich poll question).	73	10	17
5. There are many jobs in which men should be given preference over women in being hired or promoted (traditional, from Attitude Toward Women Scale).	45	7	47
6. Women rarely, if ever, read the business section of the daily newspaper (reversed egalitarian, from Attitude Toward Women Scale).	19	15	66
7. Women find it difficult to respect husbands or partners who earn less than they do (traditional).	14	14	70

Table 4. Reader responses to attitude statements, 1985—Continued

	Percent		
	Agree	Undecided	Disagree
8. In cases of divorce the mother should always receive custody of the children (traditional).	8	8	83
9. A truly feminine woman is never aggressive (traditional, from Morgan and Schlafly).	17	6	78
10. The husband of a woman who works outside the home should share in household tasks such as doing the laundry, cooking, and cleaning (egalitarian, from Attitude Toward Women Scale).	91	3	6
11. A woman should have the right to choose whether or not to have an abortion (*Woman's Day* poll question).	73	8	19
12. Women need the protection of an Equal Rights Amendment to the U.S. Constitution (*Woman's Day* poll question).	58	21	20
13. There is nothing wrong with a couple deciding not to have any children (Yankelovich and Roper poll question).	93	4	3
14. Requiring equal pay for comparable work (for example, mandating that trained nurses make at least as much as truck drivers) is necessary if women are ever going to achieve real equality in the work place (primary women's issue during the 1980s according to NOW and WEAL).	71	15	14
15. A woman with preschool children who is employed outside the home is neglecting her duties and responsibilities as a mother (traditional, from Mason and Bumpass 1975; *Woman's Day* poll question).	19	8	72

Note: Strongly agree and mildly agree responses are collected under the agree column, and strongly and mildly disagree responses under the disagree column.

Concern about job and wage inequities, found to be high among women generally, also is apparent among romance readers. Judging from volunteered comments, the equivocation shown in responses to the statement that men should be given preference over women in some job situations was due largely to the belief that a real difference in physical strength exists between men and women and therefore in their ability to perform certain jobs. A number of readers also volunteered comments about comparable work that suggest the statement may have been misinterpreted by some to mean equal pay for the same work, underscoring the results of a national poll conducted for the National Committee on Pay Equity in 1984, which found that, though 69 percent of those surveyed believed female-dominated jobs are underpaid and 79 percent supported pay equity as a solution, public familiarity with the term "comparable worth" was extremely low (in Nicholson 1985).[7]

Romance Reading-Buying Behavior

A Book Industry Survey Group study reported in *Publishers Weekly* (July 22, 1983) found that 61 percent of women were leisure-time readers compared with 39 percent of men, and that the number of "heavy readers" (those who read a book a week) had doubled since 1978. In addition, the entire book market, according to John Cole and Carole Gold (1979, 53), is "heavily female and upscale." Certainly romance readers had to have been at least partly responsible for that huge increase, since in 1982 almost 80 percent of those surveyed were reading five or more romances a month.[8] One reported, "I take twenty-one [romances per month] in the mail," and another that she has "three recipe boxes full of my books listed by alphabet." A New York woman who works part-time as an accounting clerk said she reads the "short easy reads" at work during breaks and lunch because "they don't require much attention or analysis," saving mysteries and science fiction for weekends "when I can give them the time they deserve." Only 17 percent limit their book reading to romances. In addition to mainstream fiction (48 percent), mysteries (39 percent), science fiction (14 percent), and westerns (19 percent), more than 40 percent say they read nonfiction (biographies, history, pop psychology, and how-to books).

Yankelovich, Skelly, and White reported that the "average romance reader" read nine romance novels per month in 1978, while a third of Radway's (1984) forty-two readers consumed between twenty and thirty-six per month. She found the sixty to eighty per month reported by 9 percent of her readers implausible because, she said, not that many were being issued at the time (though there were sixty new series titles alone appearing every month by the end of 1982, plus another forty or more mainstream romance titles). Radway also ignored the fact that paperback romances have been published in large numbers for more than a decade, constituting a huge backlog of titles still available in used book stores. Half of all romance readers surveyed were buying at least some of their books used, nearly a third exchange them with friends and relatives, and 16 percent obtain some titles from the library—all of which is consistent with the fact that no significant correlation between income and the number of books read per month appeared in the data. Carolyn Nichols, editorial director for Bantam's Loveswept line, told authors attending the annual Romance Writers of America meeting in 1985 that the romance industry estimates an average seven readers for each copy sold.

Nearly 80 percent of those surveyed said they read both historical and contemporary stories. In 1982, 40 percent of this group said historicals were their favorite kind, while slightly more than a quarter preferred the contemporaries. The majority also read both single-title and series books. Significant correlations do appear between reading contemporary romances, reading series romances, and the number of books read per month, which is to be expected since series contemporary romances literally flooded the market during the first half of the 1980s and since most series titles are shorter than other types, so are both less expensive and take less time to read.

Some other observed significant differences of interest are suggestively paradoxical. For instance, contemporary romance readers had a higher level of education ($p = .01$) than historical romance readers, were more active politically ($p = .01$), were more likely to trade books with friends or relatives ($p = .01$), and more of them liked books with older women as heroines ($p = .01$). At the same time, however, more of them read series books ($p = .01$), liked a simple story ($p = .05$), and purchased books in supermarkets ($p = .01$). Historical romance readers watched more television ($p = .05$) than contemporary readers, more of them read westerns ($p = .05$), and more of them had been romance readers for a longer period of time ($p = .001$).

Age is significantly correlated with how long these women have been reading romances, which also is to be expected. In 1982 more than 35 percent of all readers had been romance consumers for five years or less, confirming the huge growth that occurred in this market between 1977 and 1982. Another 31.4 percent had been readers for six to ten years, which means that by 1982 two-thirds of all romance readers surveyed had joined the romance audience since 1972, the year Kathleen Woodiwiss's *The Flame and the Flower* was published.

In spite of the pluralistic nature of the readership and the fact that some prefer historical to contemporary settings (as well as the reverse), a fairly high consensus is evident on certain story and character attributes. In 1982, for instance, two-thirds of respondents said they liked strong, independent heroines. In the words of one, "I like a woman who knows her own worth, sets her goals and goes after them. She likes men, and wants one in her life, but not dominating her. She walks with him, not behind him." Nearly half of readers liked a sensitive and compromising hero, while 43 percent liked a dominating hero. Some liked both, as did the reader who commented, "I like a dominating male and a woman strong enough to tame him." And 77 percent said they liked "a lot" of sexual description, while 55 percent liked "lots" of love scenes.[9] More than one-third liked a complex story, while 29 percent preferred a simple story, and again some said they liked both types. More than 70 percent wanted the hero's point of view better developed than it was in stories then on the market, half said they would like to see some romances with heroines who were aged forty or older, and nearly a third were looking for more humor. Passive heroines, rapes scenes, and a heroine-only point of view were at the bottom of just about everyone's list.

By 1985 the dampening effect of the high level of redundancy associated with series romances was evident in the decreased number of titles being read per month—at both ends of the scale. One reader complained, "They're all beginning to sound alike, just a different cover and background. I have a growing stack of half-finished paperbacks." One-quarter of the repolled readers were consuming fewer than five titles per month, compared to 16 percent in 1982, and only 8 percent were reading more than thirty per month, down from 20.5 percent. Nearly half said they were exploring more of other kinds of fiction (see chapter 9 for a comparison of reading-buying behavior, 1982 and 1985).

In 1985, readers were asked to rank order the story and character attributes they liked, rather than simply choose those they liked most. Their top five choices are shown in Table 5, along with those mentioned most often in 1982. Not only does the mixed heroine and hero point of view top the 1985 list of most-liked attributes, it takes this position with twice as many first-place mentions as any of the others.

Table 5.   Rank order of the five most-liked story and character attributes

1982	1985
1. detailed sexual description	mixed point of view
2. well-developed hero point of view	several love scenes
3. a strong, independent heroine	mature humor and teasing
4. "lots" of love scenes	detailed sexual description
5. sensitive, compromising hero	fairly complicated plot

That the mature, strong, independent heroine no longer numbers among the top five does not mean that readers have fallen out of love with her, however, since "adventure with the heroine participating" and "an assertive and outspoken heroine" ranked sixth and seventh (with the vulnerable, sharing hero ranked eighth). Viewed along with other information from readers, it is clear that the New Heroine now is simply assumed and has become a norm or convention common to all erotic romances, as is also the heroine's career in stories with contemporary settings. The passive heroine is still at the bottom of the list, along with the macho hero, rape scenes, and the heroine-only point of view.

In view of the number of readers who in 1985 said they were reading fewer romances and more of other kinds of fiction, and the numerous volunteered complaints about them, the selected attributes speak eloquently to a desire for better stories, characters who are more fully developed, and sexual activity that is integrated into a believable relationship. The fall of explicit sexual description from first to fourth place therefore appears to be due more to the predictable, simple, and simple-minded stories incorporating gratuitous sex (i.e., explicit sexual descriptions and events without regard to compatibility with story line or characterizations) that have saturated the market since 1982 than to disenchantment with the sexual element per se. Readers want "more story" and are tired of shallow characters who share nothing beyond a "jolt of electricity" at first sight or touch, then are overwhelmed by a mindless, compulsive physical desire and immediately fall in love and into bed. It is not so much that they want less sex, as some editors have begun to advise authors, but less sex that occurs without rhyme or reason. A concert pianist thrown into the arms of a professional football player may satisfy readers' seemingly insatiable appetite for something new, but unless a *credible* relationship between heroine and hero can be developed, the sex is gratuitous (often equated with male pornography) and the story fails as an erotic romance.

Uses and Gratifications: Why Women Read Romances

C. S. Lewis (1961, 137), in an essay on criticism in which he reversed the usual practice of judging books and then judging readers by the books they liked, asked, "Why do we occupy ourselves reading stories about what never happened and perhaps never could, at times vicariously experiencing feelings we would never want to have personally?" He suggested the answer is that "we seek an enlargement of our being. We want to be more than ourselves. Each of us by nature sees the whole world from one point of view, with a perspective and a selectiveness peculiar to himself [sic]. . . . We want to see with other eyes, to imagine with other imaginations, to feel with other hearts, as well as with our own."

In a study published twenty years ago, Jan Hadja (1967) described two different motivations for reading fiction, one passive (to pass the time, a form of forgetting) and the other active (to expand one's range of experiences, associated with the psychological need for stimulation). Peter Mann (1979, 38) also spoke of passive and active forms of leisure in comparing television viewing and reading: "The reader constructs a mental world of his [sic] own; the television viewer merely receives a world created for him and several million other viewers." Voluntary exposure implies purposeful behavior, and nearly all the survey respondents say they read romances for one or more of four reasons: entertainment, relaxation, fantasy, and escape. Inseparably linked to the need for entertainment, says Peter Kaupp (1979, 239), is a "whole series of other primary human needs that are no less basic: the need to escape from reality, the need to confront reality, the need to identify with others and to dissociate from others, the need to be curious and finally the need to [communicate] with others."

When entertainment is viewed as a human need shared by all, the selection process is seen to serve variable needs. Thus, the so-called high and low forms of culture may be selected by the same person, and the woman who attended a symphony performance early in the evening may read an erotic romance novel at bedtime, just as the man who watches a football game on television may have attended a Shakespeare play the night before and may also be reading the latest Louis L'Amour story. Yet the abiding myth is that romances fill an emotional void, and this inherently negative conclusion, which implies a lack of something, has had an especially tenacious hold on most deliberations in which the readers in question are women and the texts are romances—even when the scholars have been female. Though the human need for entertainment, for relaxation and relief from stress, is as basic and normal as the need for sleep and food, women who seek to fulfill this need through romantic fantasy are assumed to be doing so because of their impoverished intellectual or emotional lives. No empirical evidence to support this assumption is available to date.

In their comparison of two groups of women, Claire Coles and M. Johnna Shamp (1984) hypothesized that a lack of sex and/or sexual satisfaction would motivate women to find satisfaction of this need through erotica (in this case erotic historical romance novels). They found no significant differences between romance readers and non-readers, however, when it came to access to partners, sexual satisfaction, feelings of self-esteem, or sex-role orientations (traditional-liberal). Certainly there are women who read romances simply to pass time or as a substitute for something that is lacking in their lives, as seems to be the case for the young woman who responded, "Why? For what I don't have in my life—romance, love, a guy." That also may be true for the woman who reads romances "for the same reason men love to watch sports. If you can't do it the next best thing is to read about it." And a thirty-five-year-old Alabaman, holder of a master's degree, confessed that "personal experience is that firecrackers only go off occasionally, but the heroine is almost guaranteed a climactic." A California reader was at a loss to explain "why I love these books. I just know that 'their' lives are more interesting than mine. And they don't get fat, wrinkled, post-natal sag, or wear glasses. The heroes are inflamed when they see the heroine naked. My man looks politely away. Vive l'amour." Others read romances in order to help recall and relive an experience in the past, such as the woman who said, "I love my husband, but it is a mellow, comfortable, long-married feeling. With each new romance I read it brings back the excitement, the sparkle, tears and joy of falling in love."

For almost all of the readers surveyed, however, reading romance novels is primarily entertainment-seeking behavior that provides pleasure, escape, relaxation, and renewal because it stimulates and challenges the imagination. Thus the romance as a form of entertainment and escape encompasses a web of complex motivations and gratifications, serving as a means of exploring new ideas about the changing role and status of women in society—a kind of test run or sounding board for a variety of ideas, attitudes, and behavior—at the same time that it provides the security of the familiar. It is the formulaic nature of genre fiction that opens the door to the unfamiliar, and through time and repeated exposure converts unusual or new elements into the ordinary and familiar.

John Cawelti (1969) suggested that formula fiction can be defined in terms of a game that provides both patterned experience and ego enhancement through fantasy. Viewed as a game, the romance novel allows women readers to test themselves against the expert (the heroine) by putting themselves in the heroine's place and trying out their own ideas about interacting with the hero and resolving conflict, free of the constraints or dangers of the real world. This kind of role playing or identification with the heroine is confirmed by romance readers themselves, one of whom explained, "I like books where I can get involved. I imagine myself in the heroine's place, do what I can't in real life"; another said, "During the sex scenes (I love them) the hero is my husband"; and still another found herself "wondering what the characters are doing after I complete a book, as if they're real people. I also find myself comparing a lot of my dates and other men with the fictional men in romances, and they come up a very poor second or third!" A twenty-nine-year-old Louisiana reader whose formal education ended with the tenth grade described even more succinctly the way these stories work as games for her: "I imagine what I'd do and how I'd react if I were in the same situations. Reading makes me think, makes me explore how I feel about relationships, prejudices, war, personal tragedy, life itself. It builds my confidence to think out how I would handle certain situations—gives you a good feeling to conclude that you could cope with this or change that, and also helps explore your own morals and beliefs."

The results of such practicing or imaginary experience often cross over from fantasy and are put to use in everyday life. Women use romances for escape—*to* another time or new experience and *from* the constant demands being made on their time, attention, and energy. "I love to 'explore' new places in my books," wrote one, while an elementary school teacher with two young children said, "I use them to escape, but from the stress of family and job, not unhappiness." Reading romance also provides the personal privacy so many women crave: "I can come home [from work] and entirely lose myself in a book, get involved with someone else's problems, be in different situations, and end up happily. It's the same sensation I get when I listen to the stereo with headphones. There's nothing in my head except the music. I can read anywhere, even on the back of our motorcycle when the scenery isn't interesting."

Reading romances, or any other kind of engrossing printed material, is isolating, and privacy is one of the primary reasons women favor reading as a form of entertainment or relaxation. That does not mean romance readers never discuss what they read with friends, relatives, and co-workers. The testimony from readers to this effect would fill an entire chapter, ranging from the California woman who ships boxes of romance novels to her daughter in Oregon, even though their tastes differ somewhat ("My daughter reads a lot of regencies. Isn't that strange? You'd think a young modern woman with a profession would prefer something more up to date!"), to the office worker who reported what she and two of her co-workers liked in the way of a romance: "I like meticulously passionate sex scenes," she said, while the second one "likes the lust to begin right away—we both especially liked two of the scenes in Susan Johnson's *Love Storm*" (Playboy Press, 1981; see chapter 7)—while the third reads regencies. There is a lot of trading going on among readers, some of it simply to reduce the total expenditure for books and some because friends or relatives take pleasure in these books and want to share the "good ones." Certainly no one believes this happens without the readers talking about the stories or the characters, and also about authors.

A majority of readers say they incorporate into their own lives at least some of what they learn from these stories—about careers for women, history, trivial facts, and sex—but particularly the more intangible kind of enlightenment that helps them to better understand themselves or to improve their relationships with others. "They've helped me with my personal life—I've gained some backbone," said an Indiana reader, and a thirty-eight-year-old divorced Californian who works full-time as a bank officer observed that "the different types of relationships presented between the hero and heroine often provide insight into the behavior of someone you know personally." A college student was sometimes "surprised at how romance novels can help me with my personal relationship with my boyfriend, for example, being more open with him (talking it out, communicating), especially when we have disagreements." And a thirty-one-year-old New York reader added, "I've enjoyed talking about some of the sexual scenes with my husband. Some things I didn't know about." Another reader said, "I think reading these novels has made me less inhibited sexually and a more interesting sexual partner." Indeed, about half of the readers surveyed in 1985 said they use erotic romance novels as sexual fantasy.

Not all survey respondents are attracted to romance novels for all of these reasons, but the list made by a thirty-five-year-old Maryland reader (who earns more than half of her family's $40,000–49,000 income) constitutes a good summary: "(1) entertainment; (2) escape to another era (with historical romance); (3) experience different careers and lifestyles through the heroines; (4) the love scenes are sexually stimulating; (5) they usually end happily for the hero and heroine after much conflict and adversity, showing that hope does exist even when it seems very bleak; (6) [they] can be quite educational about an era, class of people, customs, countries, etc."

If there is an addictive element in romance reading as behavior, as some critics and readers claim, it appears to be an addiction to pleasure, which more than anything else is suggestive of a neurochemical response (see, e.g., Liebowitz 1984). That the huge increase in romance reading over the past decade and more took place coincidentally with changing lifestyles, which have put increasing pressures and stress on women, seems a far more compelling explanation for the observed intense need for entertainment, fantasy, and escape. In addition, this increase occurred during a time when women have been exploring and learning about themselves as sexual beings and about where the parameters of their changing self-concept lie. That they discovered a type of entertainment peculiarly suited to their needs has been due not only to the private and personal character of the medium itself but also to its responsiveness to those changing needs.

Still another reason why a number of women say they read romances (many more in 1985 than in 1982) is that they intend to or are in the process of writing one. This grassroots do-it-yourself enterprise has been fueled in part by publisher-sponsored (Silhouette and Harlequin) seminars held in department stores all around the country, as well as Cinderella stories about high school graduates who achieved not only fame but fantastic fortune (which undoubtedly has great appeal to readers like the one who wrote on her questionnaire, "I like them so good I'm writing one"). A number of romance authors have come from the ranks of readers who say they were moved by the belief that "I can do better than that!" These how-to seminars serve primarily to publicize and sell books, however, since herds of hopeful authors are instructed by editors to "read at least thirty of our books before you even attempt an outline—and be sure they're new ones so you'll know what we're looking for today."

A new grandmother living in California sent a personal letter along with her questionnaire in 1982, describing the role reading romance novels has played in her life:

> I first started reading romance novels about five years ago. My children were in their teens and giving me the usual hassles that accompany children that age. I worked a full eight-hour day and found that all my time was tied up working, being a mother and wife. There was never any time for me and I found that I needed something extra, some little escape. It started out as a diversion and became a hobby. I now own over 1200 and have given away another 300.
>
> I started out reading just historical romances. After a while, I got tired of that and mixed in a few short reads, i. e., Harlequin Presents, Regencies, etc. Later I started buying full length contemporaries. Soon I was skipping lunch, coffee breaks, whatever, just to read. . . . On the thirteenth of November I turned in my notice, giving up a stable income of $1200 a month, and with the encouragement of my husband, children and friends, I am now pursuing the field of writing—you guessed it—romance novels. Whether or not I have any talent I don't know, but succeed or fail, reading THOSE BOOKS has changed my life. At the ripe age of 42, when it's all supposed to be over but the shouting, I am starting what I hope to be a new career, and I would be lying if I said I wasn't excited.

Notes

1. A number of romance publishers have used the 1982 reader survey data reported in this chapter—Bantam in a multimedia presentation at the 1985 Romance Writers of America meeting in Atlanta, for instance, and Harlequin in a 1985 press release in which "Some Interesting Facts" about romance readers in general were summarized using figures and phrasing from Thurston (1983): "40% are university educated, 40% are employed full-time, 40% have an average family income in excess of $30,000, 20% read one romance book a day, 40% read one romance book every two days."

2. A random sample of 600 names was drawn from a name pool of approximately 3,500 readers who returned back-of-the-book questionnaires inserted into historical and contemporary romances published by Richard Gallen/Pocket Books in 1981 and early 1982 (see chapter 3). Though Gallen had been producing historical romances for Pocket Books before 1981, it was not until then that the contemporary romances and the RG cover logo first appeared. While the name pool from which the sample was drawn is not necessarily representative of all romance readers, survey responses showed that no re-

spondents read only Gallen/Pocket Book romances but in fact read romances issued by a variety of publishers. In addition, most read more than one type: single-title and series books, historical and contemporary stories. Though the entire sample is assumed to have read at least one Gallen/Pocket Book romance (since they were the source of the returned back-of-the-book questionnaires), a fifth of those responding indicated they did not, which means they were unaware of the line identity. In this sense, then, the sample represents a general rather than a specific publisher readership.

An equal number of names (300) were drawn from the questionnaires returned from historical and contemporary romance titles. The first survey was conducted in the spring of 1982 and had a return rate of 83.7 percent (502). There are probably several reasons for the unusually high return rate, one of which is that the name pool may have been biased in the sense that subjects already had demonstrated a willingness to respond. Responses to the questionnaire, including volunteered comments, letters, and phone calls, suggest that still another factor was in play—the desire to be heard, to be listened to, and to be taken seriously. Addressing the unexpectedly high return rate on the *Woman's Day* poll, Martha Lear (1984, 69) spoke of "that communal sound: the voice of women wanting passionately to be heard, to be counted, to be taken seriously as political beings," which is symptomatic of the sense women have that no one listens to, wants, or values their opinions. A resurvey of the same 600 readers was conducted in the spring of 1985, with a considerably lower rate of return—50 percent of the 440 deliverable questionnaires, or 37 percent of the original sample—which was due in part to the attrition of viable postal addresses, which in turn very likely age-biased the 1985 data since the younger members of the sample were presumably more mobile. For that reason, the demographic profile drawn here is taken largely from the 1982 survey. More information about the sample, how it was selected, and the questionnaire are located in the Appendix.

3. Unless noted otherwise, the population figures given here are from the *Statistical Abstract of the United States*, 1985 and 1986, issued by the U.S. Census Bureau. In most cases the latest figures available at the time of writing were for 1984.

4. Most women who are full-time homemakers are more than a little offended by the way the Labor Department and other sources report statistics, implying that managing a home and caring for children is not work. This assumption is given credence, however, in tax laws and the lack of retirement benefits, as for example the extremely limited contributions "unemployed" homemakers are allowed to make to an IRA.

5. Mann's data (1974) on education are difficult to compare with American statistics since they are reported as age at completion of full-time education. All of Mann's data predate the erotic contemporary series romance. As late as 1980 most Harlequin (by then the parent company of Mills and Boon) readers were reported to be between twenty-four and forty-nine years of age and held

high school diplomas but had not completed college; 49 percent were employed at least part-time, with average annual family incomes between $15,000 and $20,000.

6. The 1985 Roper Virginia Slims poll found that while 61 percent of Americans eighteen or older found nothing morally wrong with premarital sex—a nearly perfect reversal of the 1969 Gallup figures, when 68 percent thought it was wrong—extramarital sex was considered wrong by 88 percent. Two-thirds of the romance readers surveyed in 1985 agreed with the statement "Infidelity is the most unforgivable of sins in a relationship, whether on the part of the man or the woman," while 24 percent disagreed. Romance editor Star Helmer commented in 1983 that readers "don't want the heroine and hero fooling around with anyone else once they've met."

7. It is a sad commentary, indeed, that after leading the way in antidiscrimination legislation and affirmative action during the 1960s, the United States now lags behind other Western industrialized nations in closing the wage gap between males and females. A Rand Corporation study predicted that American women will be making only 75 percent of men's incomes by the year 2000 (in Bernstein 1984). American women earned only 60 percent of wages earned by men in 1983, compared with 70 percent in Great Britain, 72 percent in West Germany, 77 percent in France, and 90 percent in Sweden (Patterson 1983). The claim is frequently made that women who interrupt their careers in order to have children are a major reason for this "gap," but a Columbia University survey of women holding the M.B.A. degree found that after ten years in the work force the salaries of those who did not take leave (maternity or any other) were not significantly higher than those who did. The average salary of women with an M.B.A. was 20 percent lower than the average salary of men with an M.B.A. (Gibson 1984).

8. Romance readers surveyed in 1982 were asked about physical handicaps in order to assess whether such limitations could have any bearing on the amount of reading reported. Less than 2 percent of respondents reported any kind of physical disability.

9. None of Radway's (1984, 67) romance readers considered "lots of scenes with explicit sexual description" among the most desirable ingredients in a romance, and only one-third did when the statement was changed to "lots of love scenes with some explicit sexual description." In spite of her disclaimer of "representivity" for her so-called Smithton readers, Radway elaborated thirteen elements in the narrative structure of what she called the "ideal romance" on the basis of titles chosen by these forty-two readers, all of whom lived in the same midwestern town. "Dot," a bookseller who acted as interpreter and adviser to her customers, was both subject and intermediary in distributing Radway's questionnaires, which put her in a position to select who was eligible to respond. It is to be expected that these respondents would therefore be readers she knew well and who would tend to agree with her own values and evaluations of stories and characters. All of the titles Radway used

to formulate the narrative structure (p. 134) of what she called the ideal romance were published prior to 1981 and the appearance of the erotic contemporary series romance. None were series romances, and all were historical in setting, except for the two that contained parallel historical and contemporary narratives (Jacqueline Marten's *Visions of the Damned* and Katherine Kent's *Dreamtide*).

Chapter Seven

UPDATING THE KAMA SUTRA

The Romance as Erotica for Women

And at long last—often on the last page—there is
THE KISS. This first kiss is the erotic explosion for
which the entire rest of the book was foreplay.
  Kathryn Weibel, *Mirror, Mirror: Images of Women
  Reflected in Popular Culture*

Her fingers entwined in his thick hair, her breath
coming in tearing gasps, Mallory reveled in his
hunger, in the warm strength of the hands holding her
knees apart, so that she could not close herself to him.
As his tongue began to savor her in long strokes,
Mallory shuddered and gasped a plea and loosed her
fingers from his hair to again spread the veiled place
for his full satisfaction and her own.
  Linda Lael Miller, *Snowflakes on the Sea*

*I*n *Ways of Seeing*, John Berger
(1973, 47) examined the nude in art history and concluded that "men
look at women. Women watch themselves being looked at." At about
the same time, a host of feminists were pointing out that this pervasive
and long-standing unilateral arrangement alienated women from
their own sexuality—that female sexuality was culturally defined as
the capacity to arouse desire in someone else, thereby disfranchising
women from one of the most fundamental and inalienable human
rights. "What the double standard hurts in women (to the extent that
they genuinely, inwardly, bow to it) is the animal center of self-respect;
the brute sense of bodily prerogative, of having a right to one's bodily
feelings," according to Dorothy Dinnerstein (1976, 73). Linda Phelps
(1979, 22) argued that women are sexually alienated "because we relate
neither to ourselves as self-directed persons nor to our partners as the
objects of our desire, but to a false world of symbol and fantasy. This
fantasy world that veils our experience is the world of sex as seen
through male eyes. It is a world where eroticism is defined in terms of
female powerlessness, dependency, and submission. It is a world of
sado-masochistic sex."

139

Even as Phelps and Dinnerstein protested this state of sexual affairs, however, a significant transformation was beginning to take place in that most unlikely of places—the romance novel—that was destined to redefine female sexuality in this popular mass medium and spread the message to millions of women both at home and abroad. Still focusing largely on the thoughts and feelings of the heroine, the role model with whom women readers identify through vicarious experience, the erotic heterosexual romance by the early 1980s was portraying a female sexuality that was no longer repressed or made obtuse and mysterious through psychoanalytic symbolism and innuendo, forbidden to the heroine by the double standard.

Feminists early on rejected the simplistic assumption that sexual liberation equals women's liberation (a familiar cry being "the sexual revolution is not our revolution"), asserting that it increased the availability of pornography and in general made women more vulnerable to sexual exploitation. They also realized, as Edwin Schur (1983, 118) warned in his comprehensive work on the social control of women, that "when women's active sexuality is acknowledged, it may be misleadingly presented as the main path to full female liberation," ultimately distracting women from the pursuit of real social change. But while a fully developed sexuality does not predict a conscious sense of self, it is difficult to imagine that such a self could be achieved without it.

The view of female sexuality as dichotomous not only ties sexuality to reproduction in the "good" woman but is psychologically bizarre insofar as it assumes both sexual insatiability (justifying the need for control) and frigidity (the good woman doesn't enjoy it).[1] Mary Anne Warren (1980, 426) defines sexuality simply as "the propensity to desire sexual stimulation and sexual activity," though most feminists treat female sexuality in more complex terms, questioning the relationship between power, violence, and pleasure.[2] Catharine Stimpson and Ethel Person (1980, 2) point out that "to understand female sexuality is to explore the power of social constructions of reality and symbolic transformations of what seem to be matters of natural fact. . . . Public production and reproduction, social structures and sexuality, are linked as irrevocably as the brain and our five senses." Certainly how female sexuality is socially constructed has been the subject of considerable debate within the feminist movement, and long before the recent split over antipornography laws. Over time, however, the emphasis on social construction has resulted in devaluation of the role of biology, which in turn produces a conflict between "our experience as women and as intellectuals"—the kind of contradiction Maria Mies described as the starting point of feminist research methodology (in Bowles and Duelli-Klein 1983).

Carole Vance and Ann Snitow (Ferguson et al. 1984, 132) observed that, "ironically, the obsessive focus on androcentric dominant culture does not open up information about women's actual sexual experience. In the end, two sexual silences are created: silence about what women actually do and silence about what women find arousing." To help remedy this problem, Ann Ferguson (Ferguson et al. 1984, 111) advocated the development of "feminist erotica and sex education [to] encourage new forms of feminist fantasy production. This erotica and education must emerge in a variety of contexts (high school courses, soap operas, and Harlequin novels as well as avant-garde art) and be geared to all types of audiences."

More and more explicitly articulated after 1972, female sexuality became increasingly complex in the most evolved erotic romances (heterosexual in the genre examined here), and by 1982 it was generally being portrayed as inextricably intertwined with both economic and personal autonomy, and ultimately with a joyously feminine sense of self. The relationship between heroine and hero thereby has been transformed at more than simply the physiologic level—changes that were clearly fueled and shaped by consumer demand—which resulted in the emergence of two new archetypal characterizations.

Hundreds of these erotic romance novels have made history of Phelps's (1979, 21) assertion that "with little acceptable sexual imagery —either male or female—available in this culture for women, many do not allow themselves any sexual desires or fantasies at all." If there is any single label that fits these romances today it is female sexual fantasy, and they are available in essentially every supermarket in the land. Certainly the two "kisses" described in the epigraph to this chapter leave little doubt about the quantum leap the romance novel has taken into the what, who, and how of sexual content—and neither do hundreds of articulate readers, who for the most part are well aware of the role this erotic fiction plays in both their real and fantasy lives. The majority of comments offered to this effect by readers polled in 1985 expressed the same general idea: "Sexy books make me feel sexy or sometimes aroused"; "Love scenes give me ideas. Some put me in a more sexual mood"; and "Certain books can be a real turn-on. My husband can always tell when I've read a good one!"

One reader, a single woman with a master's degree who lives in Washington, D.C., teaches Sunday school, and works full-time as a reading specialist earning $32,000 annually, explained that "I like graphic passionate sex scenes because I'm a visualizer while I read. . . . It's also fun to have my lover act out a love scene occasionally." Another reader, a thirty-one-year-old secretary who lives in Massachusetts, reported that "reading [erotic romances] sometimes gives me ideas for fun with my husband. For example, I'm surprising him tonight by wearing garters instead of panty hose. Hmmm! I also use Romance as a gateway for fantasies, be they erotic or just material for dreams." Still another said, "I always write to Bertrice Small and tell her I *love* the orgasms. She describes them exactly the way I feel them."

More than a century after Victoria Woodhull campaigned for the presidency on a platform that included equal rights to orgasm for women, changing perceptions and expectations about equality and autonomy among consumers means that erotic romance heroines today are full partners with the men in their lives, including shared sexual initiatives and satisfaction. Readers can pretty much pick and choose what interests them most in terms of (hetero)sexual fantasy, whether it be only occasionally and somewhat vaguely mentioned or almost continuously and exuberantly described. Linda Lael Miller's *Corbin's Fancy* (Pocket/Tapestry, 1985), for instance, contains eleven separate episodes of sexual intercourse, five of cunnilingus, and four of fellatio, all within about 270 pages.[3]

The physiology of sexual arousal and descriptions of sexual responses are almost always couched in "romanticized" anatomical euphemisms and overripe phrases because, according to Star Helmer, vice president and editorial director for Harlequin North America, "what you're trying to do is create a mood . . . and correct clinical terms have a hard sound to them. You've got to remember that the flow to the whole story is very important to readers, that hard words jar the reader" (in Harrison 1984, 9). Used naturally, however, as a number of Ballantine Love and Life romances have demonstrated, anatomical terms often enhance rather than impede the flow of the story, since they tend to blend in rather than stand out because of their abject silliness. The rising redundancy factor, the result of heavy readers (about half of those surveyed) consuming one romance every three days, caused the hero's "manhood" to be replaced by a "warm shaft" and other such euphemisms, while the heroine's "femininity" is more likely to be the "core" of her desire or sensitivity.

Euphemisms do nothing to impede readers' understanding of what is going on, however, as this passage from Linda Lael Miller's *Snow-flakes on the Sea* (Silhouette Intimate Moments, 1984, 57) illustrates: "In a smooth motion born of passion and desperation, Nathan grasped Mallory's slender waist, lifted her easily and then lowered her onto the pulsing pillar that would make them each a part of the other." The reverently worshipful kiss on chastely sealed lips has been displaced by plundering tongues that lap and lick, dart and delve—his from the warm moist cavern of her mouth to the pink shell of her ear, then to the pulse in her throat before descending to the rosy crest of a passion-swollen breast and across her creamy belly to the nest of silky curls, there to find its sheltered secret; hers paints a wet trail across one muscular shoulder before discovering the tiny brown nub hidden in the wiry hair that arrows downward, to disappear below the belt of his pants, after which pants are quickly done away with and she teases a tortuous path down his firm abdomen to the warm granite of his need.

These erotic romances appropriate more than euphemisms from John Cleland's *Fanny Hill,* since the heroines are not only feisty women with a will to overcome, but are sensual and warm women who "listen" to their bodies. They embrace their own sexuality as right and natural and partake of one of life's greatest pleasures with open delight, often with playfulness and humor. Where sharing is rampant and mutuality is the norm—"I love to feel your hands on my body. . . . [And] I love it that touching me gives you pleasure, too"—the heroine is no longer limited to the role of receiver, the one always being done to, as the following passage illustrates:

> Brenna steadied herself above him. Smiling down at Guyon through the unruly mass of her glistening hair, she held herself absolutely still. Only her powerful inner muscles moved, pulsating in an ancient rhythm that quickly brought him to the edge of rapture. . . . Balanced just on the tip of his hardness, she teased him with undulating waves as the rosy peak of her breast found its way inside his mouth. Guyon was not content merely to suckle her. Unwilling to be outdone in their sweet combat, he reached an expert hand down to where she was so finely perched. Revealing the most exquisitely sensitive point of her, he began rapid, unrestrained strokes at the same time his lips and tongue continued to work her nipple. (Maura Seger, *Defiant Love,* Pocket/Tapestry, 1982, 159)

As in Johanna Lindsey's *Brave the Wild Wind* (Avon, 1984, 102), heroines in post-1981 erotic historical romances may still be young (eighteen in this case) and inexperienced, but defloration rarely comes about through rape. Lindsey's virginal Jessie exhibits an eagerness that borders on downright impatience and a full-blown sexuality suggestive of instinct, resulting in simultaneous orgasm for heroine and hero their first time together, a fantasy that is common to the genre.

> She could feel the evidence of his desire and was extremely excited by it. . . . He was too inflamed to be gentle, but so was she. She ripped a button from his shirt, trying to reach his bare flesh. . . .
>
> He tugged at her pants, and she helped him push them down to her feet. But when he moved to fight with her boots so as to remove her pants completely, she stopped him. . . . "I want you now," she whispered huskily. "Now." . . . No one had ever told her there would be any pain. But it faded, and then it was gone, the urgent need returning and washing through her like a flood. He was moving in her, and she delighted in the full length of him. He was gentler than she would have liked, slower, but she found the exquisite torture had its rewards, intensifying her need, prolonging the craving.

Once this mutually sought ecstasy cools, however, Lindsey's hero begins to feel trapped, faulting the heroine for misleading him. After all, she hadn't behaved like a virgin! " 'You're not going to expect . . . anything . . . because of this?'. . . 'What do you mean, expect anything?' she asked warily. 'Come on, Jessie, you know what I mean. I'm sure you're not like most virgins, who give themselves up just to trap a man, but. . . .' " Jessie lets him know she is not interested in marriage to such a tradition-bound, sexist jackass, then a hundred pages later spits out her "untimely" views in plain English: "It's just, being raised as I was, I see things in a different light. I see things like . . . how many men go to their wedding beds virgins? If it's acceptable for a man to have lovers before marriage, why can't a woman? As long as I'm faithful afterward, it shouldn't matter" (p. 247).

Erotic romance heroines almost without exception have forsaken denial or sublimation of physical desire in favor of enjoying what they now perceive as their rightful due, through firsthand experience with multiple orgasms, fellatio, and cunnilingus. In an almost constant state of sexual awareness, the heroine is receptive *and* assertive, often seeking out the man she desires and initiating or taking control of the events that take place between them, with neither shame nor apology for her feelings, needs, responses, and actions. Now sexual dominance emanates from both sides of the bed, with the hero taking his turn at "being done to," as in Nina Coombs's *Love So Fearful* (NAL Rapture, 1983, 165): "For a minute longer she teased him, coming near but never quite reaching the part of him she knew yearned most for her touch. When finally she took him in her mouth, his sigh of relief was so heartfelt that she almost giggled. She had never imagined a love like this—warm, tender, and amusing. It was a revelation to her. As was the fact that she enjoyed taking the initiative. She enjoyed having him, in a very real way, in her power." Nora Roberts, author of some forty romance novels since 1981, lets the reader in on the emotions of both the heroine and hero when the traditional domination scene is reversed:

> Her aggression both unbalanced and aroused him. . . . She was un-dressing him swiftly, her lips following the path of her busy hands until his mind was totally centered on her. Shivering thoughts, quick tastes, maddening touches—she gave him no time to focus on only one, but insisted he experience all in an enervating haze of sensation. . . . She was driving him beyond the point of reason, but still he couldn't find the will to stop her and take command. This time there was only response. It poured from him, increasing her strength and depleting his. Knowing he was helpless excited her. . . . With sudden clarity she smelled the lemon and beeswax polish from the desk. In some sane portion of her mind, Jessica knew the scent would come back to her whenever she thought of the first time he fully gave himself to her. For she had him now—mind, emotion and body (*A Matter of Choice*, Silhouette Intimate Moments, 1984, 167).

Though no longer sexually inexperienced—as is the heroine in the traditional romance, a disadvantage that produced not only fear of rejection but also anxiety about adequacy—today's heroine may still feel sexually insecure at times, but now the hero can too.

> Doug stood before her naked. . . . He was a bronze god, his skin a teak treasure broken only by a paler swath across his loins. It was to this paler swath that Sasha's gaze was drawn, to the essence of Doug's masculinity, long and strong and quite helplessly responding to her visual caress. . . . And he felt utterly exposed. For aware as he was of his own body and of the fact that Sasha admired it, he was abundantly aware of the broader implica-tion of what was happening. . . . with these slow moments' perusal of what he offered, she was being offered a chance to refuse him. . . . Awaiting her decision was perhaps the hardest thing he'd ever done in his life. (Barbara Delinsky, *Bronze Mystique*, Harlequin Temptation, 1984, 153–54)

When the New Heroine experiences a similar insecurity it is often the New Hero who encourages her to discovery and self-confidence:

> Sy rolled onto his back, pulling Susie above him so her open thighs were poised over his own. "You come to me, Susie," he urged her quietly. "It's your body. You're in control of it. Take me with you." He clasped her hips as Susie gazed down at him with a gleam of triumph in her eyes.

Bronze Mystique, © 1984 by Barbara Delinsky. Reproduced by permission of Harlequin Enterprises.

Christina
Crockett
A MOMENT
OF MAGIC

By the author of TO TOUCH A DREAM

> Sy issued a purring sound as Susie lowered herself, claiming the right of her own passions—inflaming his with the tension in her slim body. . . . Feeling the fullness within her, Susie gasped in tiny breaths . . . feeling the hunger Sy had wanted her to know, but also comprehending the power of her own body to enfold, to excite and to elicit a surge of desire. (Christina Crockett, *A Moment of Magic*, Harlequin SuperRomance, 1984, 329)

Readers are consciously aware of this basic change in the "doing-being done to" convention, as is sadly but clearly borne out by the fifty-two-year-old Florida woman who volunteered, "There is no intercourse or sex in my marriage so I feel through reading. Is that so wrong?" Employed full-time as a nurse and now in her second marriage, this reader made a two-column listing of "Things I would like to do" (kiss using tongues, feel all over a man with my hands, and tell a man "I need to have you") and "Things I would like to have done to me" (be kissed using tongues, be undressed, just be held, and try different positions). Another reader, a thirty-eight-year-old New Yorker who works part-time as a cashier in a liquor store, said reading erotic romances "made me wish for a better sexual partnership with my husband, and later, when I realized that wasn't going to happen, it helped me become more aggressive and playful."

In his examination of sexual literature, Maurice Charney (1981, 12) found the women's fantasies collected by Nancy Friday "surprisingly resistant to the new sexual physiology (as in Mary Jane Sherfey's *The Nature and Evolution of Female Sexuality*) and the new sexual sociology (most notably Shere Hite's *The Hite Report*). It is paradoxical that sexual biology plays so minor a role in sexual fantasizing. It is almost as if the two were antagonistic systems." In the face of the evidence presented by hundreds of erotic romance novels and readers, it would seem that Charney may simply have been looking in the wrong place. American sexual fiction written between 1955 and 1980 (Charney 1982) may be characterized by sexually oriented content, but more than anything else it is social protest, satire, and humor, none of which are sexually stimulating to most readers, whether male or female. To translate sexual experience or fantasy into literature is not necessarily to create erotica, at least not when erotica is defined as sexually arousing. Even today most overt attempts by women to produce erotica for women are fatally flawed by what Linda Phelps and others have described so eloquently as seeing and evaluating the world, even a woman's own internal physical and emotional responses, through male eyes.

Lonnie Barbach's *Pleasures: Women Write Erotica* (1984) purports to detail "real experiences" female authors found sexually arousing, but most of the pieces ape both the sound and imagery of male pornography—complete with cocks, clits, cunts, and crotches. With the exception of the lesbian accounts, which exhibit considerable sensitivity and self-knowledge, most are little different from commonly recounted male fantasies except in the gender of the narrator. In "The Fifty Minute Hour," an anonymous piece that fairly reeks of Henry Miller, the narrator sponges her underarms and crotch, "ignoring the other smells beneath her clothes." Soon "the shooting hot fluid [is] filling [her] body," and she whispers to her partner that he is "the best fuck in the world" (pp. 101–2). If the romance readers surveyed are at all representative of American women in general, and the demographic data certainly suggest that they are, the crude language used by many of Barbach's narrators does little to move most women toward an erotic frame of mind, let alone closer to the Big O.[4] One of the readers surveyed in 1985 told of urging her husband to be "more verbal" during sex, only to have him ask, "Are you ready for me to fuck you?" at the crucial moment. "It was like a bucket of cold water. I decided after that I'd rather have him silent." As sexual fantasies, many of the Barbach pieces recall Beatrice Faust's (1980, 19–20) observations about most pornography: "The social and psychological components of sexual conduct have no place in pornography: flirtation, courtship, refusal, seduction, and even mundane activities like undressing and sleeping are all left out. The men are always potent, the women always willing. That is, the women are presented as approaching sexual activity in exactly the same way as men do, living up to masculine fantasies of the sexually assertive, instantly aroused, uninhibited woman, who never has a headache, never asks for affection . . . [and] climaxes as easily as she is aroused. She is, in fact, a man in disguise."

Another recent entry into the arena of sexual literature for women, *Ladies Home Erotica,* was written by the Kensington Ladies' Erotica Society, "an improbable group of [ten] women over forty, for whom dashing off an erotic story was one more task to be sandwiched in between trips to the supermarket and visits to the dentist" (p. 3). The collection started as a sleeper from Ten Speed Press in October 1984 with a 5,000-copy print run, but within six months had become a 100,000-copy bestseller, at which time, after a mean-spirited lawsuit was threatened by the *Ladies Home Journal,* the title was changed to *Ladies Own Erotica.* Some of these stories are erotic, some are humorous, and others read as declarations of independence, but almost all are refreshingly explorative. The catalyst of the group, Sabina Sedgwick (a tongue-in-cheek pseudonym derived from the nineteenth-century author of "domestic" novels), challenged her "ladies" with the following questions: "Do you think women and men agree about what is erotic? Are our experiences different from theirs? Do we really know what turns us on, or do we just go along, accepting and acting out what male writers proclaim to be erotic?" Sedgwick's own "Address to a Penis Owner" in large measure sets both the tone and the approach of the entire volume.

> In the feminine experience the penis can add the finishing touch to satisfaction, but it is not *sine qua non.* . . . We suspect that the penis culture is a male invention from an earlier age when fertility was tantamount to the survival of the race. Understandably, then, the penis is still an important showpiece, and while it also adds much gratification to its owner, it offers comparatively less to the fulfillment of female desires. . . . We know neither the power that comes with owning this tool nor the fear of losing it. Since we don't have anything as obvious and as embarrassingly untrustworthy in our love-making paraphernalia, we share your concern for its ups and downs, so much so that we have obliterated our own needs for gratification. We are not trying to diminish your appendage, but we want to enlarge upon those parts of you that have been unjustly ignored. These are the parts that are essential to our pleasure: your hair, your eyes, your lips, your tongue, your chest, your thighs, your voice, and—most importantly—your hands. It is no accident that our stories have celebrated these greater assets. (pp. 23–24)

A different work in both conception and expression than either *Pleasures* or *Ladies Home Erotica* is Roberta Latow's *Three Rivers* (1981), which combines lush sensual description with both female and male sexual fantasies, undoubtedly the reason both sexes, including many romance readers, find it so appealing. *Three Rivers* is about a relationship (courtship), a happy love affair involving two mature people in a story that includes secondary characters (family members and friends) and subplots (the Arab-Jewish conflict).

In spite of the widespread contempt and ridicule the romance as popular culture suffers, with its presumed low culture content and consumers, these paperback novels contain more than an occasional allusion to what Maurice Charney called the "new sexual sociology," as, for instance, in the ruminations of Laura Matthews's heroine in *Emotional Ties* (Avon, 1984, 190): "Of course all being an extraordinary lover really meant was that he was a considerate lover. He paid attention to what she liked, he never pressed her, he always waited until she was ready, and never made himself look like a martyr in doing it. Surely she should have run into more men like that in her thirty years. Not that she meant to downgrade her own attraction to him, and presumably his to her, but why were all the men she knew so intent on instant gratification for themselves? It was enough to turn a woman off permanently!"

It was primarily Masters and Johnson, however, who articulated what Charney called the "new sexual physiology" with data demonstrating that the sexual capacity of females is both unique and probably superior to that of males. From their analysis of "10,000 orgasms," Masters and Johnson (1966, 45) concluded that, unlike the male, the female sexual cycle does *not* include a refractory period following orgasm during which it is impossible to respond to more sexual stimulation, which means that females exhibit a richer variety of sexual responses. Therefore, it is what females were found to be missing that makes multiple orgasms possible within a short space of time. What males are lacking, by contrast, is an equivalent to the clitoris, which Masters and Johnson described as "a unique organ in the total of human anatomy. Its express purpose is to serve both as a receptor and transformer of sensual stimuli. Thus the female has an organ system which is totally limited in physiologic function to initiating or elevating levels of sexual tension. No such organ exists within the anatomic structure of the human male" (p. 45).

Today, erotic romance heroines experience multiple orgasms—the linchpin of the new sexual physiology—with such frequency they are simply a "given." (One cannot help wondering, in fact, at the potential mischief caused by portraying multiple orgasms as the norm, since exactly how widespread this capability is among women has never been established.) In Carol Sturm Smith's *The Right Time* (Ballantine Love and Life, 1982, 75), for instance, "He stopped short of joining her as she crested the wave and splintered upon orgasm. She complained, and he laughed gently. 'No, it's all right,' he said. 'You're a greedy lady. I'll give you another one.'" This scene also demonstrates restraint and control on the hero's part, which some observers interpret as symbolic of the fantasy that the male will not ejaculate prematurely, thereby ending the event for the woman without resolution to orgasm and satisfaction.

The multiorgasmic heroine leads naturally to variety, since it is a foregone conclusion that even the most virile of heroes cannot hope to keep up with her, with the result that cunnilingus is portrayed as both foreplay and stimulation to orgasm.[5] Cunnilingus is not always delayed until the couple engage in a familiarizing experience or two, either, but often occurs during their first sexual encounter, as in Pat Wallace's *Sweetheart Contract* (1983, 121), one of Silhouette Intimate Moments' first titles: "With teasing, excruciating leisure, that unseen mouth moved open-lipped and moist over her vibrant flesh, licking her knees and her upper legs, traveling upward in an arrowing path, nuzzling the golden luxuriance of her secret body for so long that she thought a scream would be torn from her lips. Then his questing tongue found at last the key to all her frenzy. . . . she quivered, arching as his rhythmic tongue continued and continued and continued, waves of pleasure lapping at her, washing her like sea waves in a fiery dream."

Used to portray the heroine's sexual capacity and to vary her experience of sex, as well as to extend the length of foreplay-love scenes, cunnilingus as visual-emotional imagery at times takes on the trappings of a shrine at which the hero worships. Though the hero in Anne Stuart's *Catspaw* (Harlequin Intrigue, 1985, 216) is a retired cat burglar, his amorous exploits appear in no way inhibited by his wrecked knee: "She felt like a pagan goddess with Blackheart kneeling in front of her, slowly worshipping her body with his mouth and fingers. She felt decadent and sinful and gloriously alive, and when his mouth sank lower to the tangled heat of her femininity, her heart and soul emptied in a rush of pleasure, so heady that she had to brace herself against his strong shoulders or lose her balance. . . . Her body trembled against his mouth, and the world began to slip away, bit by bit, until it finally shattered in a tumbled rush, and her body convulsed in a white-hot heat of love."

Masters and Johnson also demonstrated that the female can respond more or less as quickly as men do to *effective* sexual stimulation, and concluded that the key variable in her arousal and/or satisfaction is the quality of the sexual attention she receives. This idea, too, is reflected in Linda Shaw's *Way of the Willow* (Silhouette Special Edition, 1983, 85), when a Vietnam War widow begins to wonder about her dead husband rather than continuing to doubt herself: "Jenny had always required time to reach fulfillment. Had Martin taken the care she needed? Or perhaps Jenny had needed the time only back then, only with him. Maybe it was his own clumsy inexperience."

The physiological data gathered by Masters and Johnson not only dumped the vaginal orgasm on the garbage heap of Freudian misogyny, but struck to the very heart of male sexual myths and conventions—that penetration is the ultimate source of satisfaction to the female. Instead, Masters and Johnson (1966, 133) found, "The maximum physiologic intensity of orgasmic response subjectively reported or objectively recorded [among female subjects] has been achieved by self-regulated mechanical or automanipulative techniques. The next highest level of erotic intensity has resulted from partner manipulation, again with established or self-regulated methods, and the lowest intensity of target-organ response was achieved during coition." This "reality," too, has appeared with increasing frequency in the erotic romance, sometimes in the context of the heroine's developing self-awareness, as in Carole Nelson Douglas's *Her Own Decision* (Ballantine Love and Life, 1982, 156): "It wouldn't have mattered if she hadn't come during intercourse; Dan knew how to see to it that she did afterward, anyway, and she was learning ways of her own with her own body."

Anthropologist Helen Fisher (1982, 87–94) has suggested that, at some time in the mists of prehistory, females who evolved the ability to maintain sex drive beyond the estrus in order to attract males to help care for their young were favored by natural selection. Thus, Fisher argued, females evolved brains that could be activated by LHRH (luteinizing hormone-releasing hormone) even when not ovulating, which supports evidence now available indicating that the brain is involved physiologically and exerts more control in the sexual arousal of females than in males, and that male sexual arousal is more reflexive in character. Since biological evolution proceeds toward greater and greater complexity, this in turn suggests that perhaps one of the basic sexual problems of twentieth-century heterosexual females is that they are out of phase with their sexual partners in the evolutionary sense, and that males are biologically (and therefore perhaps psychologically as well) incapable of matching the complexity of response in females. This does nothing to deny that our realized sexuality, whether male or female, is to a large degree socially constructed, or that a great many of our most entrenched cultural values and mores have acted to widen, rather than narrow, this difference between males and females.[6] What it does do is underscore the fact that sexual response without emotional involvement is considered to be superior or enviable only when the more reflexive and limited (less brain-controlled) male sexual response is considered normative.

The sexually liberated woman in the erotic romance did not waste much time exploring the world of casual encounters with multiple partners, discovering early on what *Cosmopolitan* editor Helen Gurley Brown took much longer to learn—that "sex with commitment is absolutely delicious. Sex with your date for the evening is not so marvelous—too casual, too meaningless" (in Leo 1984, 75). Thus, all the overtly sexual excerpts in the world cannot alone spell out the necessary and sufficient conditions that make a romance erotic, because they are lifted out of the stream of events and out of the context of the relationship in which they take place. Women romance readers seem to derive a sustained level of sexual awareness and pleasure from the tension built into the development of this loving relationship *over time*, and it is the process of conflict and resolution that takes place between two wills and bodies that creates the necessary tension to turn the entire story into a psychogenic stimulus.

One common device used to build and sustain sexual tension, for instance, is the Twice-Told Tale, which also illustrates restraint on the part of the hero. First he tells the heroine exactly how he wants to and is going to make love to her (verbal foreplay), thereby putting the reader in a state of anticipation and heightening the intensity of every encounter between the two characters thereafter until the event actually takes place, fifty or more pages further along, when it is described again. This time factor is not only crucial to the erotic romance but also speaks to what many women believe to be a fundamental difference between pornography and erotica—the encounter versus the relationship—and ultimately to why one is sexually stimulating to most women while the other usually is not. It takes time for the reader to become involved, to get herself into the pictures that form in her head, which in turn activate the pleasure switches in her brain. A sixty-year-old Californian who "voted for Geraldine" explained that she "just finished reading Sylvie Sommerfield's last book, and with three couples in it there's explicit sex on every other page. I like these parts, but let's have a little more story leading and building up to it. No one likes a rabbit!" Two-thirds of the readers polled in 1985 agreed that "most women become sexually aroused more slowly than men" (11 percent were undecided and 23 percent disagreed).

Does this mean that romance readers, like nearly three-quarters of the women who responded to Ann Landers's now-famous question, would "be content to be held close and treated tenderly, and forget about 'the act' "? Not likely, since 66 percent of surveyed readers disagreed with the statement "Experiencing orgasm during sexual intercourse is not very important to most women."[7] If the choice is either a "quickie," with no foreplay and no pleasure to the woman, or a little affectionate hugging, it is not difficult to explain the Landers responses, for the question then becomes which of two unsatisfying experiences a woman prefers. Landers (in Angier 1985) commented that "this says something very unflattering about men in this country. It says men are selfish. They want theirs." June Reinisch, director of the Kinsey Institute, called the Landers responses expressions of "dissatisfaction with their relationships and partners, not with sex per se." Lending additional weight to the Landers-Reinisch conclusion is the comment from Carolyn Nichols, editorial director of the Bantam Loveswept line: "I've received a lot of letters from women who ask 'Can't you persuade your company to promote these books to men, so at last they will know what women really want and need' in the way of sex" (in Harrison 1984, 8).

Certainly erotic romances share with Charney's (1981, 10) definition of sexual literature the convention of repetition (both imagery and patterns of discourse), as well as characteristic themes of sexual fantasy and wish fulfillment. A few even share both the terminology and fantasies of classic pornography, as does Elaine Barbieri's *Love's Fiery Jewel* (Zebra, 1983). Barbieri's heroine is not only insatiable but possesses a "tender slit" which releases in "gasping tribute the sweet nectar of love and total fulfillment" (p. 348). Susan M. Johnson's *Love Storm* (Playboy Press, 1981) falls back on the use of drugs to eliminate the female's supposedly natural inhibitions yet leave her faultless and free of responsibility. Kidnapped and sold to a slave trader, the heroine ends up in the harem of Ibrahim Bey, where she is first subdued with hashish-laced sweets and then given wine containing cantharides, before being taken to the Bey's tent to entertain his guests, including the hero. She is subjected to an explicitly detailed array of sexual tortures—having her "burning-hot cunt" stuffed first with plums and then a red leather dildo complete with feather-filled testicles—before the hero manages to rescue her, by which time her body is on fire as a result of the aphrodisiac in the wine. As they ride away from the Bey's tent the hero orders his men to stay back while he solves the heroine's problem via another classic pornographic device, *le coît de cheval:* "Unbuttoning his riding pants, Alex pulled out his engorged penis, raised Zena slightly, and impaled her on his erect stiffness. Wrapping her legs around his waist, he gave a gentle nudge to Pasha, and the black stallion broke into a slow gallop" (p. 190). Though set within the context of a developing relationship, descriptions of this kind have been the exception among erotic romances rather than the rule.

Making no distinction between erotica and pornography, and using a male model of sexuality, John Cawelti (1976, 14) argued that "the escape experience offered by pornography is really too immediately physical to be sustained for any substantial period of time. In effect, the only possible consequences of a pornographic episode are orgasm or detumescence, both of which lead inevitably back to the world of reality. . . . I would hazard the guess that the actual experience of pornography for most people consists of moments of pleasurable excitation interspersed with long stretches of boredom and frustration, rather than a sustained and completed experience that leaves one temporarily satisfied." Cawelti may have described quite accurately what he and males in general find sexually exciting, but he ignored the fact that females can experience sexual pleasure at many different levels and with more than one pattern of response—a continuum rather than a polarity where she is either "turned on" or "turned off"—and that women are physiologically capable of continuing to respond to sexual stimulation following orgasm, while males are not. This concept of continuum and complexity in the sexuality of women is consonant with Adrienne Rich's (1980) more global definition of female sexuality, the "lesbian continuum of sexuality," though her label seems unnecessarily limiting.

Women use all kinds and intensities of foreplay, including some that men probably would not so categorize, sometimes even the most minimal expressions of attention and caring, to achieve different levels of sexual stimulation and satisfaction. Bernie Zelbergeld (1978, 231) found in his study of more than 400 female subjects that "what is usually called foreplay is not something women see as a prelude to something better. It is valuable in its own right, and women like men who are sensual enough to enjoy this aspect of lovemaking." Comments from romance readers surveyed in 1985 make it very clear that most of them do not view hugging and touching as a substitute for but as part of "the act."

It is this complexity in the female experience of pleasure—the interpretation of many different kinds and intensities of stimuli to the brain as erotic, and her ability to sustain pleasure over relatively long periods of time—that helps explain both the attraction and satisfaction women find in the erotic romance. It also helps explain why romantic fiction has been such a popular entertainment medium among women for the past decade and a half. Katchadourian and Lunde (1976, 18) point out that "the brain can use memory and imagination to initiate sexual excitement without sensory stimuli," and that sexual stimulation through purely mental activity is, in addition, "infinitely more complex" than through the senses. The single factor that appears to be most crucial to this complex process is the extent to which the imagination is allowed to come into play.

Beatrice Faust (1980, 97) pointed out that "[women] may laugh at *Deep Throat* and *The Devil and Miss Jones*, or even say the films are good fun, but they rarely get wet pants from them. Women are less interested in epidermal friction than in emotional vibrations which, in any case, lend themselves more to words than pictures. . . . The great romantic favorites had nary a penis between them, yet they encouraged women to identify with the heroines and imagine a relationship with the hero." A number of investigations of responses to erotic material support the assertion that most males are more aroused by visual stimuli while most females are more aroused by the printed word, lending credence to the cliché that a woman falls in love with her ears while a man falls in love with his eyes. John Stauffer and Richard Frost (1976), for instance, compared interest in features in *Playboy* and *Playgirl* magazines among male and female college students and found that males were most interested in centerfold nudes, ads, cartoons, and photo essays, while females were most interested in fiction, interviews, and letters to the editor. Dealing with both sexual content and the form it takes, Byrne and Lamberth (1971) tested the reactions of forty-two married couples to three types of stimuli — photographic, literary, and imaginary representations of the same scene — and concluded that while males were slightly more aroused by the pictorial stimuli and females by the literary and imaginary stimuli, self-generated imaginary stimuli were about twice as arousing as either the visual or semantic forms of erotica. Another study, aimed directly at examining the role of the imagination (Tannenbaum 1971), tested for responses to three versions of a film and found that the details supplied by viewers' imaginations were more vivid than those explicitly described in the film itself. Both of these studies confirmed an earlier experiment by Jakobovits (1965), who concluded that females were more sexually stimulated by stories in which mental processes beyond the purely sensory are engaged. The more the imagination is activated by an erotic stimulus, according to Jakobovits, the more likely that it is women who respond to it. Glenn Wilson (1978, 78) suggested that not only does the effect of erotica depend upon the way in which it impinges on the imagination of the viewer, but that "relatively subtle stimuli lend themselves to more imaginative elaboration, and are less likely to activate the internal censor."[8]

Most of these findings are suggestive of the way the erotic romance seems to function for women readers. In addition, they help to explain the importance of cover illustration characteristics. They are consistent, for example, with the responses of readers polled in 1982 when asked if they would like to see romance novels they liked made into movies: 72 percent said yes, but almost half of them added the proviso "but not with well-known actors." Imposing a specific identity on fictional characters, through either photographic cover illustrations or famous personalities, functions to limit the imagination of the female romance consumer, impeding her ability to "identify with the heroines" or to "imagine a relationship with the hero."

While the Coles and Shamp (1984) study, which was conducted in 1978 and focused on the bodice rippers of that period, does not say that erotic romance readers make love twice as frequently as nonreaders *because* they read romances, it does establish a correlation between frequency of intercourse and reading erotic romances, and between reading erotic romances and use of sexual fantasy. According to Byrne and Lamberth (1971), if the imagination is such a powerful and easily utilized sexual stimulant, individual differences in sexuality, such as sex drive and preferred frequency of orgasm, may largely be due to the way we learn to use sexual fantasy.

Kay Mussell (1984, 139–41) set the sexuality depicted in romance novels in the context of the three stages of development in the "social mythology of sexuality" described by Masters and Johnson in *The Pleasure Bond*. "In Stage I, sex is done by the male *to* the female. In Stage II, it is done by the male *for* the female. In Stage III . . . it is performed by the male *with* the female." In Stage II, females acknowledge real sexual feelings and needs, including orgasm, but do not initiate sex. Sexual satisfaction remains the responsibility of the male. Contrary to Mussell's assertion that Stage II describes romance novels today, the passages quoted here show that considerable evolution into Stage III has taken place. This is not to say that Stage II situations do not appear in some stories, but it is far more likely that a mixture of events color the relationship, making it impossible to categorize them as one *or* the other. Mutually exclusive stages do not describe the complexity of relationships in the romance novel any more accurately than they do relationships between real people.

Literally hundreds of romances have been and are being published in which all of the following appear at some time during the course of the story: (a) the heroine initiates the sex act and satisfies the hero and herself; (b) both hero and heroine perform a sexual service for the other at one time or another, sometimes in ways that could be described as "sex done by" one to the other; and (c) the initiation and conduct of sexual activity is shared, with equal enthusiasm and pleasure. The loved one may still be the source of greatest sexual pleasure for both heroine and hero in the new romance novel, but most of the surrendering that is going on is to the erotic experience per se.

Pornography or Erotica?

That "pornographic" and "obscene" are more or less synonymous is given credence linguistically through both derivation and definition, and legally in statutes dealing with the sale and distribution of pornography that rely on the definition of obscene (explicit sexuality that is offensive to community standards). Thus pornography and erotica cannot be used synonymously unless we are prepared to agree that everything sexually explicit is negative. To do so equates what is natural, pleasurable, and healthy with what is unhealthy and detrimental to the dignity and integrity of both the individual and society. It also would deny women (and men) access to material that could aid their development as fully realized sexual beings, since all sexually explicit material would be socially unacceptable. Not unimportantly, equating erotica with pornography also plays into the hands of those elements in society that would suppress freedom of speech and expression, and particularly sexual expression in all its forms.[9]

A number of feminists have tried to spell out differences in sexually oriented material, among them Gloria Steinem (1980, 38) in a piece for *Ms.* magazine: "Erotica is about sexuality; pornography is about power and sex-as-weapon." Andrea Dworkin (1979) applauded these "honorable efforts . . . to distinguish between pornography and erotica" (which assert that erotica involves mutuality and reciprocity while pornography involves dominance and violence), then restated the radical feminist position that "in the male sexual lexicon, which is the vocabulary of power, erotica is simply high-class pornography: better produced, better conceived, better executed, better packaged, designed for a better class of consumer. As with the call girl and the streetwalker, one is turned out better but both are produced by the same system of sexual values and both perform the same sexual service."

Today the word "pornography" has become so thoroughly politicized, carrying implications that go far beyond the purely sexual, that it has lost any possibility whatsoever for neutrality, if indeed it ever had any, making value-free definitions such as "pornography means nothing more than sexually explicit materials" (Smith 1976, 16) either obsolete or specious. Beatrice Faust (1980, 17) argued that pornography "can't be defined in terms of its impact on the viewer's emotions, nor of arbitrarily selected subject matter. It must be defined in terms of its manner. . . . [It is] not what, but how it is shown that makes the difference." Maurice Charney (1981) refuted Steven Marcus's (1969) definition of pornography in the broadest terms, including the latter's assertion that literature has a beginning, a middle, and an end, while pornography does not. At least from the mid-1970s, however, feminists have been defining pornography in political terms, as "the undiluted essence of anti-female propaganda" (Brownmiller 1975, 394); "a medium for expressing norms about male power and domination which functions as a social control mechanism for keeping women in a subordinate status" (Diamond 1980, 129); and as "the cluster of sexuo-violent images which dichotomize the participants into active/passive roles" (Killoran 1983, 443).

By mid-1980, Los Angeles, Minneapolis, and several other cities had mounted feminist-led attempts to ban pornography by labeling it sex discrimination and defining it as any material that includes "graphic, sexually explicit subordination of women" (Blakely 1985, 40). In at least one of those cities, Minneapolis, that included paperback romance novels. Ironically, the attacks focused mainly on the romances with "lurid" cover illustrations, rather than on the more innocuous appearing Harlequin Romance (which has fairly consistently carried degrading depictions of women, usually without being sexually explicit). In time this definition has become more broadly inclusive, and distinctions between types (e.g., involving children or violence) have tended to drop by the wayside, resulting in an all-or-nothing mentality that damns everything (hetero)sexually explicit, whether words or images, as demeaning to women.

The result has been that those feminists who supported anti-pornography laws found themselves the uncomfortable bedfellows of fundamentalist religious and far-right political groups. Anti-abortion and anti−birth control as well, these religious right groups, under the guise of a return to "traditional" values and morality, are striving to maintain male power and male control of society. They also equate economic and social equality with Marxism and/or communism, and their stance in support of private enterprise is little more than an attempt to put a patriotic public face on their aims to limit and control civil liberties.

The water was muddied still further with the release of the *Attorney General's Commission on Pornography: Final Report* in 1986, which defined pornography as material that is "predominantly sexually explicit and intended primarily for the purpose of sexual arousal" (pp. 228–29)—reaffirming that everything sexually explicit is of negative value and socially unacceptable, and also managing to infer that even sexual arousal is somehow improper. The commission rejected the term "erotica" on the ground that it constitutes a conclusion rather than a description; erotica is the mirror image of pornography, the one differing from the other only in whether the user of the terms approves or disapproves of the material in question (p. 230). One member described the group as "hopelessly deadlocked" on the issue of whether a category of sexually explicit, designed-to-arouse material that is neither violent nor degrading exists, which he called a major failure of the commission (p. 92).

Most advocates of anti-pornography statutes—radical feminists, fundamentalists, and the majority of the Meese Commission—assert that a causal relationship exists between the sex depicted in books, magazines, and movies, and crimes against women (without clear distinction as to type of portrayal), though little, if any, research data support this sweeping claim. Edward Donnerstein and Daniel Linz found no behavioral effects among college students who viewed films with sexual content alone, but did find behavioral effects among students who viewed sexually violent films (in Savage 1985). Donnerstein, a professor at the University of Wisconsin, accused the Meese Commission of "going beyond the evidence," and said, "They are picking on pornography when the research shows quite clearly that you get similiar effects from other material" that features violence; Neil Malamuth, a psychologist at UCLA who in one study found that 30 percent of his male subjects were sexually aroused by the nonsexual violence against women depicted in the films they saw, said the commission "extrapolated" from his findings to apply them to nonviolent material (in Kurtz 1986). Two of three dissenting commission members—Ellen Levine, editor of *Woman's Day*, and Judith Becker, professor of clinical psychology and psychiatry at Columbia University's College of Physicians and Surgeons—issued a twenty-page statement objecting to the report on the basis that it described the available scientific evidence inaccurately and drew unfounded conclusions.

An attempt to stop the sale and distribution of pornography (without legal sanction) was made in the spring of 1986 by Meese Commission executive director Alan Sears, who wrote what the court deemed an intimidating letter (Stengel 1986, 17) to merchandisers handling *Playboy*, *Penthouse*, and *Hustler*—"Failure to respond will necessarily be accepted as an indication of no objection [to pornography]" —after which the Southland Corporation withdrew the magazines from the shelves of its nationwide chain of 7-Eleven stores. Though a court injunction stopped the publication of a "blacklist" of retailers of these magazines, the now famous "Meese letter" may well have had a chilling effect on other retailers. One book wholesaler reported at the annual meeting of Romance Writers of America in 1986 that some of his key accounts were refusing sensual romance covers in the wake of the pornography hearings (Douglas 1986, 31).[10]

In 1985 the anti-pornography debate cracked the feminist movement wide open, with the anti-censorship faction making it crystal clear that its objection was to the laws as written, which would restrict feminist erotica as well as pornography (MacKinnon and Hunter 1985). These laws would ultimately, as Nan Hunter suggested, "take women down the path to enhanced sexual repression and not to liberation and/or empowerment" (p. 7). Popular romance novels are a case in point, since as a genre they vary, with a great many fitting the definition of erotica ("sexual liaisons between peers who each have a right to equal sexual pleasure"), while others conform to the definition of pornography ("relations of dominance and submission") proposed by Ann Ferguson (Ferguson et al. 1984, 111). Trying to apply legal sanctions against one type of romance and not the other would be all but impossible.

Though no claim is made that erotic romance novels as a whole are fully developed as feminist erotica, certainly they have moved a long way in that direction. Alexandra Sellers's *The Male Chauvinist* (Silhouette Intimate Moments, 1985) provides one example of what a "sexual liaison between peers who each have a right to equal pleasure" means in a section of dialogue that takes place following an uninhibited, urgent sexual encounter between the heroine and hero, which the heroine worries might have given the hero the wrong idea.

> "What I'm trying to say, Andrea, is that a lot of men think that women have a rape fantasy, and it's just not true. And if last night gave you that idea about me, well, it shouldn't have." . . .
> "Kate . . . if for the rest of my life I have no control over myself with you, still I promise you one thing: Violence and sex never, *never* were connected in my mind. I will never deliberately hurt you."
> She believed him. She trusted him. . . . "And you would never think that I would want you to hurt me?" . . .
> "We can be everything to each other, Kate; we can try every sexual and

162

loving possibility with each other, and even if we live another sixty years, we don't need to scrape pain from the bottom of the barrel.

"But if you want me to chase you, if you like to feel that you fight and I win—and I am a fighter, too—please don't confuse this with rape, or pain. And when you want to be aggressive, when you want to conquer my body and do with it as you please, I will enjoy that, too. We will not think in stereotypes, you and I; we will not think what is right or wrong, or what feminists say, or male chauvinists say. We will think only of what we want, and pleasure. Because with you I want to experience everything." (pp. 206–7)

It is important to remember that romance novels constitute a dynamic mass medium that is continuing to change even as the description presented here is being written. To attempt to ban or limit their distribution by labeling them pornography, or even to continue to condemn them in the wholesale fashion most feminists have to date — as if to do otherwise might brand them "nonfeminists," as happened in the 1985 pornography debate—is to ignore or castigate what has been one of the most effective channels for communicating feminist ideas to the broad base of women who must be reached if the women's movement is to continue to effect significant social change. Whether stories and fictional characters will continue to move in this direction or at what rate, especially in the face of the increasingly atavistic sociopolitical pressures of the eighties, remains to be seen.

Notes

1. This culturally imposed schizophrenia is described in a number of "serious" fictional love triangles in which the female protagonist is strongly attracted to two men who are opposites. She is torn by indecision and unable to reconcile the opposing forces within herself, ultimately ending in madness or even death (Daleski 1984).

2. The discussion of female sexuality has been hampered by the split within the women's movement over anti-pornography laws. To have to ask what constitutes politically acceptable sexuality is laughable, but not funny, since, like the male-defined sexuality Phelps (1979, 22) spoke of—"So all-pervasive is the male bias of our culture that we seldom notice that the fantasies we take in, the images that describe to us how to act, are male fantasies about females"—it raises the specter of continued alienation, this time imposed by the sisterhood itself. As Ilene Philipson observed (Ferguson et al. 1984, 113), already "one must carefully monitor her words and actions these days in order to avoid being seen as an enemy of the women's movement, or conversely, a moralistic defender of vanilla sex."

3. One can only wonder at Suzanne Rose's (1985, 256) assertion that because "the manifest themes are nonsexual ones the romance fails to provide a model of sexual agency for women" (she apparently meant all types, since she mentioned Dell Ecstasy, Jove Second Chance at Love, and Silhouette Desire, as well as Harlequin Romances and Presents). Rose also claimed that passivity is an "exalted state [and] central to the romance's appeal," without presenting any evidence whatsoever from readers.

4. Barbach (1984, x), a sex therapist, writes in the introduction to her anthology that she has used Nancy Friday's collected sexual fantasies, the work of Anaïs Nin, *Fanny Hill,* and *The Pearl* to "assist women in creating an erotic frame of mind. . . . But, with the exception of a scene or two in romance novels, or *Fanny* by Erica Jong or *Blue Skies, No Candy* by Gael Greene, not much else could be found in local bookstores."

5. A number of studies in recent years have confirmed that oral sex is one of the most popular forms of sexual activity. Donn Byrne and John Lambeth (1971) observed the reactions of married couples to nineteen erotic themes and found heterosexual cunnilingus the most arousing theme to both sexes, while heterosexual fellatio ranked fourth among men and sixth among women. A decade later, Sandra Kahn (1981) rank ordered the sexual preferences of men and women and found that heterosexual cunnilingus ranked first among women and heterosexual fellatio ranked first among men. The highly controversial 1986 Supreme Court decision which upheld a Georgia anti-sodomy law spread far and wide the definition of sodomy contained in this and twenty-three other state laws (without specification as to the sex of the individuals involved) as "any sexual act involving the sex organs of one person and the mouth or anus of another" (see, e.g., Goodman 1986; Hight 1986; Wermiel 1986).

6. Jack Sattel (1983, 123), for example, argues that male inexpressiveness is a culturally produced temperament trait that is not only dysfunctional to the companionate, intimate American-style marriage, but works as a method for achieving control both in male-female and in male-male interaction. He suggests that it also may be used as a strategy to maintain power rather than to move toward a nonsexist equality.

7. Based on a national sample of 1,100 men and women, *Parade Magazine* (Ubell 1984) reported that having an orgasm during sexual intercourse is important to 60 percent of the women and 81 percent of the men polled.

8. Research findings about the importance of context (romantic and/or committed) to female sexual arousal have been mixed. Using genital and general systemic measures as well as subjective reports, Julia Heiman (1975) examined sexual arousal in a sample of forty-four male and seventy-seven female college students exposed to a variety of taped sequences and concluded that the erotic and erotic-romantic sequences were significantly more arousing than the simply romantic, and also that female-initiated, female-centered activity was the most arousing tape content. D. G. Steele and C. E. Walker

(1976, 272) looked at female responses to erotic films and then described the ideal erotic film from the female perspective: "The cast of the film would consist of one attractive male and one attractive female, displaying affection, 'romance' and prolonged foreplay in a bedroom setting. The film would involve a gradual process leading to a coitus involving a variety of positions. The emotional tone of the film would emphasize the 'total' relationship, and not merely genital sexual behavior." More recently, Thomas Harrell and Richard Stolp (1985) presented taped stories to sixty-five women, about women engaging in either a committed or casual sexual relationship, and found no significant differences in their responses for either context or the interaction between person and context.

9. In February 1986, the U.S. Supreme Court affirmed a lower court ruling that the Indianapolis pornography ordinance was unconstitutional on free speech grounds. The lower court had ruled that the state could not declare one perspective right and thereby silence opponents, a ruling that also attempted to speak to the difference between "demean" and "obscene."

10. K-Mart also was reported to have notified New American Library that it would not accept Bertrice Small's *A Love for All Time* because of the "lascivious" cover illustration (*Romantic Times*, no. 30, 22). In a July 1986 telephone interview, Small pointed out that the cover of her book was no different from hundreds of others, and speculated that the K-Mart buyer may have taken courage from the Meese letter to act out of his own personal views. Most erotic romance covers carry illustrations of the heroine that are highly suggestive of her physical "charms," though generally they are less revealing than the photographic covers of *Cosmopolitan* magazine. Johanna Lindsey's books have become notorious in recent years for illustrations in which the male is nude; on her December 1986 title, however, both characters are fully clothed, which implies that publishers are beginning to respond to what they perceive is a hostile marketing environment. Commenting on "lurid" covers (which many authors heartily dislike but have little, if any, say about) at the 1985 Romance Writers of America meeting, Carolyn Nichols pointed to the fact that male sales representatives tend to push those books with illustrations that appeal to them. In a highly competitive market, however, it is likely that publishers have simply used "sensational" covers both to get the attention of buyers and to imply sexual content.

Chapter Eight

GATEKEEPERS ON ROMANCE

Central Characters in the

Drama of Change

> [Serious women novelists] have more in common with
> each other than they have with their enemies, the
> popular or romantic women novelists. . . . these
> writers recognized "the woman's novel" as a perfect
> means for telling women accurately where they stood
> at a given moment.
>
> Anthea Zeman, *Presumptuous Girls*

> Romance novels today show change better than serious
> literary novels, which concentrate on discontent. . . .
> Solutions may seem easier in some than they are in
> real life, but they act as role models, if not for readers
> themselves, then for what they hope and expect for
> their daughters. Look at the careers being described in
> popular romance novels. They're way beyond what
> most women are working at today, but it is more
> important to show a goal, and ways it can be achieved.
> [Serious literary novels] don't show the change in
> aspirations, the hope.
>
> Roberta Gellis, 1985

*W*hether readers' likes and dislikes are simply inferred from sales figures and other publishers' successes or read directly through consumer research, it is romance authors who conceive and construct the product being marketed, and agents and editors who determine which unique mixture of words and ideas fit what they believe readers will buy—who sit at the manuscript "gate" and decide what to allow through.[1] Several editors were incubating ideas about a new kind of contemporary series romance in the late 1970s, with the result that the sensuous (erotic) contemporary romance appeared just as the bodice-ripper fever was cooling down. Though these early sensuous series novels carried considerable baggage from the past, they quickly evolved into stories of contemporary women who were leading actors on the stage of life, not passive members of the audience. The erotic series romance, quite simply, was a story whose time had come, and it sent a second shock wave of burgeoning sales reverberating through the romance publishing industry.

Vivien Stephens, an editor for Dell's Candlelight Romance line (an American version of the sweet Harlequin), says she received two manuscripts in 1979 that "didn't fit" content guidelines.[2] Instead of rejecting them, however, Stephens convinced her editorial director to go along with a new line she dubbed Ecstasy. "On the Wednesday before Thanksgiving in 1978," she recalls, "I stepped into a Woolworth's while waiting for a bus home after work, and I watched women load up from a freshly-stocked rack of Harlequins [Romances and Presents] as if preparing to be snowed in. Only one approached the Dell rack, and she took a Regency. I asked one of the women browsing the Harlequin rack if she ever read Dell romances. She answered, 'No—the women are insipid blue-eyed blondes with bubble brains.'" Approval for the line came easily. "The sales people said it was okay. And then my editor-in-chief said it was okay if the sales department thinks they can sell it." Stephens used Ecstasy as a working title—"it really wasn't planned or researched"—and in spite of her director's comment that "it sounds so orgasmic," the title stuck when "nobody came up with a better one by the time we were ready to go." The first two Ecstasy titles, Amii Loren's *Tawny Gold Man* and Jayne Castle's *Gentle Pirate*, appeared on the racks in December 1980, and the line was so successful that the number of titles available each month quickly increased from two to four to six and finally to eight. (In 1986 the publisher cut back to six new releases plus two reissues, called "classics," after the popularity of the line diminished.)

Stephens believes that "sensuousness" has special appeal to women readers, and at a Romance Writers of America workshop in Houston in 1981, she suggested that authors "go to stores and try on fur coats, so you know the difference between how mink and rabbit feel." She described her own foray into a jewelry store in Manhattan to try on necklaces heavy with diamonds, not simply to see how they looked, but to learn how they felt against her skin. "Ecstasy Romance heroines never shower," she advised. "They take sensuous baths. So light a scented candle or two, and get into your bathtub and think about how all this *feels!*" Later, after the redundancy of erotic series romances became so intense, Stephens complained, "I'm seeing too many nipples! Be more imaginative! There *are* other erogenous zones!"

In October 1981 Stephens was hired away from Dell to work on a new American Romance line for Harlequin, for the first time with editorial offices in New York. In 1982 she said, "We are hearing that Harlequin sales are down, but the figures don't bear that out, because of worldwide sales. American women are different than European, and the American part of the market probably is down. That's the reason they hired me to create a new line for American women." The new line, she said, would be "a cross between mainstream fiction and category. A little more realistic, with older heroines and so on." Launched in 1983 with four titles per month, the Harlequin American Romance is in direct competition with the Silhouette Special Edition and Silhouette Intimate Moments lines (both of which now are owned by Harlequin), though the stories were, at least in the beginning, more innovative. Stephens left Harlequin at the end of 1984—she says she was fired—and now is an independent producer of women's fiction.

Stephens was the editor whose erotic series romance reached the stands first, but the "handwriting was on the wall," and other editors could read it as well. Some of them moved the stories both farther and faster. The editors at Richard Gallen—Judy Sullivan, Star Helmer, Leslie Kazanjian, and Mary Jo Territo—produced contemporary romances of greater depth and breadth, and with more pages, stories exhibiting both variety and innovativeness. "With the contemporaries we did a lot of experimentation," Sullivan says (in Jennings 1985). "The books were much more mainstream in feel, in the beginning. . . . There was more latitude for the writers, fewer rules and more variety."

Candace Camp, author of one of the first erotic contemporaries issued by Richard Gallen/Pocket Books in April 1981, recalls that "Star Helmer had read my *Rainbow Season* [a historical romance published by Jove in 1979] and contacted my agent about my doing a historical for them. But she'd been wanting to do contemporaries, and when she found out I was a lawyer, she asked me to do a contemporary book instead, where the heroine was a lawyer. The result was *The Golden Sky*, which I wrote in 1980." Other notable contemporary stories from the Gallen editors include Kris Karron's *The Rainbow Chase* (1981), in which a former fat girl achieves a great deal more than a new physical identity, including close female friends for the first time in her life. Though the journalist-heroine comes to love the silent Finn who coaches a team of female marathon runners, she tells him " 'I can't leave my work or my country permanently and play the traditional role of wife and mother. That's not why I left South Dakota or why I worked so hard to lose eighty pounds' " (p. 281). In the end, these lovers work out a compromise that is characterized by both pragmatism and mutuality.

Though now dispersed, the Gallen editors are all still associated with the romance publishing business. Star Helmer is Harlequin vice president and editorial director for North America (based in Toronto); Leslie Kazanjian moved on to edit Berkley/Jove's Second Chance at Love line and then to Silhouette's Special Edition line; and Mary Jo Territo is a romance author. Judy Sullivan produced hardcover romances for Walker and Company, and in 1986 formed a partnership with Vivien Stephens (The Okra Group) to "package" women's fiction, with Richard Gallen acting as intermediary with publisher-distributors. "The demographics tell us that our readers are getting older," Sullivan says. "I want to see older heroines, in their 40s. It's really time for that." Stephens agrees and adds, "There are almost no heroines of color, in a country full of people of color."

Carolyn Nichols's conceptualization of the Second Chance line, which went on sale in June 1981, gave romance heroines some history — time to have experienced at least a little bit of life before the story opens — thereby setting the stage for greater depth of characterization (though it rarely happened). The sexually experienced woman is a given in this line, which conventionalizes the older heroine as well as the woman with a career. Like Vivien Stephens before her, Nichols was wooed away by a competitor, after Bantam's Circle of Love sweet romance line fell flat on its spine, and in 1982 she created the new Bantam Loveswept line. Today she is an associate publisher at Bantam.

Though it lasted only a year and a half (July 1982 to December 1983, with a total of thirty-two titles), the most innovative and experimental romance enterprise of the eighties was without a doubt Ballantine's Love and Life line, edited by Pamela Strickler. Gathering together a group of talented female writers, Ballantine conceived the line as "fiction for women." Much more realistic, these stories centered around problems real women are confronting today: conflicts between "her man and her career, between marriage and independence," divorce, the responsibility of being sole provider of financial and emotional support of children, or being married to a man she has outgrown. Launch ads in *Publishers Weekly* talked about "multifaceted plots, believable romance, realistic career scenes and adult sex that adult women can enjoy," but most of the titles speak for themselves, such as *Her Decision, Renewal, A New Tomorrow, In Her Prime, Searching, Separate Ways.*

Roberta Anderson and Mary Kuczkir, writing under the pseudonym Fern Michaels, were bestselling authors of a number of bodice rippers during the 1970s and already were under contract to Ballantine for historical romances when they wrote two books for the Love and Life line.[3] *Free Spirit*, a story with a strongly feminist flavor, is about a successful magazine editor who tries total domesticity with the man she loves, which turns out to be a disaster for both of them, perhaps even spelling the end of their relationship (the reader is not quite sure at the end). The heroine's mistake is largely of her own making—she misreads herself *and* the man she loves—and the lesson to be learned derives from the old adage "To thine own self be true." *All She Can Be*, which carries an even more timely universal message in the sense that the heroine is almost a stereotype of what has happened to a great many women today, is the story of a middle-aged woman's attempt to redefine herself as an individual and a woman, rather than as a wife and mother. The forty-three-year-old heroine embarks on a heroic voyage of self-discovery, ultimately becoming a strong and independent person, emotionally as well as financially, who is fully responsible for and in control of herself. Almost simultaneously she is forced to deal with her feelings about divorce and her former husband, who marries a younger woman, and to reassess her relationships with her children. Though adults or near-adult, they still expect her to arrange her life around their needs, and she manages to establish new ground rules with them, all the while continuing to work at a career that is denigrated by both her former husband and her children. When a new man comes into her life it becomes clear that he is the only kind of man possible for the woman she is becoming. He is also ten years younger than the heroine. The New Hero is in full and constant bloom in the Love and Life titles—strong, supportive, and secure enough to be a partner rather than the boss—and the New Heroine is a mover and doer as well as a sexual being who is "all woman."

All She Can Be is a landmark in the history of the romance genre, as are the Love and Life novelettes as a group. They constitute a coherent and unique set of texts in which the heroines truly come of age, growing and developing until they become fully autonomous individuals capable of decisions and resolutions that require strength and determination—and a conscious sense of self. The fantasy here, it seems, resides largely in the happy ending, in the implicit assumption that the kind of male partners these women ultimately build relationships with actually do exist.

Why did the line fail? "We came into the market at absolutely the wrong time, and we never got our packaging right," says Pam Strickler. "It seemed there were a million books coming out every month. It was a choke-out. And we went out too strongly—perhaps we should have come out with just a few and waited for readers to find us." Though the stories followed some general written guidelines initially (e.g., heroines were to be twenty-eight to forty-five years old), "we quickly threw them out," Strickler says, except for the length, which stayed at 180–85 pages. "We just weren't giving brand name buyers what they wanted," she concluded. Today, Ballantine continues to publish the work of several of the Love and Life authors, including Irma Walker, Cindy Blair, Mary Ruth Myers, and Fern Michaels, as single-title women's or mainstream fiction.

In spite of the popularity of the sweet series romance during the 1970s and the erotic series romance in the 1980s, very few series authors or titles appear on the list of favorites named by readers surveyed in either 1982 or 1985, and most of those who do are authors of both series and mainstream titles, such as Janet Dailey. The list is heavily weighted, in fact, with erotic historical "one-offs" and their authors. Certainly the names at the top of the list, Kathleen Woodiwiss and Janet Dailey, come as no surprise to anyone. Woodiwiss was named a favorite author by 27 percent of the readers surveyed in 1982 and by 23 percent in 1985. A second cluster of names, though with a big drop in the number of mentions, included Jude Deveraux, Johanna Lindsey, Shirlee Busbee, and Danielle Steel;[4] followed by a third cluster that included Rosemary Rogers, Bertrice Small, Laurie McBain, Rebecca Brandewyne, Roberta Gellis, and LaVyrle Spencer. Patricia Matthews, a multimillion-copy seller during the 1970s who is still writing today, was listed as a favorite by only one reader, and Jennifer Wilde (a pseudonym for Tom Huff), also a bestselling author during the 1970s and still writing, was named by three. Sandra Brown, Iris Johansen, Nora Roberts, and Jayne Krentz (including their pseudonyms), some of the most prolific of series romance authors today, were mentioned by between four and ten readers.

Whether among the favorites or not, however, the sales figures show that erotic series titles were purchased by readers in huge numbers between 1980 and 1985. It is likely that the emergence of favorites from among authors of these books has been retarded by their identity with so-called brand name (low-status) books, the sheer numbers published since 1980, and the way these books have been marketed. With increasing emphasis placed on authors by series publishers (which began in 1985 and is evidenced in both new cover treatment of authors' names and in how the books are promoted) and the crossover of some of these authors to single-title books, readers' lists of favorite authors are very likely in the process of changing.

Woodiwiss's *The Flame and The Flower* was the most-mentioned favorite title, followed by her *Shanna, The Wolf and the Dove,* and *Ashes in the Wind.* The favorite Dailey title was *Night Way,* followed by *The Rogue* and *Touch the Wind* (1979), all of them "one-off" historicals set in the American West. Also receiving multiple mentions were LaVyrle Spencer's *Hummingbird, Sweet Memories,* and *Twice Loved;* Celeste de Blasis's *Proud Breed;* Bertrice Small's *Love Wild and Fair* and *Skye O'Malley;* Roberta Gellis's Roselynde Chronicles; and Danielle Steel's *Palomino.* Only one of these, Spencer's *Sweet Memories,* is contemporary in setting.

These choices, along with other information gathered in the reader surveys, indicate that a sort of nostalgia factor may be at work here, since readers appear to be recalling and associating with at least some of these books and authors how they felt at the time they first encountered them. The early favorites, particularly Woodiwiss's books, seem to have had a remarkable impact on readers and probably need to be viewed in light of their uniqueness compared to what was available on the market at the time. The four Woodiwiss titles were available in bookstores, discount stores, and other mass merchandising outlets over a period of several years (as compared with the month or two that series books are available, except in used book stores), enabling readers to encounter them for the first time through most of the 1970s— whenever they "got the word" about the revolution going on under the covers of these inexpensive paperbacks. In terms of timing, these old favorites coincide with a period of rising feminist consciousness among women generally, including the women who were reading romance novels.

Most readers own their favorite romances and say they frequently reread them, particularly the Woodiwiss titles. Several explained that they read one from among their favorites from time to time because "they guarantee a good feeling." Lending support to the idea that nostalgia plays a role in the choice of these authors as favorites are comments about the recent titles of Woodiwiss (post-1979), Rogers (post-1976 historical and all of her contemporary titles), and a number of other authors. Those about Rogers were overwhelmingly negative, and a sufficient number of readers said they have long since "given up on" Rogers or "only buy her used" to suggest that most of her appeal today lies outside of the regular romance readership. Most readers continue to buy Woodiwiss's books in the hope of experiencing the "good feeling" her earlier stories provided, but they have been tolerantly disappointed so far. Many expressed similar disappointment with other former favorites: for example, "One of the first romantic novels I read was Jude Deveraux's *Enchanted Land*. Over the years I've read it several times, but suddenly Jude is sophomoric. Her writing style is high school, and I can't help but wonder what has happened. I use her only as an example of the same with many others."

The major impact Janet Dailey has had on the romance genre as we know it today was in Americanizing the Harlequin (British) heroine — which the market would have done sooner or later, as it did in forcing eroticism into the Harlequin texts after 1981 — who after 1976 began to at least develop some backbone, though she continued to operate largely in the domestic sphere. Only rarely did Dailey explore any new territory, however, as she did in her last series title, *Leftover Love* (Silhouette Special Edition, 1984). Here the hero is plain to the point of homeliness and has been conditioned by a lifetime of experience to withdraw from social intercourse generally and to expect revulsion and rejection from women. Dailey's story is about the transforming effect of love — and a woman capable of seeing what is behind the anything-but-handsome facade.[5] Though Dailey disclaimed having what she called "the Hemingway syndrome — I'm not interested in writing the great American novel. The appeal of romance spans all generations" (in Bartimus 1981) — she ended her contract with Silhouette Books in 1984 and announced that henceforth she would be writing only mainstream fiction. A number of readers surveyed in 1985 said they would buy Dailey again when "she goes back to writing romances."

All of this suggests, of course, that either the quality of recent books by these authors does not in fact match their earlier work or that similar stories being published for the first time today are not being received by readers in the same way they were earlier. Certainly readers have changed since 1972, as has the entire market context, which makes it unlikely that similar stories would have the same impact on readers or achieve the same level of popularity. (It would perhaps shed light on this question to compare the responses of two groups of readers: those who first read the Woodiwiss favorites during the 1970s and those who read the same titles after 1981.)

Roberta Gellis's historical novels have had a sustained impact on the romance genre and its readers over a relatively long period of time by virtue of both the overall quality of her work and her characterizations of women. As Gellis herself describes her women, "they dominate but are tender and full of understanding." Widely respected for both the accuracy of her depictions of historical events and for her ability to bring to life the people who affected or were affected by those events, Gellis believes "history is exciting enough and the customs of the past 'exotic' enough when portrayed accurately to need no embellishment." It was in part the quality of her work that attracted and held readers who otherwise would not have become or now be part of the universe of romance readers. But in addition, the body of work she has produced since 1964 constitutes a kind of multivolume history of women's legal rights and personal aspirations, and their determination to achieve the same respect and justice accorded men. Her novels are for the most part lively stories of earthy and brainy women who are motivated above all else to control their own destinies. If in the process they uncover men who are strong enough and fair enough to accommodate rather than dominate them, that is the fantasy of which love stories are made.

Asked if she purposefully gives her portrayals a feminist slant, Gellis laughed, then responded, "It's natural to me in the first place, but medieval women, the nobility, were *all* something, you know. They had a real place in society. They were left to keep the estate running and to defend it when the men were away. In medieval times there were no written laws saying a woman can't. They may have been considered evil, corrupt and depraved by nature. . . ." She paused briefly, obviously reluctant to let the statement slip by without an editorial comment, no matter that it might be historical fact. "I always say Eve didn't cram the apple down Adam's throat. She only said, 'Here, honey, take a bite.' Anything a woman could, she could do, up to the middle of the thirteenth century. After that, legal restrictions on women began to appear. Middle-class women could belong to guilds, for instance, though they weren't invited to the drinking parties and didn't stand watch. Women could inherit their father's, or brother's or husband's businesses. The lowest point in feminine value was the eighteenth and nineteenth century," when women had nothing to do except produce children. "Not the lower-class women, of course. They've always had a true place because they were needed for the work they performed."

In *A Woman's Estate* (Dell, 1984), a veritable textbook on the legal rights of women in nineteenth-century England, Gellis quotes Blackstone on married women: "By marriage, the husband and wife are one person in law: that is, the very being or legal existence of the women is suspended during the marriage. . . . For this reason, a man cannot grant anything to his wife, or enter into covenant with her: for the grant would be to suppose her separate existence . . . and the courts of law will still permit a husband to restrain a wife of her liberty . . ." (p. 281). Once was enough for the female protagonist of this novel, who determined that "never [again] would she permit herself to be legally less than human just because she loved a man . . . thus reducing herself to a state in which she had no more rights than a dog or a horse" (p. 140). Even though "her body and soul wished to fling themselves into his arms and cry, 'Yes, yes, I love you, too. Let us be one,' her mind stood coolly aloof and reminded her that for a woman being one with a man meant just that—he was one, and she was nothing. She had no rights, not over her property, not over her children, not even over her own body" (p. 226).

Judging from the readers she hears from, Gellis's medieval stories are the most liked of all her books, and she speculates that the reason may be because "people in the medieval books are intrinsic to, a part of, the political events going on. They move history," while in the nineteenth century "the history of the time moved the characters. Readers also are attracted to the medieval stories by the fantasy—the castles, armor, and other medieval trappings—making them even more remote from present reality." Though her work is prized generally for depth of characterization, Gellis's family of strong women portrayed in her six-volume Roselynde Chronicles endear her most to readers: *Roselynde, Alinor, Joanna, Gilliane, Rhiannon,* and *Sybelle.* All the succeeding heroines follow the pattern set by Alinor, the matriarch of the clan whom the reader comes to know, love, and admire first as a strong-willed young girl, then as wife to a knight (Simon), the mother of Joanna and Adam, wife to Ian and mother of another Simon, and finally as mother-in-law to Gilliane and Rhiannon and grandmother of Sybelle. To read Gellis's medieval chronicles is to understand this woman as well as the exigencies of life in thirteenth-century England. Alinor constantly grows and changes, as we learn, for example, at the end of the second volume of the chronicles, when Alinor tries to lay to rest the doubt that she can ever love her second husband as she loved Simon, her first husband and Ian's personal hero and best friend: " 'Ian, I loved Simon as much as a woman can love a man. I would not have you think I forget him or that I am disloyal to him. But there was, between Simon and me, thirty years. There was as much of father and daughter between us as of husband and wife. I did not see it then. I see it now only because what is between you and me is—is so very different. I love you, Ian, as a young woman loves a young man—and for me it is the first time of such loving' " (*Alinor,* Playboy Press, 1978, 539).

The author makes it clear that she has no intention of ever adding another volume to her chronicle. "Alinor is sixty in *Sybelle*," Gellis observes, "already an extended age for a medieval person, [and] she is my favorite woman, my oldest and best friend, and I don't want her to die. She is such a dominating woman! The others were all essentially another Alinor. Adam told Gilliane what he wanted in a woman. He created her [in his mother's image]. She had no choice. You either ruled or were subject—there was no middle way."

Until *The Rope Dancer* (Berkley, 1986) Gellis dealt with the top of medieval society, but here, in a story about a group of traveling players, the heroine (the tightrope walker of the title) is from the very bottom of medieval society, people whom "we don't really know much about." Next, she says, she may do a book about the guilds, the middle class. "When people ask me how I got interested in medieval literature, I tell them it was not only the stories I heard as a child, but the freedom I enjoyed to read anything and everything on the shelves of my parents' enormous library. When I was about nine, my father encouraged me to read Caxton's *Morte d'Arthur* in Middle English instead of Pyle's *Tales of King Arthur*. For a child this isn't difficult, since a child sounds out the words and isn't disturbed by strange spelling."

Gellis is still interested in science fiction or fantasy (she has written two science fiction novels under the name Max Daniels). She worked as a research chemist for ten years and holds two master's degrees, one in biochemistry and the other in medieval literature, for which she did a study of "the cultural changes forced by the increasing sophistication of society on the Tristan legend from the original Drust up to Mallory's Tristram." In an interview in *Publishers Weekly*, Gellis said, "I'm very interested in political science and in sociological developments and their effects on people. That's why the love story is so very important. You have to realize just how the great events of time, of any time, affect individuals" (Dahlin 1981b).

Bertrice Small also has involved her heroines in the mainstream of political events, be it sixteenth-century Ireland and England or fourteenth-century Byzantium. Whether behind the scenes, as in *The Kadin* (1978), or center stage, as in *Skye O'Malley* (1980), Small's heroine's usually are in the thick of it, on the land and on the sea. "I think that women can do almost anything, just like men," she says, "and I prefer women who are winners, women who are very self-reliant. Even though they have a tough time they keep getting up, keep going. I don't set out to write books with a message, but if in being a good entertainer I can educate women to stand up and say 'I can do it,' I have no objections." From a family of four generations of businesswomen, Small feels she comes naturally to her views about women. She urges her thirteen-year-old son to work hard in school, she says, telling him, "You're part of the first generation of boys who are going to be competing with girls—and you're going to have to be good!"

It was Small who turned up the burner under the erotic historical romance in 1980, rocking even long-time bodice-ripper readers back on their heels. *Skye O'Malley*, in the words of one reader, is "the romance that has everything," an apt description of a saga that includes incest, rape, the *droit de signeur*, the woman of independent means, and true love—several times over. Another reader said she found in *Skye O'Malley* "the ultimate romance novel" and had written to Small to "challenge her to outdo herself. It can't be done!" Small includes explicit sexual descriptions in her books because "sex is part of life, any man-woman relationship, and characters are more fully developed as individuals" if readers are allowed insight into this aspect of their relationship. By the end of 1985 *Skye* had sold an estimated one and a half million copies, been translated into French, Dutch, Norwegian, Swedish, Italian, and Japanese—and had been banned in South Africa ("too much sex," Small says).

In *Skye O'Malley* and the 1984 sequel, *All the Sweet Tomorrows*, Small previews within the confines of the romance novel what many sociologists predict is becoming the natural social order—serial marriages (or multiple partners), experienced one at a time as we develop and move through the various stages of life. Though still shackled to a fertility that is the ultimate proof of love (Skye has five children by the end of the first book and three more in *All the Sweet Tomorrows*) the heroine has several sexual partners during the course of the story and well and truly loves four different men. These alliances are not simply sexual encounters but depict the love of one woman for more than one kind of man, in the process describing different kinds of relationships as well. Thus, no one male is really fully developed as *the* hero, at least not until near the end of the second book, but each occupies that position for a limited time. Though all but the last of her liaisons exit via a coffin, Skye moves on to the next installment of life with vigor and enthusiasm—in full control of herself, her children, and the shipping business that has given her economic independence from the very beginning. Niall Burke is the first love of her life and, in what appears to be a closing of the circle of her adventures, the reader assumes he will be the last. As *All the Sweet Tomorrows* opens, however, Skye is mourning Niall's death, and we quickly learn that he, too, has gone the way of all the others. "Some of my readers couldn't understand how I could do that—have him die," Small says, sounding a bit surprised. "But Niall Burke was essentially a weak man. He couldn't have held a woman like Skye for any length of time. I had to get rid of him." It is Skye's last alliance, with Adam de Morisco, that the reader finally comes to understand is the mature relationship of her life.

LaVyrle Spencer's work is characterized by sympathetic portrayals of ordinary people, whether they live in New England at the time of sailing ships or in present-day Minneapolis. It is her ability to create warm and vulnerable people—especially her male characters, with whom the reader can experience a sense of intimacy and understanding—that marks her writing as unique. By her own assessment, it is the "honorable characters, basic honest, good people" in her books that appeal to readers. Though a great fan of Kathleen Woodiwiss, who sent Spencer's first manuscript to her own editor at Avon, Spencer started out to "do something different from the beginning. I was tired of the overbearing men in the bodice rippers, and I couldn't identify with those adventures on the high seas. I want my characters to be life-size. I like nice men so I try to portray nice men."

Set on a Minnesota farm in the late 1800s, *The Fulfillment* (Avon, 1979) is indeed "different" from most of the historical romances published at the time. It tells of the three-way relationship between a sterile husband, his childless wife, and the husband's brother, who the husband suggests serve in his stead to give him a son. Spencer's second book, *Hummingbird*, sets up a confrontation between contrasting types, a straight-laced Victorian female and a mustachioed lothario she believes to be a train robber. It was rejected first by Avon and then Jove, though Jove eventually published it in 1983, because "it was too different. I've bucked the system all along, I guess. The first love scene [in *Hummingbird*] was a failure, you know. It was unsatisfactory for the woman and she kept wondering what she'd done wrong. The editor at Avon said 'that can't be done.' She also thought it had too much humor in it and it was too narrow in scope. Almost the whole book took place inside of that one house. Well, I feel that drama happens within, in the emotional impact on the characters. You have to do what the story demands. I won't go along with some imposed [element] if it just doesn't work." *Hummingbird* is Spencer's most popular book to date.

Avon also rejected Spencer's third manuscript, *The Endearment*, which was published in 1982 by Richard Gallen/Pocket Books. Set in frontier Minnesota, this story about a mail-order bride is a romance with a difference, too—the hero, who is a virgin, is quite clearly the protagonist. "It needed some work. I think it sounded like a textbook on frontier life at first, but Star Helmer [her editor at Gallen] liked it, and I learned a lot from her. I reworked the whole thing from beginning to end." Spencer prefers writing historical novels, though she began writing contemporary stories "around 1980 and '81, when the bottom was dropping out of the historical market." She has written four series romances—two for Harlequin (one Temptation and one SuperRomance) and two for Berkley/Jove Second Chance at Love—though she says she will do no more because of the short shelf life of series books. Spencer decided to try a short contemporary novel for the first time when she was beset with writer's block midway into *Twice Loved* (Berkley/Jove, 1984), a historical romance set in New England.

Separate Beds (Berkley/Jove, 1985), perhaps the most traditional of all of Spencer's romances, is uncharacteristically trite and unrealistic for this author even though it is set in the context of contemporary social problems, with an abused young girl who becomes an unwed mother. The hero in *Separate Beds* is confronted with the stereotypical choice between two kinds of women: the Other Woman is career-oriented and anti-domestic (she litters the apartment with her clothes, and when the hero talks about marriage she blatantly refuses to even consider interrupting her career to have children); the Traditional Heroine wants more than anything else to stay at home and take care of her child, fathered by the hero during a single encounter after drinking too much wine. Reared in a home with an ignorant and abusive father, the heroine of *Separate Beds* arrives at her decision purposefully, deliberately, and independently, after a great deal of learning about herself, though it is apparent that her choice is largely the result of her own lack of a loving family. The hero, of course, comes to his senses and chooses the heroine, who represents and champions all the right traditional (domestic) virtues.

In *Twice Loved*, Spencer's triangle is reversed once again (with one woman and two men, as in *The Fulfillment*), with the heroine married first to a Nantucket sailor who is presumed dead when his whaler is lost at sea during a storm, and then to a childhood friend. When her first husband suddenly reappears, she is torn between the two men; she loves them both, but in different ways and for different reasons. Both men have a history with her from which she cannot escape—bringing

LaVyrle Spencer

author of
HUMMINGBIRD

A JOVE BOOK · 0-515-07622-8 · $3.50

TWICE LOVED

*"Unabashedly sensuous...
I can't remember when I've enjoyed a story more."*
—JENNIFER BLAKE, author of *ROYAL SEDUCTION*

home to the reader the agony of a dilemma in which there is simply no one good or right answer.

"I hate the word romance," Spencer says, "partly because of the stigma, but also because when you depict love only, without developing the characters as people who live and interact with other people, it's shallow. The characters are self-centered. The story has to be opened to secondary characters [who are] as interesting as the main characters." In *Sweet Memories* (Harlequin Worldwide, 1984), Spencer's talent for plumbing the internal life of her characters clearly pushes her work beyond the genre. *Sweet Memories* is the story of a young woman with abnormally large breasts and the impact of this condition on her psychological and social development during adolescence and young adulthood (especially how males have always responded). Spencer details the relationship that develops between the heroine and the first man who even tries to see the woman behind the breasts, so to speak, who ultimately is able to breach the emotional barriers resulting from her physical problem. In the end, after working through a veritable thicket of opinion from the people around her, as well as her own doubts and feelings, she makes her own decision—to chance the loss of sensitivity and function in exchange for physical and emotional health, by electing to have surgery to correct what has become more than a cosmetic problem. Spencer tells of the woman who called her the day before undergoing the same type of surgery— she had been unable to afford it before and learned from *Sweet Memories* that insurance companies were covering surgical correction of what at last has been recognized as a serious health problem for many women—then adds, "If I touch only one reader, that's enough." In a 1983 interview the author said she wanted readers to respond emotionally to her books—"I want them to laugh, to cry, even to respond sexually" (in Lowery 1983, 66). In choosing to explore the turf of ordinary people with quite ordinary but real problems, she has succeeded in touching readers with her own insight and understanding.

Though the authors described here are among the big names in terms of sales, other innovative authors and their works do get through the romance gate. Among these, certainly, is Jacqueline Marten, whose *Visions of the Damned* (Playboy Press, 1979) is first and foremost a love story, though mispackaged with an allusion to an occult novel blazoned across the top of the front cover—"Like *The Reincarnation of Peter Proud* this is the bizarre odyssey of a young woman whose past life would not stay dead." Rather than reincarnation, however, Marten uses a historical and contemporary setting to weave an elusive and provocative tale of a love that has survived the centuries since the Norman conquest of England—reminding us not only of the still-dark corners of the human psyche but of our terribly primitive awareness of all things intangible and spiritual. Though it probably never reached all the readers to whom it might have appealed, today this novel is a favorite of a great many romance aficionados.

There is also Justine Valenti's *Lovemates* (Fawcett, 1982), the story of a relationship between a young musician (aged twenty-two) and an older artist (forty-three), a combination that in itself is not unique. But it is the male who is twenty-two in this case, which presents a number of very different obstacles for love to overcome. Except for the question of children, the problems these lovers face lie more with the people around them than in themselves, including the hero's mother, who is (was!) a long-time close friend of the heroine.

Even within the constrictions of the series romance, a unique style of writing and/or unexpected insights appear from time to time (e.g., Alexandra Sellers; Elizabeth Lowell's *Valley of the Sun*), teasing the reader with thoughts of what the author might do given greater freedom and length. Certainly there are many other authors, either overlooked here or mentioned all too briefly, who have made a difference when it comes to what we are seeing in the popular romance novel today, and therefore in what readers are thinking about. It is not just a few individual stories that have captured the readers' attention and perhaps made a difference to them, however, but the potential cumulative effect of exposure to hundreds of different stories and writers who are constantly changing, adapting, and exploring new ground.

Notes

1. The term "gatekeeper" comes from a case study conducted in 1950 by David M. White, who examined how one particular daily newspaper editor (whom he dubbed "Mr. Gates") selected the stories to be printed from among all those received from three major wire services. "Gatekeeper" now is widely used to designate the person or persons who function to filter from the mass of information being generated the fewer specific items that are passed on to the public.

2. Except where noted, all quoted statements by authors and editors in this chapter come from personal or telephone interviews, most of them conducted in December 1985. Part of the Stephens interview was conducted in August 1982, and the remainder in January 1986.

3. To give the reader some idea of what a bestselling author is in the erotic

romance genre, in 1982 *Publishers Weekly* (January 15) reported that the Anderson-Kuczkir team (Fern Michaels) had signed a four-million-dollar contract with Ballantine for four historical romances due over a two-year period, a half-million dollars of which was for world English-language rights.

4. Danielle Steele is somewhat of an anomaly in this list, since quite a few readers do not even consider her a romance writer.

5. Unfortunately, Dailey also is capable of some of the most trite, cliché-ridden writing in the genre. She cranked out seventy-one books between 1976 and 1983, the shorter series books in nine days, she says. And it shows. A caricature of the genre, her *Foxfire Light* (Silhouette Special Edition, 1982) could well serve as a how-not-to manual. It includes most of the worst romance clichés ever to see the light of day — "The nearness of him was starting those funny little pitter-patters of her heart" (p. 196); is loaded with one grammatical error after another — "Her troubled brown eyes glanced toward the front door that Linc had went out a few minutes ago" (p. 236); and contains shop-worn dialogue and suggestive innuendo — " 'I'm beginning to think I'll have to send you an engraved invitation to make love to me. . . . I thought you were a man of action. But, maybe you act as slow as you talk,' " [Joanna says]. " 'Are you trying to get a rise out of me?' Linc drawled and eyed her with a complacent look. 'Now, you're getting the idea,' she murmured" (p. 197).

Chapter Nine

THE EVER-PRESENT FUTURE
OF THE POPULAR ROMANCE
The Moving Target Moves On

> Women have moved from defining themselves in terms
> of derived status, that is, as someone's wife, someone's
> daughter, or someone's mother, and are moving toward
> wanting a sense of personal identity beyond those pri-
> vate domestic roles. . . . the quiet revolution is not just
> a matter of demographic change, but represents a pro-
> found emotional and attitudinal change that will not
> be reversed.
>
> Rena Bartos, *The Moving Target*

> "Oh, the awesome power we women have, Hannah.
> No wonder the men fear us so. . . . Because they fear us
> men keep us enslaved, but only with our consent; they
> are our jailers but we are their wardens. . . . Never
> again will I let them rule me; I am my own master."
>
> Barbara Wood, *Domina*

*H*elen Papashvily (1956, xvii) in-
troduced her analysis of nineteenth-century women's fiction with the
observation, "No man, fortunately for his peace of mind, ever discovered that the domestic novels were handbooks of another kind of
feminine revolt—that these pretty tales reflected and encouraged a
pattern of feminine behavior so quietly ruthless, so subtly vicious that
by comparison the ladies at Seneca [Seneca Falls, New York, where the
first Woman's Rights Convention was held in 1848] appear angels of
innocence. . . . [Men] did not detect the faint bitter taste of poison in
the cup nor recognize that these books were rather a witches' broth, a
lethal draught brewed by women and used by women to destroy their
common enemy, man."

Today the kind of character portrayals found in these "domestic"
novels are rejected by the majority of women readers, for at least two
reasons. First, most women now believe the self-denial associated with
the traditional role of wife and mother is both unnecessary and unfair.

The heroine who achieves some vague, constantly deferred and intangible moral victory no longer satisfies; such victories seem hollow, indeed, when she must martyr herself in the process of wreaking revenge on her oppressors. Second, to view and treat males as the enemy is inconsistent either with the reality of readers' experience as women or with what they believe their experience as women *could* be. Thus, instead of man-as-enemy, heterosexual romantic fiction since 1980 has come a long way toward reconstructing the hero in the image of women by creating males who reflect female values. (For the gynocentrist feminist position, which argues for the superiority of values associated with the traditionally female experience as compared with those of males, including violence and individualism, see Young 1985.)

Heterosexual romance readers as a constituency categorically reject the idea that heterosexual relationships are inherently exploitative, unsatisfying, and potentially dangerous to women, a view that has been put forward by a number of feminists (e. g., Brownmiller 1975; Russell 1975). The new romance novel reflects the view that a sexually satisfying relationship is possible only in a relationship of equality, in which both partners can and do freely express their desires (see Shulman 1980; Diamond 1980). The New Heroine is not only intent on both social and economic equality with the man with whom she forms a sexual relationship, but it is a rare heroine who is not also gainfully employed, usually in a nontraditional job or career, and intends to remain so. In this regard she is like 60 percent of her fans.

Literally hundreds of these new romance novels, especially those published after the late 1970s, reflect egalitarian attitudes and sex-role orientations. By 1984 the most popular romantic fiction on the market was characterized by eroticism and autonomy—draped around the enduring structure of the developing love relationship with a happy ending. Romance formula conventions now demand mutuality of heroine-hero personality traits, initiatives, and responsibilities. Most heroines live the life-cycle experiences of women described by Carol Gilligan (1982), moving toward increasing autonomy *and* increasing intimacy and connectedness, and ultimately arriving at a self-confident decision that distinguishes between selfishness and self-assertion. The New Heroine is no longer the power behind the throne but through direct participation shares power with the hero in public *and* private spheres.

Examples of sex-role crossover abound, along with an increasing number of overtly feminist statements, as in Alexandra Sellers's *The*

Male Chauvinist (Silhouette Intimate Moments, 1985), with an archeologist-hero who is anything but chauvinistic. The stage for this story is set by the hero's search for new evidence of an ancient matriarchal society—a place and time when women were central to society and its symbols. The heroine sets out on a quest for "the sense of her own value as a woman that had been denied her since birth," during which she comes to realize that "most of the Western world's art, literature and artifacts reflected the masculine. And nearly anything in the modern world that reflected the feminine reflected it from the masculine point of view, and a degrading point of view at that; a point of view that allowed women to be nothing much more than sex objects. . . . In the breasted ewers Kate knew, by the response of something deep within her, that she was seeing woman from the point of view of women; women who had had a self-esteem so deep and so basic that as a product of today's culture she could barely relate to it" (p. 135–36).

Sellers's hero recognizes the heroine's quest for what it is, perhaps because he comes from a family in which his own role-model father accompanied his archaeologist-mother on her expeditions. " 'It must be very difficult to live in a world where the battle for a sense of self-worth is so arduous,' " he tells the heroine, then adds, " 'I always think that so much of women's imagination is being diverted to that battle, it is no wonder they no longer rule the world' " (p. 136)—echoing harmonics of Edwin Schur's warning (see chapter 7). When the heroine discovers that she is probably as chauvinistic as most men, she responds with what is clearly a socialist-feminist point of view: "Why did we never notice—or never admit, that men are caught in as much of a bind as we are? . . . We ought to have done it *together;* surely we ought to have declared war on our joint conditioned responses, instead of on *men*. And then perhaps the revolution would have succeeded" (p. 96).[1]

Within the space of a decade, 1972–82, these kind of content and character transformations created a highly ordered romance typology in which the genre was split along three classifying lines: *sexual content* (sweet or erotic), *setting* (historical or contemporary), and *degree to which content is shaped and controlled by publishers* (category or mainstream romance).

"Category romance" refers to titles in which content and characterizations conform to publisher-specified written guidelines. Produced and distributed as a series, these novels generally are from 180 to 300 pages long. A "mainstream romance" conforms only to the loosely defined formula associated with genre writing and ranges from 235 to 500 or more pages in length. In the romance publishing business these novels are referred to variously as single-titles, one-offs, and fat books. All trade-size (5¼ inches by 8¼ inches) paperback romance novels published to date, which today sell for between $6.95 and $8.95, have been mainstream romances, most of them historicals. Though there is considerable confusion about the difference between mainstream fiction and mainstream romance, some editors subscribe to the belief that "if men also read it, it's mainstream fiction."

Sexual content is classified as either "sweet" or "erotic," the erotic type being defined as those which contain explicit sexual acts *and* egalitarian sex-role portrayals.[2] Not only is overt sexual content absent from the sweet romance, but sex roles are for the most part traditional in orientation: the heroine's life is centered in the domestic sphere, she is emotionally and/or economically dependent on the hero, and her development as an autonomous individual is deferred in favor of her family (parents and siblings, as well as husband and children). By 1982, six major story types or subgenres had emerged as viable commercial entities:

1. the mainstream erotic historical romance (e.g., LaVyrle Spencer, *Hummingbird,* Jove, 1983);
2. the mainstream erotic contemporary romance (e.g., Justine Valenti, *Lovemates,* Fawcett, 1982);
3. the category erotic historical romance (e.g., Pocket Tapestry);
4. the category erotic contemporary romance (e.g., Dell Ecstasy);
5. the category sweet historical romance (e.g., NAL/Signet Regency);
6. the category sweet contemporary romance (e.g., Harlequin Romance).

Until 1985 the mainstream erotic contemporary romance was represented only minimally in terms of number of titles on the market, while mainstream sweet stories were never a commercially viable type, whether historical or contemporary in setting. (Barbara Cartland's story elements and characterizations are not publisher-specified but are even more formulaic and repetitive than most series books, and therefore are classified here as category sweet historical romance novels.)

It was the introduction of the category or series erotic contemporary romance in 1981 that brought nonseries romance readers and more nonromance readers into the fold, quickly and dramatically enlarging the universe of readers and speeding up the rush to saturation of the market. Consumers, too, quickly reached a saturation point in both the number of books it was physically possible to read in a month's time and in the satisfaction to be gained from such a uniform product. Tightly programmed content predicts either a relatively long-term, static, and homogeneous readership or a dynamic and pluralistic audience with a short life span. Thus, before 1981 the series romance readership was relatively homogeneous, between 1981 and 1985 it became pluralistic, and by the end of 1985 it appeared to be moving again in the direction of homogeneous segments.

Projections of market growth in the early 1980s ranged from 10 to 20 percent per year, but during 1983 that growth, at least in the American market, began to level out. By 1984, with the market saturated with category lines, redundancy was rampant and reader ennui began to mushroom. The result was that romance readers grew not only restless but began exploring other territory in their search for something fresh and more satisfying.

Turbulence and Transition in the Marketplace

While many readers point out that quality is as uneven in romances as it is in other types of popular fiction, they express a more generalized dissatisfaction with brand name or series romance. Commenting on the hackneyed stories that flourished during the "gold rush" days of the series book, Nancy Coffey, formerly editor at Avon and now an editor/publisher at St. Martin's Press, explained that "when you're on a treadmill you don't have time to reject manuscripts or ask for rewrites. [But] if women read six mediocre novels in a row, they will hesitate to pick up a seventh" (in Span 1984, 11). The major complaint of readers surveyed in 1982, after less than two years of exposure to the new erotic series romance, was redundancy, with poor quality a close second. "Quality has gone down as quantity increased" was the sentiment most often expressed, indicating that readers correctly put the two together. And poor quality, to a great many of them, is perceived as personally insulting. Readers find themselves in the position of having to defend what they read against attacks from husbands, children, friends, and co-workers, as well as newspaper and television jibes—attacks that suggest a sex-related intellectual and emotional inferiority. Under these conditions, elementary quality gaffs often are interpreted as indications that the publisher shares this broadly expressed disparagement and contempt for any woman who would read a romance.[3]

Table 6.   Changes in romance reading/buying behavior among readers surveyed in 1982 and 1985

	Percentage	
Number per month	1982	1985
5 or less	16	25
6–10	26	21
11–20	23	27
21–30	10	18
31–40	11	5
41 or more	10	3

The mistakes readers pointed to include the grammatical (nonexistent words such as indignance, and the confusion of "lie" and "lay" in a genre in which a lot of it occurs); cover illustrations that do not match settings or character descriptions; and superficial, inaccurate, or unbelievable career descriptions. One reader commented about Suzanne Simms's *Of Passion Born* (Silhouette Desire, 1982), in which the heroine takes a sabbatical after teaching only two years at a university: "Doesn't the author even know that God didn't rest until the seventh day! I suppose I'm being picky, but often it's little errors that ruin a book for me, because then I have a hard time believing anything else in the story."

Awareness of repetitiousness is proportional to both the number and the length of time readers have been exposed to the series stories; not surprisingly, dissatisfaction with sameness or redundancy is highest among heavy and widely experienced readers. As shown in Table 6, the number of readers who say they read more than thirty romance titles per month dropped from 21 percent in 1982 to 8 percent in 1985. The second highest percentage of change appears at the other end of the scale, however, among those who say they read five or fewer titles per month. This is just one of several indications that some readers appear to be moving away from series romance, to the longer mainstream stories, as well as to other types of fiction.

While the number of used book purchasers among readers surveyed increased only 2 percent between 1982 and 1985, to slightly more than 50 percent, a great many more (35 percent) of these buyers acquired up to half of their romance titles used in 1985.[4] This rise in the proportion of used books relative to the total number of books purchased is consistent with the complaints, and even anger, expressed—both of which ultimately are focused on specific authors. A number of readers agreed with the woman who said, "Once burned I will only buy that author used." One complained that "even the good authors now seem to want to sell their books by the pound—more quantity than quality." Another explained, "I buy my favorite authors new, or books that I know I'll want to keep, and wait for the unknown or less interesting authors to show up used."

Faced with a market that was quickly flattening out, several publishers launched still more romance lines, shipping more books in an attempt to sell more books. By the end of 1983 Harlequin's return rate was up to 60 percent, compared to 1978 when the company was printing half a million copies per title and less than 25 percent were being returned (Jensen 1984, 35). Harlequin added the erotic Temptation line in order to compete with Silhouette Desire and Dell Ecstasy romances, while Silhouette, with an ear to the groundswell of conservatism and "a return to traditional values" that seemed to be emerging after the 1980 presidential election, launched the Inspiration romance line, aimed at born-again Christians. Counting heavily on readers in the Bible Belt, Inspirations were distributed through religious bookstores as well as mass merchandising outlets such as Winn-Dixie.

With more players than ever before, which meant a smaller piece of the pie for everyone, including authors, and with both the readership and the market saturated, the battle between the two biggest series romance publishers was joined in earnest. Desperation displaced sophisticated marketing strategies (e.g., quality control of the product, more enlightened consumer research, innovative advertising images, and control of the supply), hastening the move away from the category romance among consumers, especially among those readers best equipped to finance their reading habits—the better-educated, more status-conscious, and assertive women, who exhibit upwardly mobile attitudes and at the time constituted the largest segment of the romance audience. Male management teams either ignored or misinterpreted the available consumer data, seeking safety in strategies based on outdated stereotypes, initiating or increasing the number of gimmicky promotions with positive appeal only to the lower end of the reader demographic scale (where the Harlequin and other series romance base had been throughout the 1960s and 1970s).

Harlequin threw more and more "pink" parties for readers across the country, getting the kind of media attention that enhanced the romance-reader-as-silly-dope image; developed their own game of Trivial Pursuit, ignoring the fact that it is largely a family and mixed-

190

gender social activity; and under its Worldwide imprint launched the costly promotion of a novel allegedly co-written by an actress who played the role of a glamorous romance writer in a television soap opera, in spite of the fact that the audience for daytime soaps, at least among romance readers surveyed in 1982 and 1985, was relatively small. Silhouette offered sheets and tablecloths stamped with the Silhouette logo for sale to women who were already being ridiculed by their husbands, children, and friends for reading these books. (Has anyone ever seen a woman carrying one of the Harlequin or Silhouette book bags advertised in virtually every one of their romances?) Some of these gimmicky ploys were abetted by parasite enterprises such as Kathryn Falk's *Romantic Times* magazine and annual Romantic Booklovers Conference, both aimed primarily at romance readers. In 1982 Falk's "love train," replete with berths covered with pink satin sheets, picked up conference goers and media attention all across the country, from California to New York, gaining her a reputation as the pied piper of romance. What these promotions succeed in most, however, is reinforcing the low-brow (poor taste—poor quality) reputation of the entire romance genre and everyone associated with it, from publishers and editors to authors and readers.

New story elements began to be introduced in the effort to stem the rising tide of returns, though most were enlightened by nothing so much as the past. The gothic was reborn as romantic suspense, mystery, or intrigue, promising erotic stories featuring "love with a mysterious stranger," as in Avon's Velvet Glove series and Harlequin's Intrigue romances. Strangely enough, this regressive mystification of the hero came just at the time when consumers were showing a high consensus on the desire for more hero point of view and better development of the hero as a character, in order to understand what and how the hero thinks and why he behaves as he does.

Then in mid-1984 Simon and Schuster sold its Silhouette Books division (twenty-six romance titles per month issued under six different line or series names) to Harlequin for $10 million and a reinstatement of its earlier U.S. distribution arrangement with the Canadian company. Harlequin was in effect buying back most of the market share it had lost, since, according to the *Wall Street Journal*, profits in Torstar's book publishing division doubled in the first nine months of 1985 due to the acquisition of Silhouette ("Torstar Executive," 1985). Seven years earlier, when Harlequin attempted to buy Pinnacle, a publisher of single-title historical romances, the U.S. Justice Department had warned that a "further significant concentration in the mass market paperback business would not be tolerated" (because the merger would have adverse effects on competition) and it threatened to challenge the acquisition on antitrust grounds (Wagner 1979). Harlequin at that time had 8.2 percent of the total paperback rack space and $35 million in U.S. sales, while Pinnacle held 3 percent of the rack space and $10.5 million in sales in 1977. In 1984 Harlequin's share of the series romance market was somewhere between 40 and 45 percent, while Silhouette's was around 40 percent.

Now a wholly owned subsidiary of Torstar, a $550 million communications giant that also publishes Canada's largest newspaper, Harlequin romances (all types) today are translated into fifteen languages and distributed in more than ninety countries, with an estimated worldwide readership of 200 million. A 1985 Harlequin press release reported the company was spending $20 million per year for advertising, promotion, and marketing in North America alone. After acquisition Harlequin quickly dropped the Silhouette Inspiration line, a loser from the beginning, and then began an experimental market-testing program in Canada, pulling the Harlequin SuperRomance, Harlequin Intrigue, and Silhouette Romance lines out of retail stores and making them available only through the mail. A similar testing program, the company announced, would begin in the United States in 1986. The company was distributing about sixty paperback titles in North America every month under the Harlequin, Silhouette, Worldwide, and Gold Eagle (three adventure series for men) imprints by the beginning of 1986 — compared to the sixty titles per year the company put out in 1960 (Dahlin 1981a).

Though many consumers had been reading both series and single-title romances for some time, by the end of 1984 a rise in the popularity of the erotic mainstream historical romance was apparent, beginning a surge of reader crossover from category to mainstream romance novels — a reversal of what happened during 1981. A number of editors and authors apparently interpreted this renewed interest in the historical romance as evidence of a return to the "good old days" of the bodice ripper, sparking a revival of titles such as *Savage Ecstasy*, *Savage Whisper*, and *Savage Heart*, and the reappearance of the virgin heroine who often is forced into a sex act that cannot be confused with seduction, as in Christine Monson's *Stormfire* (Avon, 1984).

In addition to flying in the face of widely expressed reader sentiment, this reemergence of rape also trods on intensely felt personal and ethical ground among a great many female romance authors today. Already bristling at the pro–rape scene comments made by a panel of historical romance authors at the annual Romance Writers of America conference in 1985, the audience was so thoroughly provoked midway through the program by one author's exuberant exclamation —"I love a good rape scene!"—that many of them left the room, shaking their heads in apparent disbelief and dismay. A number of other writers stayed to make strong statements from the floor about "what rape really is" and to vehemently protest what the panel members were advocating, all to the accompaniment of spontaneous audience applause. Printed material distributed to authors at the same conference described Signet historical romances as "the bodice-rippers of the 80's: adventurous, sensual stories featuring intelligent, fiesty characters," at the same time warning that "they are not stories of rape and pillage, nor are they graphically distasteful. Our historical romances are in the tradition of such bestselling authors as Bertrice Small, Rosemary Rogers, Rebecca Brandewyne and Johanna Lindsay." Admirable as this stated ban on rape might seem, the allusion to the "tradition" of Rosemary Rogers is certainly misleading (unless this publisher was intentionally speaking with a forked tongue).

With a historical romance revival seemingly underway, several publishing houses also began to resurrect the classic gothic and regency romances (Warner, Zebra, NAL/Signet, and Fawcett) but with "a more modern, independent heroine," and by late 1985 "sexy" regencies and gothics were in full bloom. New American Library instructed authors to "leave the light on in the turret so we can see what is going on during the love scenes. No rape or violence, though." The hero is "still very mysterious, but not quite as macho" (*Romance Writers Report*, 1985). This neomodern gothic/regency also resurrected the old Forced Marriage plot device (e.g., Kasey Michaels, *The Lurid Lady Lockport*, Avon, 1984), reducing the male-female relationship to one dimension by projecting the idea that sexual chemistry is everything and that "good sex" is possible between two people who have nothing else in common. Gothic/regency elements also began to reappear in romances not designated as such, as in Sheila O'Hallion's *Fire and Innocence* (Pocket Tapestry, 1984), in which the heroine is forced to marry her uncle-guardian for "protection" after her father dies. The hero is twice her age, distrusts all women as a result of his dead wife's infidelity, and is suspected throughout not only of having killed his first wife in a jealous rage but also of being a smuggler. In true *Rebecca* style, the heroine helps to save him in the end, at which time she also learns that he has loved her all along. Such plot devices were rejected by most readers surveyed in both 1982 and 1985.

A few romance lines (Harlequin SuperRomance, Dell Ecstasy, and Berkley/Jove Second Chance at Love) modified their covers at about this time in order to visually diminish the logo and emphasize authors' names. Harlequin made a half-hearted attempt at category-mainstream hybridization in the American Premier Romance, an occasionally issued longer novel written by better-sellers among its American Romance series authors, and increased the number of "Bestsellers" being published (initiated in 1982 under its Worldwide imprint), also written by well-known series romance authors. Because of the double stigma—the Harlequin label plus authors whose reputations were tied to series books—most of these titles failed to attract consumers outside the existing romance readership.[5] Panicked by a flat market, the Silhouette-Harlequin merger, and fast-flying rumors of cutbacks in the number of titles that would surely result, authors and editors began to see these hybrids as "break-out" books—the means by which the series author could escape the stigma associated with that lowest and now apparently endangered species of romance novel. Serving as one more example of the bandwagon mentality that has been the single most salient characteristic of the romance publishing business, by mid-1985 most category romance authors were scrambling for break-out book contracts and the series romance became suddenly déclassé among authors who had never written anything else. Late in 1984 Harlequin created its Ventures Group for the express purpose of competing directly with other mainstream paperback publishers, and several other publishers began to rethink their own series publishing activities, putting them on hold with announcements that they were "full up" on manuscripts for the time being.

At last, it seemed, publishers were recognizing the single-most promising and heretofore largely untapped market (Thurston 1984), the contemporary mainstream novel such as those exemplified by La-Vyrle Spencer's *Sweet Memories*, Judith Michael's *Possessions*, and the works of Charlotte Vale Allen. These stories are peopled by warm, human, intelligent characters, including ordinary women with the kinds of problems a great many women face today and a sympathetic and understandable hero, not the glamorous-but-immoral bitch and the macho-sadist stud. Up to now, many of the same editors who acted as gatekeepers for mainstream historical romances had been producing an entirely different kind of book when it came to contemporary stories (such as Shirley Conran's *Lace*), which most romance readers surveyed in 1982 and 1985 called trash. (As with the contemporary efforts of Rosemary Rogers, these novels often are likened to the work of Jacqueline Susann). Today the contemporary mainstream romance is being referred to more and more often as women's fiction, again muddying the classification waters for both students and readers of the romance genre.

In 1984, Zebra, an imprint of the Kensington Publishing Corporation, began evolving a historical romance that masqueraded as mainstream while content was being more tightly structured and prescribed. A fat book with about 150,000 words (approximately 450 pages), the Zebra historicals are packaged under cover illustrations that vary from book to book yet are stylistically so similar that they operate as a logo. In mid-1985 Zebra began applying a small plastic hologram to its covers (which alternately reflects a heart and the word Zebra), an irrefutable identification as a brand-name book. Though Zebra gained a reputation for producing the sexiest of the historical romance crop, and also for being so trashy that some authors fear they may taint the entire historical romance subgenre, the 1985 Zebra tip sheet demonstrates a return to some of the traditional romance conventions that have been rejected by most readers, along with the admonition "Don't forget: there must be passion, passion, passion."

> The heroine must be a strong, appealing woman: lovely, young, innocent, intelligent, independent, and adventurous. Generally, she is orphaned or has somehow been separated from her family, having to rely on her own resources. She is opinionated and of a passionate nature, but only the hero can provoke her love—and her hate—as no other can. Rarely is she willingly untrue to the hero—but there are always exceptions.
>
> The hero is always older and more experienced than the heroine. He is a handsome, virile man of action in business and in love. He usually has either earned or inherited a fortune by the time he meets the heroine. Only the heroine can infuriate or excite him as no other woman has.

While some of these recent events and changes are both regressive and confusing, they are symptomatic of a period of transition in which the relatively sharp lines between category and mainstream romance, and between erotic and sweet romance, are becoming increasingly indistinct, which in turn indicates that another major shift in the market is underway.

Noise in the Communication Channel

Though the earlier significant subgenre changes (the erotic historical and then the erotic series romance) were initiated largely through individual intuition and advocacy, without specific quantitative consumer data or planned strategy, the romance business had come to be run largely by marketing people. Why, then, did such chaos set in, instead of purposeful and controlled change?

Part of the explanation lies with the number of players muscling their way into the game and the effect this had on publishers and consumers alike, as well as the big unknown—how long the market would continue to grow. Most businesses adhere to an operating philosophy and practices that are inherently conservative (trading off profits for reduced risks) and most management (including marketing) personnel are male, a combination that often results in an ultra-conservative approach in marketing to women, especially when it comes to taking the risks associated with unproven, low-competition markets. It also means that information-seeking strategies usually are both formulated and interpreted by males, and that even with quantitative data indicating change or pointing to a potential new market, male marketers and management may disbelieve or ignore some information because the picture it paints is not consonant with their own personal beliefs, attitudes, or opinions. Instead, they seek evidence to support their impulse toward conservatism elsewhere, from the mass media and other sources of demographic information as well as from within their personal networks. At certain times, therefore, there is a huge increase in the amount of extraneous "noise" pouring into the communication channel, which reduces the clarity of the messages being sent from readers to publishers.

An illustrating case is the romance publisher who initiated a new romance line (which failed) after obtaining survey data from a conservative political action group. At the same time he rejected the concept of an "upscale" romance line with content, packaging, and promotion aimed at professional women, because "I couldn't print less than 100,000 copies [and] I doubt we could identify them." In addition, "most of them live east of the Mississippi." Was this manager-marketer unaware of Labor Department statistics (in Greer 1986) showing that "white women now fill 48 percent of all professional positions held by white Americans" while "black women account for 66 percent of all black professionals"? His comments reflect not only a regional ego-centricity but a resistance to certain kinds of information, resulting in the selective acceptance of data. This gender-specific conservatism is, in addition, reinforced by a don't-rock-the-boat-when-you're-making-money, no-matter-what-the-market-research-says mentality, as seems to have been the case at Harlequin in the early 1980s.

Publishers also find succor for their conservative impulses in qualitative data that are highly subjective and therefore open to varying interpretations. Harlequin, for example, uses consumer panels or "focus groups" to test products and ideas (largely due to the prohibitive cost of one-on-one interviews, according to Brian Hickey, Harlequin president for North America). This research technique has limited usefulness, however, because the influence of one panel member on another or on the entire group can never be accurately assessed. In addition, the lack of anonymity, along with eye-to-eye confrontation, operates to inhibit most interviewees when it comes to expressing their real feelings or opinions on controversial or intimate subjects. Janice Radway (1984), whose interviews with readers were in the main conducted in groups, reported that none of her forty-two readers admitted that romance novels serve any sexual fantasy function whatsoever. Because of the group situation, in which subjects usually provide what they believe to be an expected and/or socially acceptable response, it is impossible to assess whether that was a true response peculiar to her small sample or whether the information was simply inaccessible to her. Fear of disparagement or disapproval from other members of the group and/or the interviewer operates negatively in group situations, while the desire for peer approval and group identity may create an artificial consensus.

Another source of noise that distorts the messages from consumers are romance editors, most of whom are women, and the limitations of the role they play as currently structured. Like the women who read the books they select and edit, these editors catch a lot of critical flack, even from colleagues in publishing houses where it is romance sales that subsidize the more "serious" books. Judy Sullivan commented at a 1984 Texas writers' conference that "people in the publishing business treat me as if I'm doing 'school girls in chains'." Another editor summarized, "We're at the absolute bottom of the heap around here." Some are surprisingly young and inexperienced (yet as one commented, "Here they are editing stories about 'relationships' when they haven't even had one!"). Others, apologetic and defensive about their work, exhibit a kind of patronizing contempt for readers, as if by joining the crowd of elitist disparagers they might achieve absolution and legitimation. "There are a lot of editors who don't like [this kind of reading matter] and who read it because they have to," Sullivan says (in Jennings 1985). "One reason you get so much bad stuff today is that some editors don't know the difference between a good one and a bad one. They think if it has the familiar so-called category elements and it's written fairly legibly, then it must work."

197

Romance editors operate in a hierarchical structure that generally keeps the three M's—managers, marketers, and men—together at the top. Functioning at the interface between readers and authors on the one side, and management, including marketing and promotion personnel, on the other, they are responsible for a product that is unique yet at the same time conforms to a fairly specific pattern believed to fit the desires and needs of the largest possible number of consumers. (Though imitation is rife, particularly among series romance authors, some of the most annoying redundancy appears to be the result of heavy-handed copyediting, resulting in one "wanton" heroine after another who is plagued with "melting bones" during love scenes. One reader expressed her opinion about this in a question: "Why is the heroine who enjoys sex always described as wanton?")

By virtue of both experience and education, largely in the humanities, few editors have much if any comprehension of or even familiarity with concepts that are fundamental to quantitative research methodologies and statistical analysis, such as representativeness, probability, power, and validity. These quantitative illiterates are "informed," then, by men whose knowledge has a higher value in the commercial literature environment and who report market research findings in ways that most editors understand only vaguely or as conclusions already drawn. Certainly it is a rare editor who is able to refute such interpretations on quantitative grounds or to evaluate the methods by which the information was obtained. Yet because they are responsible for generating the product, editors are the first line of defense, so to speak, and when something goes wrong they are the first to be hit by fire, whether from within or without. Thus, editing can be an extremely hot seat, and it is not surprising that an adversarial relationship exists between many editorial and marketing departments in the romance publishing business. The result is a classic gender-related confrontation, with the male/quantitative entity occupying the ascendant position and the female/qualitative entity in the position of needed but devalued underdog. It is also a rare romance editor who makes the decision to purchase a manuscript alone; consensus among some varying number of editorial personnel is the usual procedure, followed by the decision of an editorial board, which acts as a measure of protection for the individual editor but also limits her power within the hierarchy.

Problems can arise when there is a difference between what editors hear from the marketing gurus and their own perceptions of what readers want, which is based largely on letters from readers (plus information from a few booksellers). Such volunteered responses tend toward extreme expressions, however, since it generally requires strong sentiment to provoke the consumer to action. Letters may come from 5,000 readers who "absolutely hated" a story and only 20 who "loved" it, but because they are not from a statistically random sample these opinions cannot be considered representative of the universe of readers for any particular book. Yet even when editors are aware of the bias inherent in this kind of data they often act as if it were representative, simply because they have been exposed to it.[6]

The way new ideas are tested also can be a source of miscues. When the Dell Ecstasy line published a story about a fifty-three-year-old grandmother and fashion model, a considerably older than usual heroine, were negative reader comments considered as evaluations of the older heroine or of the overall quality of the story (which painted a portrait and used dialogue so trite and phony as to be entirely without credibility)? Editors tend to draw sweeping conclusions from such negative responses—a generalized reader refusal to accept over-fifty heroines, for instance—which further reduces the variety readers are clamoring for.

Some editorial departments also use freelance readers as initial filters, distancing the product even farther from time-dependent consumer research findings. Literary agents constitute still another filter, and another echelon of gatekeepers, one that varies from being more distant in terms of time and substance from research findings to being considerably more enlightened than the editors with whom they work.[7] A surprising number of publishers of commercial literature do not engage in any consumer research as such, which means they rely on the subjective judgment of editors and agents, reports from booksellers and sales representatives (which often include heuristic judgments as well as numbers), new product testing, and sometimes even the editors of romance newsletters and review magazines. Buyers for big chainstores also have become increasingly influential in recent years.

Good editors may be capable of insights that are both different and more astute in certain areas than those of male marketing personnel, though the record suggests that their opinions rarely carry much weight. When the Silhouette Romance line was being launched in 1980, for instance, management faced a decision as to which male image to use in a television advertising campaign, Ricardo Montalban or Tom Selleck. Judging by the 1982 reader responses, the editor who pushed for Selleck, a relative unknown at the time, was right on target. A congenial salesman for the line, Montalban was too well known to ever be anyone but himself and therefore could never call forth that slightly hazy, ideal male that existed in the imaginations of thousands of women. Though the campaign undoubtedly succeeded at the most elementary level, spreading the word that the product existed and giving it some legitimacy by virtue of the national medium that carried the message, because Montalban could not bring the reader's imagination into play, he could not suggest that the product he was promoting would either.[8] The high-confidence entity may be a tried and true strategy in the launch of new products, but the romance novel is not an ordinary consumer product, either in the way it is used or in the gratifications consumers derive from it.

A more tangential problem than noise entering directly into the communication channel is the technologically unnecessary time lapse between manuscript acquisition and publication. Buying behavior and most other consumer measures describe the world as it is, not where it is headed, so the romance product may be a year or more out of phase with changing consumer likes and dislikes. Another tangential problem is a merchandising system that is shackled by returns, which means that sales reports cannot be assessed for at least eight to ten months after distribution and may not be complete for as long as three years (one of the reasons why copies in print usually are cited, rather than copies sold).

The Changing Sociopolitical Milieu

The national mass media by 1983 were beginning to trumpet one story after another about the massive resurgence of "traditional" values and lifestyles. *U.S. News & World Report* (June 20, 1983) discovered, on the basis of new statistics showing that the number of marriages was up while the number of divorces was down, that marriage was "back in style!" *Time* (April 9, 1984) decided "The Revolution Is Over" and commitment, marriage, and babies were "in." Neither magazine bothered to mention that along with the increase in the number of marriages there was a continuing increase in the number of unmarried couples living together. Even *Ms.*, the mouthpiece of establishment feminists, began sounding like *Cosmopolitan*, hyping stories on its cover with titles such as "Staying in Love—Secrets of Marriages That Last" and "Still Surprising Each Other."

"Backlash" became a buzzword to describe how white males were beginning to resist efforts to achieve equal opportunity and treatment for women. Newspaper pieces like the one headlined "Men Lose Out

When Women Enter Job Race" (Hacker 1984) fed the flames of misogyny, while the Moral Majority and other religious right groups, with help from the president of the United States, lobbied for a return to "traditional morality," resting their case on both the Bible and economic necessity. The Reagan administration launched a concerted effort to combat "the excesses of the women's movement," dismantling federal regulations requiring affirmative action and proposing tax reforms that would benefit the traditional or nuclear family (i.e., income-earning father and stay-at-home-with-two-children mother, which according to the Census Bureau now describes only 10 percent of all families). It also rejected the concept of equal pay for jobs of comparable worth on the premise that it would lead to "massive wage redistribution and, ultimately, to widespread job dislocation" (and a federal appeals court reversed the earlier Washington state employees decision). When the president met with Soviet leader Mikhail Gorbachev in Geneva, White House Chief of Staff Donald Regan relegated half the American population to duncehood with his comment that most women would not understand the issues at stake in the summit meetings, whether it be missile throw-weights, Afghanistan, or human rights.

Women, too, joined the backlash, some of them because they had come to realize that equal opportunity and equal justice carried a hidden thorn—equal responsibility. Groups such as Concerned Women for America presumed to define matters of both conscience and constitution for everyone else, launching a "counterfeminist women's movement" organized around prayer cells that bombarded legislators with letters that were anti-abortion, anti–gay rights, and pro–school prayer. Members of the "righteous right" began bombing abortion clinics all across the country, twenty-four of them in 1984 alone, and in November 1984 Colorado became the first state to constitutionally prohibit public funding of abortion. Federal funding to international family planning organizations providing abortion counseling and services was cut off, and in 1985 the Justice Department filed a brief with the U.S. Supreme Court seeking a reversal of *Roe* vs. *Wade*, the 1973 decision making abortion legal. William Bradford Reynolds, U.S. assistant attorney general for civil rights, denounced Supreme Court Associate Justice William Brennan on the ground that he was trying to achieve "a radically egalitarian society," which Reynolds called "perhaps the major threat to individual liberty in the United States today" (Pear 1986).

A survey of single women in their twenties commissioned by the

National Institutes of Health (conducted in 1983 but not released until 1986) found that unmarried twenty-year-olds have had sexual relations, on average, with 4.5 men; one out of three single women in her twenties has been pregnant at least once, and one out of six habitually risks pregnancy by engaging in intercourse without contraceptives (in Brenna 1986). By the end of 1985, Colorado physicians were reporting an increase in "infected abortions," a phenomenon that had virtually disappeared after the decriminalization of abortion in Colorado eighteen years earlier. At about the same time, a Louis Harris–Planned Parenthood poll ("Public Attitudes About Sex Education," 1985) showed that 49 percent of the population saw some merit to arguments on both sides of the abortion issue, 78 percent would like to see messages about birth control on television, 85 percent were in favor of sex education in the schools, and 67 percent wanted schools to establish links with family planning clinics to enable teenagers to learn about and obtain contraceptives.

Preparing to campaign for president, television evangelist Pat Robertson argued that the Constitution does not guarantee the separation of church and state, and that neither Congress nor the president is bound by decisions of the Supreme Court (Hume 1986). Beverly LeHaye's "concerned women" supported attacks on textbooks mounted by fundamentalists, against not only Darwin's theory of evolution but also "feminism, satanism, pacifism and secular humanism" ("Religious Right Attacks Textbooks," 1986). Not to be left behind, Phyllis Schlafly's Eagle Forum contributed to this latest censorship movement her own list of forbidden instruction topics, which included nuclear war, all aspects of human sexuality, and "antinationalistic, one-world government curricula" (in Hechinger 1986, 25).

In the summer of 1986 the Meese Commission report on pornography and the Supreme Court decision on state sodomy laws lent further impetus to the left-right debate of free speech and the right to privacy (see, e.g., Schneider 1986). In Tyler, Texas, a city ordinance banning nudity below the navel (temporarily) stopped sales of *Cosmopolitan* magazine because it carried an article with illustrations of tummy-tucking operations for women (Stengel 1986, 21), while in Maine, an anti-pornography measure was resoundingly defeated in a state voter referendum. In Boulder, Colorado, a feminist group mounted a six-woman "Sodomy Patrol," carrying binoculars, cameras, and clipboards, to look for evidence of "unlawful sexual behavior" ("Sodomy Patrol," 1986).

Polls of the American people, by Gallup for *Newsweek* and Yankelovich for *Time*, showed that only a minority (38 percent) agreed with the commission that "pornography in general is harmful to society," while 78 percent agreed that people should have the right to buy it ("Pornography: A Poll," 1986). A nationwide telephone poll of 2,400 adults conducted by the *Los Angeles Times* showed that 38 percent thought there should be laws against the distribution of pornography; 35 percent were against using federal funds for abortions; and 61 percent favored the ERA. The general conclusion drawn from the *Times* poll: "Americans retain not only their historic regard for separation of church and state, but also their traditional reluctance to let government meddle in their personal lives" (Skelton 1986, 1).

In an environment filled with such mixed messages, it is perhaps not surprising that some romance authors began to talk out of the other side of their mouths. Möeth Allison, the same author who in 1983 created a career-woman heroine earning $400,000 a year—who called the hero an "insecure, small-minded bastard!" and then added, " 'You don't need a wife—you need a lame duck to make you feel superior' "—tried a different tune in 1984:

> *Her* main interest was Sasha, his hopes and fears, his aspirations and his well-being. It might be quaint and old-fashioned [but] she was born to be a wife and mother, and if it made her vulnerable, so be it. It was a talent in itself, and she had the man who made her want to shine at it. Maybe when she got this career out of her system, there'd be time for a second one, but right now it didn't matter. Columbia's school of law didn't matter, and neither did the catalogue job. Someone else could [do that]. But no one, no one else on God's green earth, could ever love Sasha and make him happy the way she knew she could. Her vacillating days were over. She was going to go for it even if it made a travesty of all her struggling over the last three years, even if it put the women's movement back twenty years. (*Russian Roulette*, Silhouette Intimate Moments, 1984, 246)

Is it the romance industry that will be put back twenty years by stories like *Russian Roulette*, or does Allison's new-old heroine suggest that still another change is taking place among women—a sliding back into old attitudes and domestic aspirations, to a life experienced vicariously? Nothing in the 1985 survey data suggests that such a conservative-traditional reversion is underway among readers, whether it be in attitudes, values, or lifestyles. A few readers expressed a specific desire for stories about women who are not involved in careers outside the home, but one who explained her statement leaves no doubt that it was variety she was seeking: "Some professional women stories are okay, but as a housewife, I enjoy heroines that aren't professionals as well. I also like blue collar men, farmers and policemen, as well as rich men." That most editors are aware of and indeed strive mightily to satisfy readers' desire for variety is evident in the fact that it was the same romance line, Silhouette Intimate Moments, that published both Allison's *Russian Roulette* and Sellers's *The Male Chauvinist* in 1985, with heroines who are about as different as any two people can be.[9]

What is evident in the data is a mindset about equality and autonomy that assumes or demands for women the rights, privileges, and respect due everyone in our supposedly one-class society—the kind of change that is irreversible. Women have not so much exchanged values, attitudes, and aspirations as they have added to or modified old ones, and women all across the country, at all socioeconomic levels, are exhibiting at least some feminist consciousness, whether they call themselves feminists or not. An example is the woman who wrote to a local newspaper in response to a letter from a man suggesting that if women would behave according to "God's plan" and stay home and take care of their husbands and children, unemployment would be almost nonexistent: "I know many women, myself included, who take care of children, keep a clean house, gladly take care of a husband and work outside the home 40 or more hours a week! We have the right to have other interests just like men. I'm not pushing for any women's rights movement either. Personally, I love being a wife—but don't feel that God frowns on me just because I am working in this world (along with my husband) to be able to accomplish a dream—to eventually be able to buy our first house!" Thomas Barry, a professor of marketing, says his studies show that "marketing aimed at stereotypical women misses half the time" (in Gamboa 1985). The others—Barry calls them "neutral women"—are "hard to characterize because they are neither housewives nor career women, or at least they don't see themselves as either one"; they respond best to generic ads which advertise to "women as women," rather than those in which women are depicted in specific roles.

Most women today are, in a word, eclectic. They want to and do play many roles, not one *or* another, and their experiences and feelings are complex and mixed. One way to describe such broadly based change is to simply say that most American women want and expect to have *more*. Certainly the sociopolitical climate of the eighties, which makes no apologies for elitism (one of the most frequently heard buzzwords is "upscale"), rather than inhibiting this progression toward self-development and autonomy in fact makes it even easier for women to justify upwardly mobile attitudes and expectations. American women also want *better*, a quality they perceive as compatible with their enhanced sense of personal worth, and this more and better mind-set is a crucial and central consideration in marketing to women today.[10] It is because of the quality-status factor, for instance, that many women do not now and probably never can be induced to read a brand name or series romance, with its generalized negative associations (i.e., mass-produced trash for housewives). Others have already begun to move away from them, to something they perceive as better in quality and also more satisfying, and these readers generally are the ones with more education and more income. Exhibiting greater security and confidence, they are the first to explore new territory rather than accepting only the familiar and predictable, and they are willing to try almost anything that appears on the market at least once, which they can afford to do.

In 1985, romance readers, including a big majority of series romance readers, expressed an overwhelming desire for stories with greater complexity of plot and characterization. It is along this complexity-simplicity continuum that readers are most likely to be spread in the near future, with the demand for increasing complexity correlating positively with increasing self-awareness and autonomy among women consumers. It is paradoxical, then, that this irreversible change among women is probably responsible for a reversal to old compositional patterns in the romance readership. Rather than a pluralistic mass readership, with most demographic and genre classification lines being crossed, the audience for paperback romance novels appears headed toward greater segmentation along demographic lines similar to those existing before 1981, when the lower end of the scale showed a high correlation with sweet series romance novels while the upper end was associated with single-title erotic historical romances, though these demographic characteristics may be more confounded by other factors this time around.

In spite of Harlequin's near monopoly of the series romance market, by the end of 1986 the romance publishing business as a whole seemed mired in trial-and-error ploys that succeeded most in simply spreading the chaos. The time had arrived for far more sophisticated consumer research, for more attention to differences between groups of consumers (see, e.g., Alsop 1986), and to creating differing products aimed at specific target groups. For the business to move beyond the chaotic, transitional holding pattern it seems to be in, this probably means appealing to the same type of women who led the revolution after 1972—the most eclectic, upwardly mobile segment of the female population—for it is these consumers who are capable of fueling the kind of fluctuation in the system that could move it to a far-from-equilibrium state, which is described in the next chapter.

Notes

1. For a recent history and description of the diverse ideological orientations operating within the New Feminist Movement, see, for example, Ferree and Hess (1985).

2. Confusion about romance types abounds. Kay Mussell (1984, 5), for example, said, "Today, series romances dominate the market but other romance formulas—especially the erotic formulas—continue to do well," leaving one to wonder how she classified the six new erotic series romance lines introduced in 1983, which she named two paragraphs later.

3. Elizabeth Noelle-Neumann (1984) hypothesized that most people who perceive their (opinion) position to be waning or in the minority reduce their overt support for that position in fear of isolation from the majority position in society. This reduction of overt support further strengthens perceptions of decline, leading to further reduction in support, which amounts to a Spiral of Silence that accounts for major shifts in public opinion, both actual and perceived. Romance readers appear to be one group that does not fit Noelle-Neumann's theoretical construct, since they are both strongly aware and resentful of the criticism and disparagement directed toward them from those in the majority position. Judging by the hundreds of comments volunteered by readers in both 1982 and 1985, these women are fiercely determined to resist or ignore such disparagement, which seems to indicate that fear of isolation as a motivating factor is either inoperative or is overridden by some other, more important motivation.

4. Most readers surveyed in 1982 obtained romances from more than one source: 83.5 percent from new book stores, 48.5 percent from used book stores, 56.6 percent from supermarkets, 17 percent by mail, 16 percent from libraries, 30 percent from friends and family members, 4 percent from discount stores, and 10 percent from a miscellany of drugstores and other retail outlets (percentages total more than 100 because readers were asked to choose all applicable responses).

5. The word "Harlequin" has entered the language as a generic term synonymous in the public mind with junk literature for women—paperback romance novels—thereby "branding" any woman who reads romances as a reader of "Harlequins." When a colleague recommended what she had found to be an interesting paperback novel, she mentioned that it was put out by Worldwide, a publisher she had never heard of before. When I told her World-

wide was a Harlequin imprint, her response was a "knee-jerk" denial. Then she laughed and said, "Oh! Well, if I'd known that I wouldn't have bought it."

6. Faced with the current transition in the market, a growing number of authors have begun to express concern and even alarm about what they believe to be misguided or mistaken opinions on the part of editors as to what readers want. In 1986 the monopolistic control Harlequin feels it has on the industry was evident in part in the $10,000 limit Silhouette placed on advances to authors, and in the fact that all Harlequin-Silhouette author contracts called for a reserve on royalties of 60 percent against returns. For more about these and other problems authors have had or are having with publishers, see *Romance Writers Report*, the bimonthly publication of Romance Writers of America. Romance authors as a group have only recently begun to think about protective measures similar to those advocated by other professional groups.

7. During the decade of rapid market growth, most editorial departments accepted unsolicited manuscripts from authors, reducing the impact of the role of agents. By 1985, due to both the market condition and the sheer numbers of manuscripts they were receiving, almost every romance publisher had instituted some kind of procedure to limit the number of manuscripts they had to process, ranging from a query letter and short synopsis to accepting only agented manuscripts.

8. In 1986 videocassettes were being touted in the press as the next blossoming of romance. Shades of Love videos, scheduled for debut late in the fall, were to star famous leading men (such as Ed Marinaro) and unknown females, so women viewers "can easily fantasize falling in love with the male stars," according to Kenneth Atchity of L/A House, coproducer with Karl/Lorimar (in Zack 1986). Atchity called them "original programming for women's fantasies" and said plans were underway for a paperback romance line of the same name to follow. A more apt title would seem to be Shades of Past Mistakes, since the video concept as described seems to ignore two of the most important gratifications successful romance novels provide their audiences—the opportunity to use their imaginations and privacy, both of which are essential to the escape so many readers say they seek. It is more likely that romance videos will compete with the increasingly popular X-rated videos now being designed by and for women (and couples), perhaps attracting an audience that wants this type of content but under a more "innocent" label.

9. This romance line did exhibit regression, however, in the questionnaire inserted into the books in 1985; among the elements readers could choose that "you feel best describe this book" were "wholesome/not too sexy" and "too wholesome/not sexy enough." Equating wholesomeness with some specific amount of sex is not only regressive in terms of social mores but indicates a lack of understanding of what readers are saying about sex in general and about sex in romance novels in particular.

10. Women, and romance readers, also are increasingly aware that society continues to devalue the role and accomplishments of mother, wife, and manager of the home, and with this "raised consciousness" has come a simmering anger—no less an anger than that seen in women who also work outside the home, most of whom in spite of all the rhetoric continue to experience discrimination when it comes to access to both jobs and pay. A National Academy of Sciences report (see Noble 1985) found that half of all men and women work in jobs dominated by one sex, and that while sex segregation declined significantly during the 1970s, any further decline through 1990 is expected to be slight. The report concluded that 40 percent of the disparity in earnings between men and women is due to sex segregation.

Chapter Ten

THE EVOLUTIONARY PARADIGM

A New Conceptual Framework for the

Study of Popular Culture

> What makes the Prigoginian paradigm especially
> interesting is that it shifts attention to those aspects of
> reality that characterize today's accelerated social
> change: disorder, instability, diversity, disequilibrium,
> nonlinear relationships (in which small inputs can
> trigger massive consequences), and temporality—a
> heightened sensitivity to the flows of time.
> Alvin Toffler, in the foreword to
> Prigogine and Stengers, *Order Out of Chaos*

*H*ow are we to reconcile the dilemma of opposing views set out in the Introduction as to how mass media and/or popular culture function, the one depicting mass culture as conservator of the status quo, acting to dampen any perturbations that may arise in the social system, and the other as both reflector and instrument of sociopolitical change? The obvious answer is to place them within a conceptual framework in which both are possible and then describe the conditions under which variations from the norm produce instabilities in a social system that can evolve into a new synthesis, as opposed to the conditions under which such perturbations are likely to be damped, losing both potency and identity through diffusion and assimilation. In order to do this, however, we need a framework capable of dealing with the complexity associated with the interaction of multiple social, political, and economic forces over time.

Whatever form it takes, popular culture is a phenomenon that derives life and form from human behavior and is therefore time-directional, or evolutionary, in character. All forms of popular culture in this sense appear to obey a single law: if it cannot or does not change with time it eventually dies. The word "popular" in combination with "culture" has at least two different connotations. One is the idea of mass or "massification" (the latter a word that was popular during the heyday of Marshall McLuhan's ideas about the social consequences of certain mass media), which in turn is value-loaded by virtue of being the opposite of a small group or an elite. The second connotation is that of time, implying a waxing and waning of favor with consumers, as for example the change in the composition of movie theater audiences and therefore in the kind of films being offered in theaters that occurred after home television sets became as common as radios.

Nobel laureate Ilya Prigogine's "order through fluctuations" paradigm incorporates concepts capable of organizing the observations about popular romance novels, producers, and consumers presented in this text (and perhaps the behavior of other forms of popular culture as well), and also offers a way of modeling qualitative change. It provides a way to explain, for instance, how purely quantitative growth can lead to qualitative change, and how very small changes or unique innovations can have very large effects. That it already has been adapted to studies of urban growth and development, ecological systems, decision making, and biological species exhibiting social behavior, to name only a few areas outside of thermodynamics, is testimony to its emerging usefulness.[1] Prigogine's theoretical construct carries profound implications when applied to political systems because it suggests that sociopolitical phenomena traditionally labeled "alternative," "underground," "deviant," "revolutionary," or "utopian" are naturally occurring processes that are necessary to health, since it is only when little change is possible that a system moves toward disorder (and to convert isolation to nonlinear interactions is a strategy-laden concept).

The Prigogine model is described in general terms of what happens to a *system* in respect to *fluctuations* acting to disturb and possibly restructure that system. When the system is in *equilibrium* these fluctuations are rapidly damped, regressing in time to eventually disappear; when the system is *far from equilibrium* and when *nonlinear relationships* are present, fluctuations above a critical size can destabilize the system, which can then undergo *bifurcation*. This leads to the development of one or more *dissipative structures* within the system, after which a new state of equilibrium is established.

Defining these key concepts, we can say that fluctuations, or variations from average behavior, are always present in complex systems but will not grow in the absence of nonlinearities. Broadly used, feedback refers to any information or reaction to a process or product; positive feedback is any reaction that produces either more of the same or qualitative change in the process or product that spawned the reaction, and this kind of feedback constitutes a nonlinear relationship. When diffusion is very rapid, the system becomes homogenized before the fluctuation can grow large enough to destabilize it, and only fluctuations that exceed a critical size escape being damped by interaction with the rest of the system and can resist the system's power of integration. When the system is in a far-from-equilibrium state, bifurcations (branchings or situations of choice) occur which introduce the element of randomness, or chance, and lead ultimately to variety in behavior or form. The distance from equilibrium is determined by the amount and rate of exchanges of matter and energy (goods and information) with the environment. With a great deal of exchange a system is far from equilibrium and with very little it is at or near equilibrium. The behavior of systems at equilibrium might be thought of as predetermined by initial conditions and therefore predictable in terms of behavior; when the system is far from equilibrium what is not predictable is *when* the next bifurcation will appear or exactly what type of new "structure" or pattern of organization will emerge (the latter depends on the conditions under which bifurcation occurs).

The introduction of a new technique or product may break a kind of social, technological, or economic equilibrium, and that appears to be what happened with the introduction of the erotic historical romance in 1972. The system for our purposes is defined as including all individuals and groups associated with producing romance novels, as well as the novels themselves; the environment is the American social, political, and economic environment, with special focus on the consumers of paperback romance novels. The erotic historical romance fluctuation was quickly amplified by pricing, promotion, and advertising (from the very beginning promoted as bestsellers by Avon); a distribution system that placed the product in mass merchandising retail outlets where it could catch the eye of female impulse buyers; and a large number of positive responses from readers and booksellers. All of this resulted in increasing the amount and rate of exchange of both goods and information. At the same time, very little integration or assimilation was taking place within the system. Instead, existing romance products either disappeared as a commercially significant type (i.e., first the modern gothic and then the regency) or continued unaffected (i.e., the sweet series romance represented by the Harlequins of this period).

Positive consumer responses produced quantitative change — publication of more titles and larger print runs of each title—but with the appearance of increasingly negative responses, qualitative change began to appear as well. Sources of feedback included sales figures, letters from readers, promotional activities of booksellers, and reports from booksellers to publishers, consumer research data, informal reader networks, and eventually a number of parasite enterprises. Feeding off the system as a whole, including romance consumers, the latter operated as mediators, filtering and coloring information as they passed it from publishers to readers (an inexpensive form of advertising) and from readers to publishers (through reports from retailers, book reviews, and letters from readers).

Readers were undergoing considerable change themselves at this time, and qualitative change in the stories continued through the second half of the 1970s, with positive responses affirming certain qualities in these novels while negative responses suppressed others. As the product changed it attracted new consumers, who in turn effected more change. Thus, the conditions required to move the system away from equilibrium—the presence of nonlinear relationships, and a high rate and amount of exchanges of goods and information—were met. By 1978 or 1979 this giant fluctuation had pushed the system far from equilibrium, where branchings, or new choices, occur, and a new type of romance was in the planning stages in several publishing houses.

The erotic contemporary series romance novel that appeared at the end of 1980 and the beginning of 1981 constitutes a new synthesis which is not only a fundamentally modified romance formula but also a new form of popular culture: erotica for women. This new romance —in Prigogine's lexicon a dissipative structure because it must have established a high level of energy exchange with its environment in order to have evolved and must continue to do so—stabilized the system once again. Now the assimilation and homogenization that characterizes equilibrium systems was taking place and a new norm emerged, with most other romance novels being patterned after the new entity.

It perhaps needs to be emphasized that a nonequilibrium condition is likely to occur only when one part of the system is doing something different from other parts—in the context of the paperback romance, when more than one kind of romance novel is successfully being produced and sold. Thus, the erotic historical mainstream romance, the fluctuation, flourished during the 1970s in part because the sweet

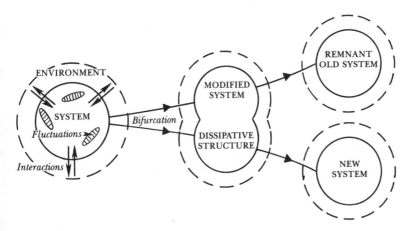

Figure 6. A schematic representation showing how a system can bifur-
cate to produce two new systems. Bifurcation depends on amplification of
a fluctuation through nonlinear interaction with the environment when
the system is far from equilibrium.

contemporary series romance continued to sell very well as a distinctly
different product, which also implies groupings (segmentation) within
the universe of romance consumers. By 1983 the sweet romance was no
longer sufficiently successful in the American marketplace to survive
without at least some modification, at which time it adopted some of
the qualities of the most successful product. The fluctuation had not
only become too large for the far-from-equilibrium system to damp,
but it evolved into a new entity—the contemporary series romance
with erotic content and egalitarian sex-role portrayals—which became
the primary activity of the system. In effect, the sweet romance itself
had become a variation from average behavior and was in danger of
being damped by a system that was once again in an equilibrium state.
The erotic historical romance continued to be published but in considerably diminished quantities, and most of these, too, adopted the
new norm. Another possible result of bifurcation is the modification
of the system itself into more than one system (see Figure 6), which
may be what is now happening to the romance system as defined
earlier.

In summary, (1) a state of equilibrium exists when all romance
publishers are producing fundamentally similar products and small
changes that are initiated by one publisher are either quickly adopted

by all the others or fail to establish sufficient exchanges of material and information with the environment; (2) under nonequilibrium conditions and in the presence of nonlinear relationships, one or more publishers can fluctuate products while others do not or cannot adapt to this change; and (3) when the nonequilibrium condition is sufficiently advanced the fluctuation can cause a bifurcation of products, with one or more evolving into a new equilibrium dissipative structure, representing a new synthesis.

Today the romance system appears to be characterized by assimilation and homogenization. Some recent fluctuations, such as the introduction of new plot elements (intrigue, sexy gothics), have been quickly integrated while others simply died out (most inspirational romances). With the system again in an equilibrium state the reduction of competition, through both the elimination of some romance lines and the Silhouette-Harlequin merger, has the effect of enhancing the system's power to damp fluctuations, making it even more unlikely that anything very interesting will happen in the series romance business in the near future. In addition, the optimization drive that characterizes the commercialization of popular culture—as intense in the case of series romance novels as television programs, resulting in product redundancy and almost instant audience satiation—is a source of instability in the system for the very reason that it ignores or subverts diversity.

Euphemizing the romance as "women's fiction" also is an act of integration, involving other types of fiction that appeal to women readers and resulting in a further loss of identity *as a romance*. The fact that women make up bigger and bigger percentages of other fiction readerships (50 percent of the readers of westerns, for instance, where they already have had considerable impact on sex-role portrayals and male-female relationships) predicts a new pluralistic mass of readers who cross formula or genre lines, which in turn means a change in what constitutes the system of interest. Should that eventuality become sufficiently advanced, some exciting possibilities would exist, with the system itself being transformed into a new system having new internal equilibrium characteristics.

Nina Baym (1978, 296) described the flowering and then waning between the 1820s and 1870s of what she called women's fiction, which is suggestive of the phenomena described here, and speculated that the reason the popularity of this fiction fell off was that "adult women's experience in America may have become too heterogeneous and complex to be reasonably represented by the formula of feminine heroism." The likely scenario for the popular romance in the near future is that packaging attributes and distribution strategies will more and more function to at least implicitly define demographic differences between consumers, which in turn will probably speed up the movement of upscale readers away from series romances (though new imprint names may be used to try to shake the stigma associated with old identities, especially the Harlequin name). Because impulse buying goes down as prices go up, new promotion and distribution strategies may further define separate consumer segments. Both the readership and the market, in other words, appear to be moving in the direction of a hierarchical configuration, away from the amorphous but pluralistic mass readership for romance that developed during the late 1970s and early 1980s and toward Baym's complex and fragmented heterogeneity.

The new romance that has evolved out of this revolutionary decade could rightfully be called the American Romance, as opposed to most previous models which in modern times have been either British imports or heavily influenced by a seemingly rigid British formula, since it is very much the product of the American social milieu of the 1960s and 1970s. It is nearly impossible to speculate about the potential long-term effects of the new erotic romance—containing ideas about equality and autonomy for all women, not as privilege but as every woman's due—on either our own society or others. American it may be, but it is very popular right now in the supermarkets and department stores of France, Australia, and Japan. Might the new romance turn out to be the second most important American export of this century (after Planned Parenthood), affecting the aspirations and expectations of women everywhere, in part because it reaches not the elite but the masses of women? Certainly it would seem the height of foolhardiness to assume that it will have no effect at all.

Suggestions for Future Research

Many gaps in our knowledge of the romance as popular culture remain, about both the processes that shape these cultural artifacts and their producers and consumers. To view the romance as popular culture means continuing studies of erotic and other types of romances in order to follow the evolution of the species, so to speak, since the stories and the market are constantly changing.

The so-called sweet Harlequin romances present more than classification anomalies, for while most other sweet series products have
either disappeared from the market or been modified to include at least
some of the qualities characteristic of the new romance—the Dell
Candlelight Romance disappeared and the Silhouette Romance has
been modified—most of the titles issued under the Harlequin Romance and Harlequin Presents lines continue to confuse sexuality
with violence and cruelty, and to portray a surprising number of
submissive and masochistic heroines—suggesting antecedents such as
The Story of O and that their roots lie more in so-called classic pornography than in romantic fiction. That these two romance lines have
been the cornerstone of Harlequin's empire also suggests a difference
in the socioeconomic development of British female consumers (as it
appears to delineate a similar difference among American readers).[2]
Certainly the books, their producers (authors and publishing organizations), and their readers deserve much more rigorous and enlightened inquiry than the investigations offered to date.

The Ballantine Love and Life stories tease the imagination and
constitute one of the most interesting romance fluctuations of the post-
1980 period. It is difficult to imagine that scholars will overlook this
coherent group of female, and distinctly feminist, bildungsroman for
long. The thirty-two titles in the series by fourteen authors were published by Ballantine from July 1982 through December 1983, and
these romances—which very likely will become collector's items, at
least until they physically self-destruct—now are available only in
used book stores or libraries.

A number of other inquiries would enrich both our knowledge and
our appreciation of the social and political role played by various
segments of this still relatively unexplored mass medium. Young adult
romances have appeared in astounding numbers in the space of just a
few years, have undergone considerable change in content over a short
period of time, and are already long past due serious scholarly attention. Are they contributing to sex education and/or to sexual activity
among teenagers today, to redefining sex roles, and if so, how and in
what ways? Microlevel data on romance authors are another almost
entirely overlooked area of serious inquiry. We know very little, for
instance, about what factors, internal and external, have influenced
certain authors in their progression from writing bodice rippers to
what can only be described as neofeminist fiction, as was the case with
Roberta Anderson and Mary Kuczkir (Fern Michaels), from *Vixen in
Velvet* to *All She Can Be*. The lack of in-depth studies of the develop-

ment of authors and their work vis-à-vis the opportunities and constraints placed on them by editors and the marketplace at any given time leaves a gap in our understanding of how individuals operate within the system, and therefore of how the individual experience contributes to and perhaps shapes the system.

Conclusion

In recent years we have seen the beginning of a reconstructed history that makes women visible to us as they have never been before, in work such as Cathy Luchetti and Carol Olwell's *Women of the West* and Antonia Fraser's reappraisal of seventeenth-century women in *The Weaker Vessel*. What we have learned has not only changed our own reality but also should engender an uneasy skepticism about some of our other most cherished assumptions—about romance novels and the women who read them, for instance. Lynn Carmichael (1985, 160) pointed out that changes in the nature of the heroine of romantic fiction may well go unnoticed "in a society that tries to ignore the very existence of the genre," but to continue to ignore the wealth of evidence available today, at least of the pluralistic character of both the romance genre and readers, requires a blind eye, indeed. Evidence of change in women is widespread in American society, yet the commonly projected image of the romance heroine and reader has remained static, defying everything we know about the successful marketing of commercial products and about the relationship between popular culture and its consumers. In order to accept that the romance is still the same old story, we must first accept that the social forces at work in society and women in the mass have not changed either—and that clearly is not the case!

Rather than supporting rampant claims that one effect of romance reading is to divert or dilute "real" action on the part of readers to change their lives, the quantitative and qualitative data presented here suggest just the opposite—that many readers have been spurred by the stories they read to seek change in their own lives. In addition, the fact that romance readers mirror so closely the attitudes and values of other groups of women (see chapter 6) constitutes hard data contravening the assertion that all manner of dire effects are associated with this "nasty habit." Readers for the most part lead busy, participatory lives, not the passive, derivative existence envisioned by some "experts."

Almost everything that has been written in the past about the female sexuality portrayed in romance novels became instant history after 1972, when the bodice rippers appeared. Evolutionary as it was, however, that era is now history, too, and to describe the romances of that period as the current state of the genre or subgenre is equally misleading; the erotic romance continued to evolve during the early 1980s, when it moved into stories with contemporary settings, which in turn influenced the historical romances that were published after 1980. And to describe the bodice rippers as purveyors of the myth that women (heroines) wish to be raped, as some critics have done, is evidence of the yawning gap between two realities—that of readers contrasted with most critics. Though erotic romance novels still present a number of misleading social messages to women consumers (or at least some of them do), they changed dramatically in that respect in only ten years, a phenomenon in itself. The historical romance heroine of the 1970s frequently was a victim, a situation she struggled to overcome in spite of her society's very real legal and social constrictions and a state of affairs that usually left her economically dependent. After 1980 that changed. Yet most critics have continued to castigate heroines as weak or even masochistic, while others fault the genre for ignoring the "real" problems of women today, such as the feminization of poverty —even though that is exactly what so many of these stories, whether historical or contemporary, have been and are really about. The romance, it would seem, is damned if it does portray a world in which women are oppressed and damned if it does not.

Popular romances dwell on overcoming, on winners rather than losers, because that is what their consumers want to read about, even though they are well aware that not every woman overcomes the problems she faces in real life. "Why," the women who responded to the surveys asked repeatedly, in one form or another, "should I choose to read a book about drug addiction and herpes when I need entertainment and relaxation? I can get plenty of that in the newspaper and on TV. In a romance I can always count on a happy ending, no matter how bad things might get before you arrive there. I want to believe that it *is* possible for women to be 'winners'."

Certainly the erotic romance novel is, more than anything else, a social phenomenon. And it is as such that we need to try to understand the forms of popular culture which are so much a part of the world we live in, reflecting how and what we are thinking about, even as they help shape the way we live with—and love—each other.

Notes

1. Prigogine's interpretation of developments in modern science, as well as his vision of "a possible future," are presented with persuasive eloquence in *Order Out of Chaos*, published in the United States in 1984 (in France as *The New Alliance* in 1979). Prigogine suggests that his order through fluctuations model allows for "a more precise formulation to the complex interplay between individual and collective aspects of behavior . . . [which] involves a distinction between states of the system in which all individual initiative is doomed to insignificance on the one hand, and on the other, bifurcation regions in which an individual, an idea, or a new behavior can upset the global state. Even in those regions, amplification obviously does not occur with just any individual, idea, or behavior, but only with those that are 'dangerous' — that is, those that can exploit to their advantage the nonlinear relations guaranteeing the stability of the preceding regime" (p. 207).

2. According to one report, Japanese romance publishers are "churning out 50 titles a month — most of them translations of American novels — and selling 12 million copies a year, all since Harlequin- and Silhouette-style romances landed there 6½ years ago" (Lynn 1986, 2). Romance novels by Japanese authors generally have Japanese heroines, says Sanrio author Chieko Mulhern, but among heroes "Western blood outstrips pure Japanese stock three to one" (in Lynn 1986, 2). Mulhern's historical romance, "like its counterparts, is full of violence, including rape scenes," which the author defends as part of the formula of the genre and "a metaphor for the battle of the sexes that defies a simple, happy ending in real life" (p. 3). It will be interesting to see if the evolution of the Japanese romance consumer follows the pattern of the American consumer, particularly whether most Japanese readers also will in time reject the rape fantasy and violence.

Appendix

1. Examples of publisher's tip sheets for authors of brand name or series romance novels: Harlequin American Romance, 1984; Silhouette Desire Romance, 1982; and all Silhouette romance lines, 1985.

2. Reader surveys, 1982 and 1985: reader sample; 1982 survey questionnaire.

APPENDIX

HARLEQUIN AMERICAN ROMANCE

Editorial Guidelines

<u>Length</u>: 70,000–75,000 words or approximately 275–300 manuscript pages.

Harlequin's American Romances are contemporary stories of attraction, passion, idealism and love . . .

WITHIN THE REALM OF REALITY.

This romance line distinguishes itself from the traditional Harlequin romances by featuring heroes and heroines who are American. The settings are in the United States and its territories and should give the reader a sense of place and culture that is uniquely American. (Just as the Harlequin Romances and Presents give the reader a sense of place and culture that is uniquely English and/or European.)

The books are sensuous novels involving realistic characters who confront the normal and often provocative problems of modern relationships. While the novels should contain some sex, the books should not be overly sexy or sensual, and NEVER carnal. The level of sensuality should be determined by the individual characters within each story.

In general, the locale should be interesting, with enough description to give the reader the feeling of being there. The characters of the hero and heroine should be fully developed; they should emerge as mature adults engaged in the interesting, diverse occupations of today's world.

LET YOUR IMAGINATION BE YOUR GUIDE.

<u>Heroine:</u>

She should be a mature American woman of 26 years or older. She may have been married, widowed or divorced. If she has never been legally married, her previous sexual experiences need not be discussed. She should typify the average middle-class American woman so that the reader can identify with her more easily. She need not be beautiful in the traditional sense of Anglo-Saxon beauty: tall, blond and willowy. In her career, she should be assertive and goal-oriented.

<u>Hero:</u>

He should be a mature American man of any age compatible with that of the heroine, either younger or older. He should be an achiever and upwardly mobile in his job. He does not have to own his own company, nor does he have to be rich. He should be a recognizable American male. He does not have to be tall, dark and handsome.

EP6/22/10   . . ./2

It must be the United States or its territories. Characters may travel, and parts of the plot may take place in any part of the world, provided that eighty percent of the novel takes place in the United States. Remember that even your own hometown may be exotic to someone who has never been there before.

Plot:

It should be clearly defined and complex enough to keep the reader involved. Contrived plotting, such as marriages of convenience, trite misunderstandings and mistaken identities, should be avoided.

Look to your everyday life for ideas and inspiration.

Style:

The writing should be of the highest quality. Use your five senses to enhance the writing.

The dominant viewpoint may be that of either the heroine or hero, or a combination of both.

The dialogue must be mature and realistic.

Sex:

Love scenes should be fairly explicit without being graphic, and NEVER carnal.

Submission Format:

Send the complete manuscript. Priority consideration is given to submissions from agents and/or those specifically requested.

For unagented and unsolicited submissions, we do, however, prefer to see a "query letter" first, in which you should ask if we are interested in seeing your complete or partial manuscript. Your letter should clearly state how many words are in your manuscript, and include a brief story synopsis as well as pertinent information about yourself, such as whether you have ever been published (and if so, what, where and when), how long you've been writing, how familiar you are with romance novels, whether you belong to any writers' groups, and why you feel your novel is right for us.

Please clearly mark "American Romance" on your submission and direct it, or questions, to:

> Debra Matteucci
> Senior Editor
> Harlequin Books
> 300 East 42nd Street, 6th Floor
> New York, NY 10017
> U.S.A.

Dec. 18/84
EP6/22/11

Silhouette Books

SILHOUETTE DESIRE

THE HEROINE: The Desire heroine is a mature, capable woman of 25–32 who has a strong sense of her own individuality and an unshakable resolve to be happy no matter what obstacles she encounters. She need not be a virgin and is definitely not a naive young girl. Rather, she is a vulnerable, sensitive woman looking for a partner to share to the fullest the joys and challenges of life.

THE HERO: The hero must be a realistic, believable modern man, one any woman could imagine herself falling in love with. He should be strong, caring, sexy and warm. He will tend to be in his mid to late thirties.

THE SETTING: Both international and American locales are encouraged, providing the setting is presented in a romantic and appealing way.

WRITING STYLE: The writing should be extremely sensuous, providing vivid, evocative descriptions of lovemaking and concentrating on the characters' reactions to each other and the sexual tension between them.

THE PLOT: A Desire book centers on the developing relationship between the hero and heroine. The book should open with their meeting or the events leading up to it and end with their decision to make a lifetime commitment to one another. The tension and excitement in the book stem from the fact that neither protagonist is certain of the other's love until the end. Each scene must contribute to the process of discovery they're going through. The plot should not consist of a series of chance encounters, coincidences or filler scenes in which nothing substantial happens.

EMPHASIS: Desire books will emphasize innovative, unique plots, exploring realistic relationships which have been ignored up to now in other romance lines. They should depict the fears, doubts and problems, as well as the exhilarating wonder of falling in love. Because Desire intends to mirror the real lives of modern women, marriages of convenience and similarly contrived situations are inappropriate for this line. For the same reason, realistic love scenes will be possible, providing they are tastefully handled. Sexual encounters—which may include lovemaking even when the protagonists are not married—should concentrate on the highly erotic sensations aroused by the hero's kisses and caresses rather than the mechanics of sex. A celebration of the physical pleasures of love, as well as its emotional side, should be an important part of these books.

LENGTH: 53–56,000 words.

Copyright © 1982 by Silhouette Books

300 East 42nd Street
Sixth Floor
New York, NY 10017

212-682-6080

APPENDIX

TIP SHEET

This tip sheet is designed to be a guide, not a substitute for extensive reading. Your goal in writing a category romance is to come up with a story that is effective, romantic, and satisfies our readers' expectations. To have a solid understanding of what our readers are looking for and what they enjoy, you must read. Only then will you have a clear idea of what works and what doesn't within the category framework.

Your story should be told in the third person, primarily from the heroine's point of view. However the hero's perspective may be used to enhance tension, plot or character development, but must always be appropriate and work within the context of your plot and word length.

SILHOUETTE ROMANCES: 53–58,000 words
Silhouette Romances require crafty authors able to portray modern relationships in the context of romantic love. Although the hero and heroine don't actually make love unless married, sexual tension is a vitally important element. Writers are encouraged to try new twists and creative approaches to this winning formula. Our ultimate goal is to give readers a romance with a heightened emotional impact—books that make them laugh or cry, books that touch their hearts.

SILHOUETTE DESIRES: 55–60,000 words
Sensual, believable, compelling, these books are written for today's woman. Innocent or experienced, the heroine is someone we identify with; the hero irresistible. The conflict should be an emotional one, springing naturally from the unique characters you've chosen. The focus is on the developing relationship, set in a believable plot. The characters don't have to be married to make love, but lovemaking is never taken lightly. Secondary characters and sub-plots need to blend with the core story. Innovative new directions in storytelling and fresh approaches to classic romantic plots are welcome.

SILHOUETTE SPECIAL EDITIONS: 75–80,000 words
Special Editions promise our readers longer, sophisticated romances featuring the realistic plots and well developed characters that made them special. The greater length gives the author time to create tension-filled stories that enhance and prolong the reader's enjoyment. The romantic and sensuous tone of the books takes on an increased importance in the love scenes. In keeping with the sophistication of these stories, the plots must be complex and believable—and above all, they must be romantic.

SILHOUETTE INTIMATE MOMENTS: 80–85,000 words
An Intimate Moments novel never loses sight of the most valuable aspects of category romance. At the same time, these larger than life stories incorporate elements from the mainstream: adventure; suspense; Gothic intrigue; melodrama; glamour. These stories return us to the world of fantasy where category romances began, but never include a heroine who is shallow, sexually free, or too sophisticated for the reader to identify with. Here you are swept up into a special world where life is exciting and dreams do come true.

Our current submission policy requires authors to submit a query letter, rather than a full or partial manuscript. In your letter be sure to mention the line you feel your book would be most appropriate for, what you think makes it special, and any previous publishing experience. Also include a synopsis of your story that gives a clear idea of both your plot and characters and is no more than two pages long. A self-addressed, stamped envelope will ensure a reply.

300 East 42nd Street
Sixth Floor
New York, NY 10017
212-682-6080

3/85

226

READER SURVEYS, 1982 and 1985

The romance readers initially surveyed in 1982 were selected by stratified systematic random sampling. A pool of 3,488 names of readers who had returned a back-of-the book questionnaire to Richard Gallen during 1981 and early 1982 were grouped, or stratified, by whether the book questionnaires had come from a historical or contemporary romance title; 300 names were drawn by systematic random selection from each of these two groups. The sampling error for this data is ±4 percent, which means that the sample can be considered to be representative of the larger pool of readers, with the possibility that findings could vary by as much as 4 percentage points higher or lower than the figure given. Though the name pool from which this sample was drawn is not necessarily representative of the entire population of romance readers, survey responses showed that none of the respondents read only Gallen romances; all read romance novels of different types and/or from various publishers. In this sense, the sample represents a general rather than a specific readership (such as Harlequin readers) and as a group cannot be said to constitute either single-publisher or one-type romance readers. A fifth of the respondents were, in fact, unaware of the Gallen books as a type or of the producer-publisher's identity. In addition, only 17 percent of survey respondents said their book reading was limited to romance novels. Returns were received from every state and the District of Columbia.

The return rate for the 1982 survey was 83.7 percent (502). Likely explanations for this unusually high return are suggested in note 2, chapter 6, one of which is that the name pool consisted of responders (by virtue of having voluntarily returned the book questionnaire). There was, in addition, an articulated desire on the part of many respondents to "have their say" about both the books and why they read them. Some comments indicated a more sympathetic response to a request for information from a university faculty member or a graduate student than from the mass media or publishing industry; for many, the belief that this time they were "going to get a fair shake" because they were giving their opinions to an unbiased researcher probably enhanced their willingness to respond. Quite a few readers added their names to the returned questionnaires, along with a comment to the effect that "I'm not worried about giving my name. Romance readers are finally coming out of the closet!" Many did so along with a request for information about survey findings and included stamped, self-addressed envelopes for that purpose. Some wrote personal letters (one included photographs of herself and family) and a few even indulged in personal telephone calls to express their interest. Readers were guaranteed anonymity in the survey cover letter; the only identification returned questionnaires carried was the respondents' group identity (whether the name had been drawn from historical or contemporary book questionnaires), which was accomplished by using different postage stamps on the return envelopes. In 1985, only 440 of the original sample addresses were still viable, and the response rate dropped to 50 percent of the deliverable questionnaires (or 42 percent of the 1982 responses). Because generally we can expect the younger end of the age range to be the most mobile (students, renters, etc.), responses to the second survey probably are age-biased compared with the 1982 responses. (In both 1982 and 1985 readers were provided with a stamped and addressed return envelope.)

The 1982 questionnaire was pretested with and without illustrations (100 without and 100 with small black-and-white photographs of romance novel covers along the left or right margin of each page), but no statistically significant differences were found between the two forms either in the percent returned or in responses to questions. (Tests for significant differences focus on the likelihood that the observed difference could have happened by chance, and therefore test results are presented in terms of probability. Generally, $p = .001$ is the highest level of confidence sought, and $p = .05$ is the lowest acceptable level. When we say that $p = .01$, we mean that the difference between the two groups on that question is significant because the likelihood of finding the observed difference by chance is 1 in 100.) Since some readers added comments about the illustrated titles, the illustrated form was chosen for the survey because it offered the opportunity to acquire more information. The illustrated titles covered an extended period of time and were intended to convey the unstated message that the study was not limited to any particular type of romance novel. (Illustrations are not included on the questionnaire reproduced in the Appendix.)

Only three significant differences in demographic characteristics appeared between the stratified groups (names drawn from contemporary or historical romance book questionnaires): (1) in the education level achieved, with the contemporary group mean being significantly higher than that of the historical group ($p = .003$); (2) in the number of romances read per month, with the contemporary group reading more titles than the historical group ($p = .001$); and (3) in the percentage of family income earned by readers, again with members of the contemporary group earning a higher percentage of the family income than the historical readers ($p = .05$). There was no statistically significant difference between the two groups in questionnaire return rate. Three of the 1982 survey respondents were male: a thirty-eight-year-old married airline pilot, father of one young child, with a B.S. degree, who has been reading "all kinds" of romance novels (historical and contemporary, series and single titles) for "about 15 years"; a twenty-six-year-old unmarried television news reporter who also holds a bachelor's degree; and a forty-two-year-old married father of two who works in "management."

What seems paradoxical is that though the mean contemporary romance group education level is significantly higher than that of the historical romance group (the former also are more politically active), they are more likely to look for "a simple story," to read series romances such as the Harlequin,

228

Silhouette, Ecstasy, and Second Chance at Love lines, and to purchase romances by mail and at the supermarket (all at the $p = .01$ level or higher). The historical romance readers, on the other hand, watch more television, especially movies and evening soap operas, read more westerns, and are more likely to keep the books they read.

The survey data also were subjected to cross-correlation analysis using the SPSS (Statistical Package for the Social Sciences) computer program (see Nie et al. 1975). Correlation coefficients describe the amount and kind of relationship existing between two variables, with values ranging between 0 and ± 1; $+1$ is a perfect positive correlation while -1 is a perfect negative correlation. Generally a correlation coefficient value of .4 or .5 is interpreted as "real" or significant, though when there are a large number of cases (such as the readers in this data) it is possible to find significant correlations with relatively low coefficient values. There is a minimally significant negative correlation in the 1982 survey data, for instance, between family income and watching television ($r = -.10$; $p = .05$), which means that as family income goes up the amount of television viewing goes down. Age is positively correlated with voting, watching television news, and liking older heroines, while it is negatively correlated with participation in sports and watching television soap operas. Education is negatively correlated with watching television ($r = -.15$; $p = .001$) and positively correlated with choosing books by author ($r = .14$; $p = .001$), reading nonfiction and mainstream fiction ($r = .25$; $p = .001$), voting ($r = .16$; $p = .001$), and liking "a strong and independent heroine" ($r = .10$; $p = .01$). A number of other significant correlations appear in the data, most of them not surprising, such as the positive correlation between reading a daily newspaper and voting.

A P P E N D I X

Please check the square beside all answers that apply. For example, if you buy books at a used bookstore and a supermarket, check the square to the left of <u>both</u> answers.

1) How many paperback romances do you usually read in a month's time? ____

2) What kind of romances do you read?
   - ☐ Historical romances only
   - ☐ Contemporary romances only
   - ☐ All kinds of romance stories (but my favorite kind is _____).

3) Where do you usually obtain the books you read?
   - ☐ New bookstore
   - ☐ Used/exchange bookstore
   - ☐ Library
   - ☐ Supermarket or grocery store
   - ☐ Friend or relative
   - ☐ Other _____

4) What do you feel influences you the most in selecting a book?
   - ☐ Author
   - ☐ Cover illustration
   - ☐ Publisher or series name
   - ☐ Back cover description of story
   - ☐ Excerpt inside of front cover
   - ☐ Price
   - ☐ Size of print
   - ☐ Other _____

5) If you read one (or more) particular series of romances, which of those listed below do you read? (If you do not read this type of romance, please go to question number 7.)
   - ☐ Silhouette Romances
   - ☐ Silhouette Special Edition Romances
   - ☐ Harlequin Romances
   - ☐ Harlequin Presents or SuperRomances
   - ☐ Candlelight Romances
   - ☐ Candlelight Ecstasy Romances
   - ☐ Richard Gallen Romances
   - ☐ Second Chance at Love
   - ☐ Coventry Romances
   - ☐ Rhapsody Romances (tabloid format)
   - ☐ Barbara Cartland Romances
   - ☐ Other _____

6) If you do buy any of the above series, do you usually buy <u>all</u> titles issued per month?
   - ☐ Yes
   - ☐ No

7) Have you purchased any of the larger-size paperback romances, called trade paperbacks, which generally range in price from $4.95 to $6.95?
   - ☐ Yes
   - ☐ No

8) What do you usually do with the books you buy after you finish reading them?
   - ☐ Keep
   - ☐ Trade or sell to a bookstore
   - ☐ Trade with or give to a friend or charity

9) How long have you been reading paperback romances? _____

10) What types of books <u>in addition</u> to romances do you read?
    - ☐ Mysteries
    - ☐ Science fiction
    - ☐ Western stories
    - ☐ Nonfiction
    - ☐ Contemporary mainstream fiction
    - ☐ Other _____
    - ☐ None

PLEASE TURN OVER. QUESTIONS ARE CONTINUED ON THE BACK OF THIS PAGE.

11) Have you read a book by any of the authors listed below?
☐ Kathleen Woodiwiss   ☐ Janet Dailey   ☐ Charlotte Vale Allen
☐ Roberta Gellis   ☐ Rosemary Rogers   ☐ Louis L'Amour
☐ Sergeanne Golon   ☐ Linda Shaw   ☐ Robert Ludlum
☐ Stephanie Blake   ☐ Kristin James   ☐ Judith Krantz
☐ Bertrice Small   ☐ Danielle Steel   ☐ Harold Robbins
☐ Jennifer Wilde   ☐ Mary Stewart   ☐ John Forsythe
☐ Jeanne Williams   ☐ Victoria Holt   ☐ Your favorite author(s) of any
☐ Patricia Matthews   ☐ Dorothy Dunnett   kind of books _____
                                                          _____

12) Do you think paperback romances generally are
☐ Well written
☐ Mixed in quality of writing
☐ Poorly written

13) What do you particularly like to find in romance stories?
☐ A simple story
☐ A complex story with several subplots
☐ Lots of love scenes
☐ A specific setting or time period (if so, do you have a favorite? _____)
☐ A strong and independent heroine
☐ A heroine who wants the hero to protect her and take control of her life
☐ A dominating hero
☐ A sensitive and compromising hero, one who doesn't feel he must always
    have his own way
☐ Other _____

14) What would you like to read about in romances that you don't find now? _____
_____

15) Do you like romances that provide a lot of details and descriptions of sex in the love
scenes?
☐ Yes
☐ No

16) Would you like to be able to find romance stories with middle-aged (40 and older)
heroines?
☐ Yes
☐ No

17) Would you like to read stories written from the hero's point of view?
☐ Yes
☐ No

18) Do you think you learn anything from reading romances that you can use in your own
life, in your relationships with other people?
☐ Yes
☐ No

19) If you like historical romances best, what do you not like about contemporary
romances, OR, if you like contemporary romances best, what do you not like about
historical romances? _____
_____
_____

20) Can you summarize briefly why you like to read romance stories? _____
_____
_____

21) Would you like to see romance stories made into movies and/or television programs?
☐ Yes
☐ No

22) When do you read?
☐ At various times all through the day   ☐ During my lunch hour
☐ In the evening after dinner   ☐ In the car while waiting for family or friends
☐ In bed at night before going to sleep   ☐ Other _____
☐ On the way to and from work   _____

23) What do you do in addition to reading for entertainment?
☐ Television   ☐ Theater (plays)   ☐ Sports
☐ Radio   ☐ Dancing   ☐ Visit with friends
☐ Movies   ☐ Musical concerts   ☐ Other _____

24) If you watch television, what kind of programs do you like and watch regularly?
(The programs shown in parentheses are examples of the type; to check the category does
not mean that you must watch the particular programs named.)
☐ Comedies (Archie Bunker, Barney Miller)   ☐ Daytime soap operas (General Hospital)
☐ News reports (local and national)   ☐ Documentaries (NOVA, National Geographic)
☐ News magazines (60 Minutes, 20/20)   ☐ Sports
☐ Early morning news and entertainment   ☐ Movies
    (Today Show, Good Morning America)   ☐ Game shows
☐ Phil Donahue   ☐ Evening "soap operas" (Dallas, Dynasty)
☐ Dramatic series (Hill Street Blues,   ☐ Other _____
    Lou Grant)   _____

25) If you watch television, about how much do you watch in an average day?
☐ 2 hours or less   ☐ 6 to 8 hours
☐ 2 to 4 hours   ☐ more than 8 hours
☐ 4 to 6 hours

26) Do you read a daily newspaper regularly?
☐ Yes
☐ No

27) Did you vote in the last (1980) presidential election?
☐ Yes
☐ No

28) Do you have a physical handicap of any kind?
☐ Yes
☐ No

PLEASE COMPLETE THE QUESTIONS ON THE BACK OF THIS PAGE

APPENDIX

(1) SEX
- ☐ Female
- ☐ Male

(2) AGE
- ☐ Under 16
- ☐ 16 to 25
- ☐ 26 to 35
- ☐ 36 to 45
- ☐ 46 to 55
- ☐ 56 to 65
- ☐ 66 to 75
- ☐ 76 to 85
- ☐ Over 85

(3) MARITAL STATUS
- ☐ Single
- ☐ Married (if yes, how many times? ____)
- ☐ Single but living with partner
- ☐ Divorced
- ☐ Widowed

(4) CHILDREN
- __ How many?
  (Ages: _____)
- __ How many living with you now?

(5) RESIDENCE
- ☐ Rural area
- ☐ Small town
- ☐ Mid-size city
- ☐ Large city
- ☐ Own house or apartment
- ☐ Rented house or apartment
- ☐ Other _____
- __ How many people live with you?

(6) EDUCATION
- ☐ High School (completed)
- ☐ Vocational School
- ☐ Some college
- ☐ University degree
  (Please indicate highest degree _____)
- ☐ Other _____

(7) OCCUPATION
- ☐ Full-time homemaker
- ☐ Full-time paid employment
  (Kind of work: _____)
- ☐ Part-time paid employment
  (Kind of work: _____)
  If you are employed, what percent of your family's income do you earn?
  - ☐ Under 25%
  - ☐ Between 25 and 50%
  - ☐ Between 51 and 75%
  - ☐ Between 76 and 99%
  - ☐ 100%
- ☐ Retired
- ☐ Student
- ☐ Other _____

(8) RELIGIOUS AFFILIATION OR PREFERENCE
- ☐ Protestant
- ☐ Catholic
- ☐ Jewish
- ☐ Other _____

(9) POLITICAL AFFILIATION OR PREFERENCE
- ☐ Democrat
- ☐ Republican
- ☐ Other _____

(10) RACE OR ETHNIC IDENTITY
- ☐ Caucasian (white) ☐ American Indian
- ☐ Black ☐ Oriental
- ☐ Hispanic ☐ Other _____

(11) FAMILY INCOME PER YEAR
- ☐ Under $10,000 ☐ $40,000–$49,000
- ☐ $10,000–$19,000 ☐ $50,000–$75,000
- ☐ $20,000–$29,000 ☐ $76,000–$100,000
- ☐ $30,000–$39,000 ☐ Over $100,000

Please use the space below for additional information or comments about paperback romances:

THANK YOU FOR YOUR HELP

Fiction Bibliography

(Authors' given names appear in parentheses.)

Allison, Möeth (Molly Aghadjian). *Love Everlasting*, Silhouette Intimate Moments, 1983.

———. *Russian Roulette*, Silhouette Intimate Moments, 1984.

Allyn, Jennifer. *Forgiveness*, Ballantine Love and Life, 1983.

Archer, Jane (Nina Romberg Andersson). *Tender Torment*, Ace, 1978.

Ashley, Jacqueline (Jacqueline Casto). *Love's Revenge*, Harlequin American Romance, 1983.

Austin, Stephanie. *Only a Housewife*, Ballantine Love and Life, 1983.

Barbieri, Elaine. *Love's Fiery Jewel*, Zebra, 1983.

Barrie, Monica (David Wind). *Island Heritage*, Silhouette Intimate Moments, 1983.

Barroll, Clare. *The Iron Crown*, Ballantine, 1975.

Bartlett, Lynn. *Courtly Love*, Warner Books, 1979.

Baxter, Mary Lynn. *Tears of Yesterday*, Silhouette Special Edition, 1982.

Black, Jackie (Jacqueline Casto). *Payment in Full*, Dell Ecstasy Supreme, 1984.

Blake, Jennifer (Patricia Maxwell). *The Storm and the Splendor*, Fawcett, 1979.

Blake, Stephanie (Jack Pearl). *Secret Sins*, Playboy Press, 1980.

Bode, Margo. *Jasmine Splendor*, Richard Gallen/Pocket Books, 1981.

Bonds, Parris Afton. *Sweet Golden Sun*, Popular Library, 1978.

———. *Widow Woman*, Silhouette Intimate Moments, 1984.

Boswell, Barbara. *Sensuous Perception*, Bantam Loveswept, 1985.

Bramsch, Joan. *The Sophisticated Mountain Gal*, Bantam Loveswept, 1984.

Bremer, Joanne. *Flirting with Danger*, Dell Ecstasy Supreme, 1985.

Bretton, Barbara. *No Safe Place*, Harlequin American Romance, 1985.

Bright, Elizabeth (Robert Liston). *Passion's Heirs*, Richard Gallen/Pocket Books, 1981.

Bronson, Maureen (Maureen Woodcock and Antoinette Bronson). *Tender Verdict*, Harlequin SuperRomance, 1985.

Brown, Sandra. *Relentless Desire*, Berkley/Jove Second Chance at Love, 1983.

———. *Tomorrow's Promise*, Harlequin American Romance, 1983.

Browning, Pamela. *Cherished Beginnings*, Harlequin American Romance, 1985.

Busbee, Shirlee. *Gypsy Lady*, Avon, 1977.

———. *Lady Vixen*, Avon, 1980.

Campbell, Drusilla. *The Frost and the Flame*, Pocket Books, 1980.

Carew, Jocelyn (Jacquelyn Aeby). *Golden Sovereigns*, Avon, 1976.

Carey, Suzanne. *Kiss and Tell*, Silhouette Desire, 1982.

Cartland, Barbara. *Love Is Mine*, Pyramid Books, 1972/1952.

———. *Love Leaves at Midnight*, Bantam, 1978.

———. *The Perfection of Love*, Bantam, 1980.

Castell, Megan (Jeanne Williams). *Queen of a Lonely Country*, Pocket Books, 1980.

Castle, Jayne (Jayne Krentz). *Gentle Pirate*, Dell Ecstasy, 1980.

Clay, Rita (Rita Estrada). *Wise Folly*, Silhouette Desire, 1982.

Coombs, Nina (Nina Pykare). *Love So Fearful*, NAL Rapture, 1983.

Crockett, Christina. *A Moment of Magic*, Harlequin SuperRomance, 1983.

Curtis, Tom and Sharon. *Lightning That Lingers*, Bantam Loveswept, 1983.

Dailey, Janet. *Foxfire Light*, Silhouette Special Edition, 1982.

———. *Leftover Love*, Silhouette Special Edition, 1984.

———. *Touch the Wind*, Pocket Books, 1979.

Delinsky, Barbara. *Bronze Mystique*, Harlequin Temptation, 1984.

Deveraux, Jude (Jude White). *The Black Lyon*, Avon, 1980.

———. *The Velvet Promise*, Richard Gallen/Pocket Books, 1981.

de Winter, Michelle. *Janine*, Fawcett, 1979.

Douglas, Carole Nelson. *Her Own Decision*, Ballantine Love and Life, 1982.

Drake, Bonnie (Barbara Delinsky). *The Silver Fox*, Dell Ecstasy, 1983.

duMaurier, Daphne. *Rebecca*, Pocket Books, 1943.

Dunnett, Dorothy. The Lymond Chronicle: *Checkmate*, 1975; *Pawn in Frankincense*, 1969; *Queen's Play*, 1964; *The Disorderly Knights*, 1966; *The Game of Kings*, 1961; *The Ringed Castle*, 1971; Popular Library.

Elliott, Emily (Emily Mims). *A Dangerous Attraction*, Dell Ecstasy Supreme, 1984.

Erickson, Lynn (Carla Peltonen and Molly Swanton). *The Silver Kiss*, Pocket Books, 1981.

Fitzgerald, Julia (Julia Watson and Julia Hamilton). *Royal Slave*, Ballantine, 1978.

Ford, Jessie. *Searching*, Ballantine Love and Life, 1982.

Garner, Chloe. *The Image and the Dream*, Dell, 1980.

Gellis, Roberta. *Bond of Blood*, Avon, 1965.

———. *Knight's Honor*, Doubleday and Curtis, 1964.

———. The Roselynde Chronicles: *Roselynde*, 1978; *Alinor*, 1978; *Joanna*, 1978; *Gilliane*, 1979; *Rhiannon*, 1981; *Sybelle*, 1983; Playboy Press.

———. *The Sword and the Swan*, Playboy Press, 1977

————. *A Woman's Estate*, Dell, 1984.

Gluyas, Constance. *The House on Twyford Street*, Signet, 1976.

Golon, Sergeanne (Serge and Anne Golon). *Angelique*, Bantam, 1960.

Graham, Heather (Heather Pozzessere). *Night, Sea and Stars*, Dell Ecstasy Supreme, 1983.

Granger, Katherine. *Private Lessons*, Berkley/Jove To Have and To Hold, 1984.

Green, Billie. *The Last Hero*, Bantam Loveswept, 1984.

Gregory, Lisa (Candace Camp). *Analise*, Jove, 1981.

Grice, Julia (Julia Haughey). *Lovefire*, Avon, 1977.

Haley, Jocelyn (Sandra Field). *Shadows in the Sun*, Harlequin SuperRomance, 1984.

Hammett, Lafayette (Lalette Douglas). *The Captain's Doxy*, Leisure Books, 1980.

Harris, Marilyn. *Women of Eden*, Ballantine, 1980.

Hiller, Flora (Florence Hurd). *Love's Fiery Dagger*, Popular Library, 1978.

Holland, Cecilia. *Great Maria*, Warner Books, 1975.

Holt, Victoria (Eleanor Burford Hibbert). *Mistress of Mellyn*, Crest, 1960.

Hooper, Kay (Kay Robbins). *Something Different*, Bantam Loveswept, 1984.

Hudson, Meg (Margaret Hudson Koehler). *Love's Sound in Silence*, Harlequin SuperRomance, 1982.

Hughes, Cally (Lass Small). *A Lasting Treasure*, Berkley/Jove Second Chance at Love, 1983.

Hughes, Samantha (Susan Hufford). *Diamonds in the Sky*, Dell Ecstasy Supreme, 1984.

Hull, E. M. *The Sheik*, Amereon Ltd., 1976/1921.

Ingram, Grace. *Gilded Spurs*, Fawcett, 1978.

James, B. J. *More Than Friends*, Bantam Loveswept, 1984.

James, Kristin (Candace Camp). *The Golden Sky*, Richard Gallen/Pocket Books, 1981.

James, Robin (Tom and Sharon Curtis). *The Testimony*, Berkley/Jove To Have and To Hold, 1983.

Johansen, Iris. *The Golden Valkyrie*, Bantam Loveswept, 1984.

Johnson, Susan M. *Love Storm*, Playboy Press, 1981.

Karron, Kris (Carolyn Norris). *The Rainbow Chase*, Richard Gallen/Pocket Books, 1981.

Katz, Carol. *Then Came Laughter*, Harlequin SuperRomance, 1985.

Kent, Kathryn (Jean Salter Kent). *Silk and Steel*, NAL Rapture, 1984.

Lancaster, Lydia (Eloise Meeker). *Her Heart's Honor*, Warner Books, 1980.

Latow, Roberta. *Three Rivers*, Ballantine, 1981.

Layton, Andrea (Iris Bancroft). *So Wild a Rapture*, Playboy Press, 1978.

Leigh, Susanna. *Glynda*, Signet, 1979.

Lindsey, Johanna. *Brave the Wild Wind*, Avon, 1984.

————. *Captive Bride*, Avon, 1978.

————. *Fires of Winter*, Avon, 1980.

Loren, Amii (Joan Hohl). *Tawny Gold Man*, Dell Ecstasy, 1980.

Lowell, Elizabeth (Ann Maxwell). *Valley of the Sun*, Silhouette Intimate Moments, 1985.

McBain, Laurie. *Chance the Winds of Fortune*, Avon, 1980.

————. *Devil's Desire*, Avon, 1975.

McKenna, Tate (Mary Tate Engels). *Enduring Love*, Dell Ecstasy, 1983.

McNaught, Judith. *Double Standards*, Harlequin Temptation, 1984.

Marten, Jacqueline. *Visions of the Damned*, Playboy Press, 1979.

Matthews, Laura (Elizabeth Walker Rotter). *Emotional Ties*, Avon, 1984.

Matthews, Patricia. *Love's Avenging Heart*, Pinnacle, 1976.

————. *Love's Wildest Promise*, Pinnacle, 1977

Michael, Prince. *Sultana*, Avon, 1983.

Michaels, Fern (Mary Kuczkir and Roberta Anderson). *All She Can Be*, Ballantine Love and Life, 1983.

————. *Captive Passions*, Ballantine, 1977.

————. *Captive Splendors*, Ballantine, 1980.

————. *Free Spirit*, Ballantine Love and Life, 1983.

————. *Vixen in Velvet*, Ballantine, 1976.

Michaels, Judith. *Possessions*, Pocket Books, 1984.

Michaels, Kasey (Kathie Seidick). *The Lurid Lady Lockport*, Avon, 1984.

Miles, Cassie (Kay Bergstrom). *Tongue-Tied*, Harlequin Temptation, 1984.

Miller, Linda Lael. *Banner O'Brien*, Pocket Tapestry, 1984.

————. *Corbin's Fancy*, Pocket Tapestry, 1985.

————. *Snowflakes on the Sea*, Silhouette Intimate Moments, 1984.

Mitchell, Margaret. *Gone with the Wind*, Macmillan, 1936.

Monson, Christine. *Stormfire*, Avon, 1984.

Morgan, Alice. *Impetuous Surrogate*, Dell Ecstasy, 1982.

Myers, Mary Ruth. *Insights*, Ballantine Love and Life, 1983.

————. *An Officer and A Lady*, Ballantine, 1984.

Neggers, Carla. *Heart on a String*, Bantam Loveswept, 1983.

O'Brien, Sallie. *Captain's Woman*, Pocket Books, 1979.

O'Hallion, Sheila (Sheila Allen). *Fire and Innocence*, Pocket Tapestry, 1984.

Parker, Laura (Laura Castoro). *Silks and Sabers*, Dell, 1980.

Peters, Natasha. *Savage Surrender*, Ace, 1977.

Phillips, Patricia. *Anise*, Jove, 1978.

Pickart, Joan Elliott. *Look for the Seagulls*, Bantam Loveswept, 1985.

Radcliffe, Janette (Janet Louise Roberts). *Stormy Surrender*, Dell, 1978.

Riefe, Barbara (Alan Riefe). *So Wicked the Heart*, Playboy Press, 1980.

Robb, JoAnn (JoAnn Ross). *Wolfe's Prey*, NAL Rapture, 1985.

Roberts, Leigh. *Love Circuits*, Harlequin Temptation, 1984.

Roberts, Nora (Ellie Aufdem-Brinke). *A Matter of Choice*, Silhouette Intimate Moments, 1984.

Rogers, Rosemary. *Sweet Savage Love*, Avon, 1974.

FICTION BIBLIOGRAPHY

———. *The Wildest Heart*, Avon, 1974.

St. Clair, Erin (Sandra Brown). *Not Even for Love*, Silhouette Desire, 1982.

Savage, Christina (Kerry Newcomb and Frank Schaeffer). *Dawn Wind*, Dell, 1980.

Seger, Maura. *Defiant Love*, Pocket Tapestry, 1982.

———. *Silver Zephyr*, Silhouette Intimate Moments, 1984.

Sellers, Alexandra. *Captive of Desire*, Harlequin SuperRomance, 1982.

———. *The Male Chauvinist*, Silhouette Intimate Moments, 1985.

———. *The Old Flame*, Silhouette Intimate Moments, 1986.

Seton, Anya. *Katherine*, Fawcett Crest, 1975/1954.

Shaw, Linda. *Way of the Willow*, Silhouette Special Edition, 1983.

Simms, Suzanne (Suzanne Guntrum). *Of Passion Born*, Silhouette Desire, 1982.

Small, Bertrice. *All the Sweet Tomorrows*, Ballantine, 1984.

———. *The Kadin*, Avon, 1978.

———. *Skye O'Malley*, Ballantine, 1980.

Smith, Carol Sturm. *The Right Time*, Ballantine Love and Life, 1982.

Speas, Jan Cox. *Bride of the McHugh*, Avon, 1978.

———. *My Lord Monleigh*, Avon, 1978 (hardcover, 1956).

———. *My Love, My Enemy*, Avon, 1978.

Spencer, LaVyrle. *The Endearment*, Richard Gallen/Pocket Books, 1982.

———. *The Fulfillment*, Avon, 1979.

———. *The Hellion*, Harlequin SuperRomance, 1984.

———. *Hummingbird*, Berkley/Jove, 1983.

———. *Separate Beds*, Berkley/Jove, 1985.

———. *Sweet Memories*, Worldwide, 1984.

———. *Twice Loved*, Berkley/Jove, 1984.

Stuart, Anne (Anne Stuart-Ohlrogge). *Catspaw*, Harlequin Intrigue, 1985.

Summers, Dianne. *Wild Is the Heart*, Playboy Press, 1978.

Taylor, Abra (Barbara Brouse). *End of Innocence*, Harlequin SuperRomance, 1980.

Valenti, Justine. *Lovemates*, Fawcett, 1982.

Vayle, Valerie. (Janice Young Brooks and Jean Brooks-Janowiak). *Seaflame*, Dell, 1980.

Wallace, Pat (Pat Wallace Strother). *Sweetheart Contract*, Silhouette Intimate Moments, 1983.

Weger, Jackie. *Winter Song*, Harlequin Temptation, 1984.

Wellington, Kate (Hertha Schultze). *A Delicate Balance*, Berkley/Jove To Have and To Hold, 1984.

Westcott, Jan. *The Border Lord*, Bantam, 1976.

———. *Captain for Elizabeth*, Bantam, 1977.

Whittenburg, Karen. *A Distant Summer*, Dell Ecstasy, 1985.

Wilde, Jennifer (Tom Huff), *Love's Tender Fury*, Warner Books, 1976.

Williams, Claudette. *Blades of Passion*, Fawcett, 1978.

Winsor, Kathleen. *Forever Amber*, NAL/Signet, 1971/1944.

Wisdom, Linda Randall. *Caution: Man at Work*, Dell Ecstasy Supreme, 1984.

Wood, Barbara. *Domina*, NAL/Signet, 1984 (hardcover from Doubleday, 1983).

Woodiwiss, Kathleen. *Ashes in the Wind*, Avon, 1979.

———. *The Flame and the Flower*, Avon, 1972.

———. *Shanna*, Avon, 1977.

———. *The Wolf and the Dove*, Avon, 1974.

Wright, Cynthia. *Silver Storm*, Ballantine, 1979.

Zide, Donna Comeaux. *Caress and Conquer*, Warner Books, 1979.

———. *Lost Splendor*, Warner Books, 1981.

Reference List

Alsop, Ronald (1986). "Agencies Zero In on Segments of the Baby Boom Generation," *Wall Street Journal,* June 26, p. 27.

Angier, Natalie (1985). "Finding Trouble in Paradise," *Time,* Jan. 28, p. 76.

Attorney General's Commission on Pornography: Final Report (1986). vol. 1. Washington, D.C.: U.S. Justice Department.

"The Average American Family Then and Now" (1983). *U.S. News & World Report,* Nov. 21, pp. 78–79.

Barbach, Lonnie, ed. (1984). *Pleasures: Women Write Erotica.* New York: Doubleday and Co.

Bartimus, Tad (1981). "Writer Has Lifestyle Her Characters Would Envy," *Denver Post,* Aug. 16, Contemporary section, p. 18.

Bartos, Rena (1979). *The Moving Target: What Every Marketer Should Know About Women.* New York: Macmillan.

Baym, Nina (1978). *Women's Fiction: A Guide to Novels By and About Women in America, 1820–1870.* Ithaca: Cornell University Press.

Bem, Sandra L. (1974). "The Measurement of Psychological Androgyny," *Journal of Consulting and Clinical Psychology* 42:155–62.

——— (1976). "Probing the Promise of Androgyny," in Alexandra G. Kaplan and Joan P. Bean, eds. *Beyond Sex-Role Stereotyping.* Boston: Little, Brown and Co., pp. 48–61.

——— (1981). "Gender Schema Theory: A Cognitive Account of Sex Typing," *Psychological Review* 88(4): 354–64.

Berger, John (1973). *Ways of Seeing.* New York: Viking Press.

Berman, Phyllis (1978). "They Call Us Illegitimate," *Forbes,* Mar. 6, p. 37.

Bernstein, Harry (1984). "Wage Gap Report Outrages Women's Groups," *Austin American-Statesman,* Nov. 7, p. F1.

Bird, Sara (1983). "Passion Pit," *Third Coast,* Feb., pp. 72–74.

Blakely, Mary Kay (1985). "Is One Woman's Sexuality Another Woman's Pornography?" *Ms.,* Apr., pp. 37–47.

Blumler, Jay G., Michael Gurevitch, and Elihu Katz (1985). "Reaching Out: A Future for Gratifications Research," in Karl E. Rosengren, Laurence A. Wenner, and Philip Palmgreen, eds. *Media Gratifications Research.* Beverly Hills, Calif.: Sage Publishers, pp. 255–73.

241

REFERENCE LIST

Blumler, J. G., and E. Katz, eds. (1974). *The Uses of Mass Communications: Current Perspectives on Gratifications Research.* Beverly Hills, Calif.: Sage Publishers.

Boston Women's Health Cooperative (1966). *Our Bodies, Ourselves.* New York: Simon and Schuster.

——— (1985). *The New Our Bodies, Ourselves.* New York: Simon and Schuster.

Bowles, Gloria, and Renate Duelli-Klein (1983). *Theories of Women's Studies.* London: Routledge and Kegan Paul.

Brand, Leslie (1983). *The Wilder Shores of Love.* New York: Carroll and Graf.

Brenna, Susan (1986). "Unmarried Women in 20s Surveyed on Sex Experience," *Austin American-Statesman,* June 1, p. A1.

Brownmiller, Susan (1975). *Against Our Will.* New York: Simon and Schuster.

Brownstein, Rachel (1982). *Becoming a Heroine: Reading About Women in Novels.* New York: Viking Press.

Byrne, Donn, and John Lamberth (1971). "The Effect of Erotic Stimuli on Sex Arousal, Evaluative Responses, and Subsequent Behavior," in *Technical Report of the Commission on Obscenity and Pornography,* vol. 8, pp. 41–67. Washington, D.C.: U.S. Government Printing Office.

Cantor, Muriel G., and Elizabeth Jones (1983). "Creating Fiction for Women," *Communication Research* 10(1): 111–37.

Carmichael, Lynn P. (1985). "A Romantic Past: A Study of Historical Romance as a Form of Recreational Fiction in Public Libraries." M.A. thesis, South Australian Institute of Technology.

Castro, Janice (1985). "More and More, She's the Boss," *Time,* Dec. 2, pp. 64–66.

Cawelti, John G. (1969). "The Concept of Formula in Popular Culture," *Journal of Popular Culture* 3(3): 381–90.

——— (1976). *Adventure, Mystery and Romance: Formula Stories as Art and Popular Culture.* Chicago: University of Chicago Press.

"Census Figures Show Cohabitation Popularity Swelling" (1982). *Austin American-Statesman,* Aug. 29, p. E7.

Chafe, William Henry (1972). *The American Woman: Her Changing Social, Economic and Political Roles, 1920–1970.* New York: Oxford University Press.

Charney, Maurice (1981). *Sexual Fiction.* New York: Metheun and Co.

——— (1982). "Sexual Fiction in America, 1955–80," in Alan Bold, ed. *The Sexual Dimension in Literature.* Totowa, N.J.: Barnes and Noble Books, pp. 122–42.

Cole, John Y., and Carol S. Gold (1979). *Reading in America, 1978.* Washington, D.C.: Library of Congress.

Coles, Claire D., and M. Johnna Shamp (1984). "Some Sexual, Personality and Demographic Characteristics of Women Readers of Erotic Romances," *Archives of Sexual Behavior* 13(3): 187–209.

Coles, K. C. (1982). *Between the Lines*. Garden City, N.Y.: Anchor Press.

Dahlin, Robert (1981a). "The Editors: Giving Readers the Goods," *Publishers Weekly*, Nov. 13, pp. 34–39.

——— (1981b). "Roberta Gellis," *Publishers Weekly*, Nov. 13, pp. 6–7.

Daleski, H. M. (1984). *The Divided Heroine*. New York: Holmes and Meier.

Diamond, Irene (1980). "Pornography and Repression: A Reconsideration," in Catharine R. Stimpson and Ethel Spector Person, eds. *Women: Sex and Sexuality*. Chicago: University of Chicago Press, pp. 129–44.

Dinnerstein, Dorothy (1976). *The Mermaid and the Minotaur: Sexual Arrangements and Human Malaise*. New York: Harper and Row.

Douglas, Ann (1980). "Soft-porn Culture," *New Republic*, Aug. 30, pp. 25–29.

Douglas, Carole Nelson (1986). "Digesting the 'Minne-Apple,'" *Romance Writers' Report* (a publication of the Romance Writers of America, Houston, Tex.), July–Aug., pp. 29–32.

Dowd, Maureen (1983). "U.S. Women Increasingly Prefer Work Outside the Home, Poll Shows," *International Herald Tribune*, Dec. 6, p. 1.

Dworkin, Andrea (1979). *Pornography: Men Possessing Women*. New York: G. P. Putnam's Sons.

Edwards, Margaret (1985). "But Does the New Woman Really Want the New Man?" *Working Woman*, May, pp. 54–56.

Eisenstein, Zillah (1985). "Against the New Right," *Texas Humanist*, Apr., pp. 15–17, 46 (excerpted from *Feminism and Sexual Equality, Crisis in Liberal America*. New York: Monthly Review Press, 1984).

Falk, Kathryn, and Elene M. Kolb (1981). "Telling the Romance Styles Apart," *Publishers Weekly*, Nov. 13, p. 39.

Fallon, Eileen (1984). *Words of Love*. New York: Garland Publishing.

Faust, Beatrice (1980). *Women, Sex and Pornography*. New York: Macmillan.

Ferguson, Ann, Ilene Philipson, Irene Diamond and Lee Quinby, and Carole S. Vance and Ann Barr Snitow (1984). "The Feminist Sexuality Debates," *Signs* 10(1): 106–35. (*Also see* Estelle B. Freedman and Barrie Thorne, "Introduction to the Feminist Sexuality Debates," *Signs* 10 [1]: 102–5.)

Ferree, Myra Marx, and Beth B. Hess (1985). *Controversy and Coalition: The New Feminist Movement*. Boston: Twayne Publishers (G. K. Hall).

Fichtner, Margaria (1984). "Heroine of the Harried Housewives," *Austin American-Statesman*, Apr. 8, p. C1.

Fish, Stanley (1980). *Is There a Text in This Class? The Authority of Interpretive Communities*. Cambridge: Harvard University Press.

Fishburn, Katherine (1982). *Women in Popular Culture: A Reference Guide*. Westport, Conn.: Greenwood Press.

Fisher, Helen E. (1982). *The Sex Contract: The Evolution of Human Behavior*. New York: William Morrow and Co., pp. 87–94.

Flynn, Trisha (1982). "Best of Two Worlds—Home and a Career," *Denver Post*, Feb. 14, Contemporary section, p. 2.

Fraser, Antonia (1984). *The Weaker Vessel*. New York: Random House.

Frenier, Mariam Darce (1981). "Harlequins: The 'Traditional' Woman Takes on the Sexual Revolution." Paper presented at the annual meeting of the Popular Culture Association.

Friedan, Betty (1981). "Being 'Superwoman' Is Not the Way to Go," *Woman's Day*, Oct. 13, p. 53.

Friedl, Ernestine (1975). *Women and Men: An Anthropologist's View*. New York: Holt, Rinehart and Winston.

Gamboa, Suzanne (1985). "Closing the Advertising Gap," *Austin American-Statesman*, Aug. 25, p. E18.

Gerson, Mark (1983). *A Choice of Heroes: The Changing Faces of American Manhood*. New York: Houghton Mifflin.

Gibson, Elise (1984). "Statistics Belie Ideal of Equality," *Austin American-Statesman*, Dec. 8, p. F1.

Giele, Janet Zollinger (1978). *Women and the Future: Changing Sex Roles in Modern America*. New York: The Free Press.

Gilbert, Sandra (1984). "Feisty Femme, 40, Seeks Nurturant Paragon," *New York Times Book Review*, Dec. 10, p. 11.

Gilligan, Carol (1982). *In a Different Voice: Psychological Theory and Women's Development*. Cambridge: Harvard University Press.

Goodman, Ellen (1986). "Homosexuals Now — Next, Heterosexuals?" *Austin American-Statesman*, July 8, p. A7.

Gough, H. G., and A. B. Heilbrun (1965). *Adjective Checklist Manual*. Palo Alto, Calif.: Consulting Psychologists Press.

Greer, William R. (1986). "Women Found to Gain Upper Hand with Increase in Professional Jobs," *Austin American-Statesman*, Mar. 19, p. A1.

Grier, Barbara (1985). Personal communication, Mar. 12.

Grover, Stephen (1980). "The Bodice-Busters: A Sure-Fire Formula for Literary Success," *Wall Street Journal*, Nov. 5, pp. 1, 17.

Guiley, Rosemary (1983). *Love Lines: The Romance Reader's Guide to Printed Pleasures*. New York: Facts on File.

Hacker, Andrew (1984). "Men Lose Out When Women Enter Job Race," *Denver Post*, Dec. 9, pp. 1C, 10C.

Hadja, Jan (1967). "A Time for Reading," *Transaction*, June, p. 45.

"Harlequin Operating Profit Down" (1984). *Publishers Weekly*, July 13, p. 29.

Harrell, Thomas H., and Richard D. Stolp (1985). "Effects of Erotic Guided Imagery on Female Sexual Arousal and Emotional Response," *Journal of Sex Research* 21(3): 292–304.

Harrison, Claire (1984). "Love at First Sight: Romance Novels and the Romantic Fantasy." CBC Radio series transcript.

Haskell, Molly (1976). "The 2,000-Year-Old Misunderstanding: Rape Fantasy," *Ms.*, Nov., p. 10.

Hechinger, Fred M. (1986). "Censorship Found on the Increase," *New York Times*, Sept. 16, pp. 17, 25.

Heiman, Julia R. (1975). "Responses to Erotica: An Exploration of Physiological and Psychological Correlates of Human Sexual Response," *Dissertation Abstracts International* 36(8b): 2472-B.

Henley, Nancy M. (1985). "Psychology and Gender," *Signs* 11(1): 101–19.

Hight, Bruce (1986). "Sodomy Law Survives in Texas Case," *Austin American-Statesman,* July 8, p. A1.

Holland, Norman (1975). *Five Readers Reading.* New Haven: Yale University Press.

Holsti, O. R. (1969). *Content Analysis for the Social Sciences and Humanities.* Reading, Mass.: Addison-Wesley.

"How Their Lives Are Changing" (1982). *U.S. News & World Report,* Nov. 29, p. 55.

"How America Will Change in the Next Decade: Interview with Bruce Chapman, Director of the Census Bureau" (1982). *U.S. News & World Report,* Mar. 22, pp. 51–53.

Howe, Florence (1973). "Feminism and Literature," in Susan Koppelman Cornillon, ed. *Images of Women in Fiction: Feminist Perspectives.* Bowling Green, Ohio: Bowling Green University Popular Press, pp. 253–57.

Jakobovits, L. A. (1965). "Evaluational Reactions to Erotic Literature," *Psychological Reports* 16:985–94.

Jennings, Lane (1983). "Why Books Will Survive," *The Futurist,* Apr., pp. 5–11.

Jennings, Vivien Lee (1984). "The Romance Wars," *Publishers Weekly,* Aug. 24, pp. 50–55.

———— (1985). *Boy Meets Girl* (a newsletter published by the author), Nov. 8 and 15.

Jensen, Margaret Ann (1984). *Love's $weet Return: The Harlequin Story.* Bowling Green, Ohio: Bowling Green University Popular Press.

Kahn, Sandra (1981). *The Kahn Report on Sexual Preferences.* New York: St. Martin's Press.

Katchadourian, Herant, and Donald T. Lunde (1976). "The Physiology of Sexual Function," in Chad Gordon and Gayle Johnson, eds. *Readings in Human Sexuality: Contemporary Perspectives.* New York: Harper and Row, pp. 16–23.

Katz, Elihu (1959). "Mass Communication Research and the Study of Popular Culture," *Studies in Public Communication* 2:1–6.

Kaupp, Peter (1979). "The Misunderstood Bestseller: The Social Function of Entertainment Literature," in Heinz-Dietrich Fischer and Stefan R. Melnick, eds. *Entertainment: A Cross-Cultural Examination.* New York: Hastings House, pp. 234–46.

Kelly, Lee (1981). "Between the Generations," *Austin American-Statesman,* June 9, p. E1.

Kensington Ladies' Erotica Society (1984). *Ladies Home Erotica.* Berkeley, Calif.: Ten Speed Press. (Later titled *Ladies Own Erotica.*)

Killoran, M. Maureen (1983). "Sticks and Stones Can Break My Bones and

Images Can Hurt Me: Feminists and the Pornography Debate," *International Journal of Women's Studies* 6(5): 443–56.

Klapper, Joseph T. (1960). *The Effects of Mass Communication.* New York: The Free Press.

Kurtz, Howard (1986). "Researchers Claim Porn Panel Jumped to Wrong Conclusion," *Austin American-Statesman*, June 1, p. A15.

Lear, Martha Leinman (1984). "What Women Voters Really Want," *Woman's Day*, Oct. 2, pp. 67–69, 110–14.

Leibowitz, Michael R. (1984). *The Chemistry of Love.* New York: Berkley.

Leo, John (1984). "The Revolution Is Over," *Time*, Apr. 9, pp. 74–83.

Lerner, Gerda (1982). "The Necessity of History and the Professional Historian," *Journal of American History* 69(1): 7–20.

Levy, Mark, and Sven Windahl (1985). "The Concept of Audience Activity," in Rosengren et al., pp. 109–22.

Lewis, C. S. (1961). *An Experiment in Criticism.* Cambridge: Cambridge University Press.

Lowery, Marilyn M. (1983). "The Bankable Ladies of Paperback Romance," *West Coast Review of Books* 9(12): 65–67.

Luchetti, Cathy, and Carol Olwell (1982). *Women of the West.* St. George, Utah: Antelope Island Press.

Lynn, Andrea (1986). "Love Bug Bites Japan; Harlequin Fever Rises," *Illiniweek* (a publication of the University of Illinois at Urbana-Champaign), July 24, pp. 2–3.

MacKinnon, Catharine, and Nan Hunter (1985). "Coming Apart: Feminists and the Conflict Over Pornography," *Off Our Backs* 15(6): 6–8.

McCombs, Maxwell E., and Donald Shaw (1977). *The Emergence of American Political Issues: The Agenda-Setting Function of the Press.* St. Paul, Minn.: West Publishers.

McCombs, Maxwell E., and David H. Weaver (1985). "Toward a Merger of Gratifications and Agenda-Setting Research," in Rosengren et al., pp. 95–108.

Mann, Peter H. (1974). "A New Survey: The Facts About Romantic Fiction" (pamphlet). London: Mills and Boon.

——— (1979). "Romantic Fiction and Its Readers," in Heinz-Dietrich Fischer and Stefan R. Melnick, eds. *Entertainment: A Cross-Cultural Examination.* New York: Hastings House, pp. 34–42.

——— (1981). Personal communication, Nov. 27.

Marcus, Steven (1969). *The Other Victorians.* London: Corgi.

"Marital Rape" (1985). *Parade Magazine*, Mar. 10, p. 16.

"Market Update" (1986). *Romance Writers' Report* (a publication of the Romance Writers of America, Houston, Tex.), July–Aug., p. 19.

"Marriage, Young-American Style" (1984). *U.S. News & World Report*, July 30, p. 12.

Maryles, Daisy, and Allene Symons (1983). "Love Springs Eternal," *Publishers Weekly*, Jan. 14, pp. 53–58.

Mason, Karen O., and Barry I. Bumpass (1975). "U.S. Women's Sex Role Ideology, 1970," *American Journal of Sociology* 80:1212–19.

Masters, W. H., and V. E. Johnson (1966). *Human Sexual Response.* Boston: Little, Brown and Co.

"Michigan Employees Seek Equal Pay" (1984). *Austin American-Statesman,* Sept. 3, p. A5.

Modleski, Tania (1980). "The Disappearing Act: A Study of Harlequin Romances," *Signs* 5(3): 435–48.

——— (1982). *Loving with a Vengeance: Mass Produced Fantasies for Women.* Hamden, Conn.: Shoestring Press.

Morgan, Ellen (1973). "Humanbecoming: Form and Focus in the Neo-Feminist Novel," in Susan Koppelman Cornillon, ed. *Images of Women in Fiction: Feminist Perspectives.* Bowling Green, Ohio: Bowling Green University Popular Press, pp. 183–205.

Morgan, Marabel (1978/1976). *Total Joy.* New York: Berkley Medallion Books.

Morris, Betsy (1984). "If the Damsel Is in Distress, Be Sure It's Career-Related," *Wall Street Journal,* Feb. 17, pp. 1, 12.

Mouat, Lucia (1983). "Stronger Laws, New Attitudes Toward Rape in the U.S.," *Christian Science Monitor,* Apr. 18, p. 12.

Mussell, Kay (1975). "Beautiful and Damned: The Sexual Woman in Gothic Fiction," *Journal of Popular Culture* 9(1): 84–89.

——— (1978). "Gothic Novels," in M. Thomas Inge, ed. *Handbook of American Popular Culture.* Westport, Conn.: Greenwood Press.

——— (1981). *Women's Gothic and Romantic Fiction: A Reference Guide.* Westport, Conn.: Greenwood Press.

——— (1984). *Fantasy and Reconciliation: Contemporary Formulas of Women's Romance Fiction.* Westport, Conn.: Greenwood Press.

Nelson, Martha (1983). "Sweet Bondage: You and Your Romance Habit," *Ms.,* Feb., pp. 97–98.

Nicholson, Liz (1984). "Public Support for Pay Equity High in New National Poll," *Women's Political Times,* Apr., p. 1.

Noble, Kenneth B. (1985). "Sex Bias Still Exists on the Job," *Austin American-Statesman,* Dec. 12, p. K3.

Noelle-Neumann, Elizabeth (1984). *The Spiral of Silence: Public Opinion— Our Social Skin.* Chicago: University of Chicago Press.

Nye, Russel (1970). *The Unembarrassed Muse: The Popular Arts in America.* New York: Dial Press.

O'Neill, Nena, and George O'Neill (1972). *Open Marriage.* New York: M. Evans.

O'Toole, Patrica (1979). "Paperback Virgins," *Human Behavior,* Feb., pp. 62–67.

Papashvily, Helen W. (1956). *All the Happy Endings.* New York: Harper and Row.

Pasztor, Andy (1986). "Pornography Commission's Report Calls for Nationwide Crackdown on Obscenity," *Wall Street Journal,* July 10, p. 5.

Patterson, Judith (1983). "Women Hard at Work," *Europe*, May/June, pp. 49–50.

Pear, Robert (1986). "Justice Brennan Blasted for Stand on Equity," *Austin American-Statesman*, Sept. 13, p. A3.

Phelps, Linda (1979). "Female Sexual Alienation," in Jo Freeman, ed. *Women: A Feminist Perspective*. Palo Alto, Calif.: Mayfield Publishing Co., pp. 16–23.

Prigogine, Ilya, and Isabelle Stengers (1984). *Order Out of Chaos*. New York: Bantam.

"Public Attitudes About Sex Education, Family Planning, and Abortion," *Austin American-Statesman*, Nov. 15, p. E3.

Radway, Janice (1981). "The Utopian Impulse in Popular Literature: Gothic Romances and 'Feminist' Protest," *American Quarterly* 33(2): 140–62.

——— (1984). *Reading the Romance: Women, Patriarchy and Popular Literature*. Chapel Hill: University of North Carolina Press.

"Rape of Wife Found in 'Landmark' Case" (1984). *Austin American-Statesman*, Sept. 1, p. A12.

Reiss, Ira (1980). *Family Systems in America*. New York: Holt, Rinehart and Winston.

"Religious Right Attacks Textbooks Used in Schools" (1986). *Seattle Times/Seattle Post-Intelligencer*, July 27, p. A3.

Rich, Adrienne (1980). "Compulsory Heterosexuality and Lesbian Existence," *Signs* 5(4): 631–60.

Robinson, Lillian (1978). "On Reading Trash," in Lillian Robinson, ed. *Sex, Class and Culture*. Bloomington: Indiana University Press, pp. 200–22.

Romance Writers Report (1985). Houston, Texas.: Romance Writers of America, Jan./Feb., p. 9.

Roper Organization (1980). *The 1980 Virginia Slims American Women's Opinion Poll*. New York.

——— (1985). *The 1985 Virginia Slims American Women's Opinion Poll*. New York.

Rose, Suzanne (1985). "Is Romance Dysfunctional?" *International Journal of Women's Studies* 8(3): 250–65.

Rosengren, Karl E., Laurence A. Wenner, and Philip Palmgreen (1985), eds. *Media Gratifications Research*. Beverly Hills, Calif.: Sage Publishers.

Rothman, Sheila (1978). *Woman's Proper Place: A History of Changing Ideals and Practices, 1870 to the Present*. New York: Basic Books.

Rudolph, Barbara (1982). "Heartbreak Comes to Harlequin," *Forbes*, Mar. 29, pp. 50–51.

Ruggiero, Josephine A., and Louise C. Weston (1977). "Sex-Role Characterization of Women in 'Modern Gothic' Novels," *Pacific Sociological Review* 20:279–300.

——— (1983). "Conflicting Images of Women in Romance Novels," *International Journal of Women's Studies* 6(1): 18–25.

Russ, Joanna (1973). "Somebody's Trying to Kill Me and I Think It's My Husband: The Modern Gothic," *Journal of Popular Culture* 6(4): 666–91.

Russell, D. (1975). *The Politics of Rape: The Victim's Perspective*. New York: Stein and Day.

Sanoff, Alvin P. (1983). "Marriage: It's Back in Style!" *U.S. News & World Report*, June 20, pp. 44–50.

Sattel, Jack (1983). "Men, Inexpressiveness, and Power," in Barrie Thorne, Cheris Kramerae, and Nancy Henley, eds. *Language, Gender and Society*. Rowley, Mass.: Newbury House, pp. 118–24.

Savage, David (1985). "Insensitivity Traced to Film Sex Violence," *Austin American-Statesman*, June 2, p. A12.

Sayers, Dorothy L. (1947). "Are Women Human?" and "The Human-Not-Quite-Human," in *Unpopular Opinions*. New York: Harcourt, Brace and Co., pp. 129–41, 142–49.

Schlafly, Phyllis (1986). Personal communication, Aug. 18.

Schneider, William (1986). "Being Good or Being Free," *Los Angeles Times*, July 20, p. VI 3.

Schur, Edwin M. (1983). *Labeling Women Deviant: Gender, Stigma and Social Control*. Philadelphia: Temple University Press.

Scully, Diana, and Pauline Bart (1973). "A Funny Thing Happened on the Way to the Orifice: Women in Gynecology Textbooks," in Joan Huber, ed. *Changing Women in a Changing Society*. Chicago: University of Chicago Press, pp. 283–88.

Shulman, A. K. (1980). "Sex and Power: Sexual Bases of Radical Feminism," *Signs* 5(4): 590–604.

Skelton, George (1986). "Voters in No Mood for Moral Crusade," *Los Angeles Times*, Nov. 20, p. I1, 28–29.

Smith, Don D. (1976). "The Social Content of Pornography," *Journal of Communication* 26(1):16–24.

Smith, M. Dwayne, and Marc Matre (1975). "Social Norms and Sex Roles in Romance and Adventure Magazines," *Journalism Quarterly* 52:309–15.

Snitow, Ann Barr (1979). "Mass Market Romance: Pornography for Women Is Different," *Radical History Review*, Spring/Summer, pp. 141–61.

"'Sodomy Patrol' Makes Fun of Supreme Court Ruling" (1986). *Austin American-Statesman*, Aug. 23, p. A13.

Span, Paula (1984). "Romance Writers Chase the Elusive Happy Ending," *Wall Street Journal*, July 5, p. 11.

Spence, Janet T., and Robert L. Helmreich (1978). *Masculinity and Femininity*. Austin: University of Texas Press.

Spence, Janet T., Robert L. Helmreich, and Joy Stapp (1974). "The Personal Attributes Questionnaire: A Measure of Sex-Role Stereotypes and Masculinity-Femininity," JSAS *Catalog of Selected Documents in Psychology*, 10, 87, MS 2123.

Spence, Janet T., and Linda L. Sawin (1985). "Images of Masculinity and

Femininity: A Reconceptualization," in Virginia E. O'Leary, Rhoda Kes-
ler Unger, and Barbara Strudler Wallston, eds. *Women, Gender and Social
Psychology*. Hillsdale, N.J.: Lawrence Erlbaum Associates, pp. 35–66.

Starr, Bernard, and Marcella B. Weiner (1981). *The Starr-Weiner Report on
Sex and Sexuality in the Mature Years*. New York: Stein and Day.

Stauffer, John, and Richard Frost (1976). "Male and Female Interest in
Sexually-Oriented Magazines," *Journal of Communication* 26(1): 25–30.

Steele, D. G., and C. E. Walker (1976). "Female Responsiveness to Erotic
Films and the 'Ideal' Erotic Film from a Feminine Perspective," *Journal
of Nervous and Mental Disease* 162:266–73.

Steinem, Gloria (1980). "Erotica and Pornography: A Clear and Present Difference," in Laura Lederer, ed. *Take Back the Night: Women on Pornography*. New York: William Morrow, pp. 35–39.

Stengel, Richard (1986). "Sex Busters," *Time*, July 21, pp. 12–21.

Stevenson, Florence (1984). "The Regency Romance," in Eileen Fallon, *Words
of Love: A Complete Guide to Romance Fiction*. New York: Garland
Publishing, pp. 31–50.

Stimpson, Catharine R., and Ethel Spector Person , eds. (1980). *Women: Sex
and Sexuality*. Chicago: University of Chicago Press.

Stone, Lawrence (1985). "The Strange History of Human Sexuality: Sex in
the West," *New Republic*, July 8, pp. 25–37.

Tannenbaum, Percy (1971). "Emotional Arousal as a Mediator of Erotic Communication Effects," in *Technical Report of the Commission on Obscenity
and Pornography*, vol. 8, pp. 326–56. Washington, D.C.: U.S. Government Printing Office.

Thornton, Arland, and Deborah Freedman (1979). "Changes in the Sex Role
Attitudes of Women, 1962–1977: Evidence from a Panel Study," *American
Sociological Review* 44:831–42.

Thurston, Carol M. (1982). "Romance Reader Survey: What Readers Want,"
Magazine & Bookseller, Nov., pp. 20–22.

——— (1983). "The Liberation of Pulp Romance," *Psychology Today*, Apr.,
pp. 14–15.

——— (1984). "Where, Oh Where, Is the Romance Market Going?" *Romance
Writers Report* (a publication of the Romance Writers of America, Houston, Tex.), Oct./Nov., p. 6.

——— (1985). "Popular Historical Romances: Agent for Social Change?"
Journal of Popular Culture 19(1): 35–49.

Thurston, Carol, and Barbara Doscher (1982). "Supermarket Erotica: 'Bodice-
Busters' Put Romantic Myths to Bed," *The Progressive*, Apr., pp. 49–51.

"Torstar Executive Sees Net Income for 1985 Rising to $2.40 a Share" (1985).
Wall Street Journal, Nov. 21, p. 58.

Townend, Annette (1984). "Historical Overview," in Eileen Fallon, *Words of
Love: A Complete Guide to Romance Fiction*. New York: Garland Publishing, p. 3–29.

"Trade News: Millions of Women Avid for Avon's Erotic Historial Romances" (1975). *Publishers Weekly*, Oct. 6, p. 44.

Trafford, Abigail K. (1984a). "She's Come a Long Way—or Has She?" *U.S. News & World Report*, Aug. 6, pp. 44–51.

——— (1984b). "Women on the Move," *U.S. News & World Report*, Mar. 19, pp. 46–48.

Turner, Alice K. (1978). "The Tempestuous, Tumultuous, Turbulent, Torrid and Terribly Profitable World of Paperback Passion," *New York*, Feb. 13, pp. 46–49.

20 Facts on Women Workers (1985). U.S. Department of Labor, Women's Bureau Bulletin. Washington, D.C.: U.S. Government Printing Office.

Ubell, Earl (1984). "Sex in America Today," *Parade Magazine*, Oct. 26, pp. 11–13.

Wagner, Susan (1979). "Justice Warns Harlequin on Pinnacle Acquisition," *Publishers Weekly*, Feb. 26, p. 97.

Warren, Mary Anne (1980). *The Nature of Women: An Encyclopedia and Guide to the Literature*. Inverness, Calif.: Edgepress.

Weibel, Kathryn (1977). *Mirror, Mirror: Images of Women Reflected in Popular Culture*. New York: Anchor Press.

Weitzman, Lenore (1985). *The Divorce Revolution: The Unexpected Social and Economic Consequences for Women in America*. New York: The Free Press.

Wermiel, Stephen (1986). "Justices Uphold Georgia's Law Barring Sodomy," *Wall Street Journal*, July 1, p. 4.

White, David M. (1950). "The 'Gate Keeper': A Case Study in the Selection of News," *Journalism Quarterly* 27:383–90.

Wilson, Glenn (1978). *The Secrets of Sexual Fantasy*. London: J. M. Dent and Sons.

"Women's Ideal Lifestyle" (1980). *Parade Magazine*, Dec. 28, p. 9.

Virginia Woolf (1981/1929). *A Room of One's Own*. New York: Harcourt Brace Jovanovich.

Yankelovich, Skelly and White, Inc. (1972, 1981). *Yankelovich Monitor*. New York.

——— (1978). *Consumer Research Study on Reading and Book Purchasing*. Darien, Conn.: The Group.

Young, Iris Marion (1985). "Humanism, Gynocentrism, and Feminist Politics," *Women's Studies International Forum* 8(3): 173–83.

Zacks, Richard (1986). "Romantic Love Is Blooming Like Violets on Home Videos," *Denver Post*, July 25, Weekend section, p. 26.

Zelbergeld, Bernie (1978). *Male Sexuality*. New York: Bantam.

Zeman, Anthea (1977). *Presumptuous Girls: Women and Their World in the Serious Woman's Novel*. London: Weidenfeld and Nicolson.

Index

INDEX

Note on the Author

Carol Thurston has a Ph.D. in mass communication from the University of Texas and currently is a writer and market research consultant in Austin, Texas. A former member of the journalism faculty at UT-Austin and the University of Houston, she also has been a newspaper reporter and political speech writer. Her work has been published in the *Journal of Communication, Journalism Quarterly, Gazette: International Journal for Mass Communication Studies, Public Telecommunication Review, Psychology Today,* and the *Christian Science Monitor.* She is coauthor of the National Association of Educational Broadcasters monograph *Case Studies in Institutional Licensee Management.*